ANALECTA BIBLICA
INVESTIGATIONES SCIENTIFICAE IN RES BIBLICAS

127

MICHAEL KOLARCIK, S.J.

THE AMBIGUITY OF DEATH IN THE BOOK OF WISDOM 1–6

A Study of Literary Structure and Interpretation

EDITRICE PONTIFICIO ISTITUTO BIBLICO – ROMA 1991

Vidimus et approbamus ad normam Statutorum

Pontificii Instituti Biblici de Urbe
Romae, die 22 mensis maii anni 1990

R. P. Maurice Gilbert, S.J.
R. D. Richard Taylor

ISBN 88-7653-127-0

Editrice Pontificio Istituto Biblico
Piazza della Pilotta, 35 - 00187 Roma

TABLE OF CONTENTS

INTRODUCTION

1) *Reasons for the Study*

The first six chapters of the Book of Wisdom contain some rather daring and bold declarations on the nature of death. "God did not make death (1:13)"; "Through envy of the adversary, death entered the world (2:24)". Within the entire opening section of Wis 1–6, which consists of an exhortation to love justice and to seek God, death is presented as a crucial obstacle to be overcome. Death is the prime negative motivation in the exhortation. From this perspective, death becomes the critical theme which the author employs and exploits to ground the exhortation in an issue of capital importance to the reader.

Because the author treats death in such an explicit manner, it is only natural to find that numerous scholars have dedicated entire works or specific studies to the clarification of the understanding of death in Wisdom. For the most part, scholarly interest in Wisdom's presentation of death began with the preoccupation to clarify the idea of death within larger theological issues, such as original sin (A.-M. DUBARLE, 1950) or the belief in an after-life (R.J. TAYLOR, 1966). Other works included a focus on Wisdom's place in the development of the presentation of death within the entire OT, from a thematic view (L. WÄCHTER, 1967).

These works engendered a lively, if not a harmonious, debate on Wisdom's presentation of death. Positions varied as to what type of death the author had in mind when constructing some of the more memorable phrases within the sustained argument against injustice. Some scholars defended the surface level meaning of physical death; others totally excluded this possibility and opted for the reading of a second or final death as distinct from physical death; still others opted for a more complex interpretation whereby both physical and spiritual death are understood to have been intended by the author of Wis.

No clear, convincing solution has been found for the ambiguity of the concept of death employed in Wis. Recently, a few scholars have concluded that the author was to some extent "confused" in the treatment of death (J.J. COLLINS, 1978), or "careless" in conjoining a personal, mythological construction to that of the Genesis accounts (Y. AMIR, 1979). Nonetheless, Wisdom's presentation of death continues to generate interest in thematic studies on death in Scripture as a whole (O. KAISER,

E. Lohse, 1977; O. Knoch, 1977; L.R. Bailey, 1979; A. Marchadour, 1979). The Wis author treats the theme of death in a creative and dramatic context that defies simplistic solutions on the one hand, but at the same time challenges the reader to reflect on the reality of death from different points of view.

Side by side with the thematic studies on life and death in Wis, multiple literary studies have flourished which focused on the structure of Wis (A.G. Wright, 1967; M. Gilbert, 1973, 1986; U. Offerhaus, 1981; P. Bizzeti, 1984). The study of the literary structure of Wis proved to be most fruitful. The author composed this literary masterpiece with a sense of craft and a gift of artistry. Perhaps in no other single work in the OT have the techniques of parallelism and concentric structure been employed with such perfection.

Only in brief and cursory fashion have the results of literary criticism been brought to bear on the clarification of the author's exposition of death in Wis. In this work, I propose to re-examine the presentation of death in the first six chapters of Wis with the aid of an attentive reading of the text through a study of its literary structure. Precisely because the author has exerted so much effort to construct the dramatic argument on death in a tight, literary structure, it is reasonable to expect that close attention to the argument in light of this structure will aid the reader to penetrate the author's notion of death.

2) *Methodology and Structure of the Study*

The methodology employed in the works on Wis, which focused on the thematic issue of death, consisted primarily in philology and word studies. Through careful analyses of the use of words and phrases and their comparisons with paradigms and syntagmas in other Scriptural and Pseudepigraphal passages, these works clarify the semantic field available for the interpretation of the specific phrases in Wis. The study of philology, which clarifies the semantic range of syntagmas (the concrete expression), remains indispensable for an intelligible understanding of phrases regarding death in Wis.

However, in interpreting a literary work, it is always important to apply methods that are suitable to the unique techniques employed by the author of the composition. Philology alone cannot do justice to a work such as Wis which is composed with intricate parallel and concentric structures that mediate a concrete argument. The phrases pertinent to the issue of death must be studied not only in their immediate contexts but also within the structures that mediate the argument. The study of the literary structure of Wis 1–6 will provide an analysis that will highlight the intricate parallelism of the various units and the concentric structure of the whole.

The analysis of the literary structure is not an end in itself. The purpose of such an analysis is to enable a more attentive and deeper reading of the poetic work itself. The method of examining the literary structure does not provide a magical key of interpretation that unlocks meaning that otherwise cannot be found. But the re-reading of the text, with attention given to its literary structure, provides the reader with a new set of tools and with a richer stock of imagery and relations with which to appreciate the work. In our case, the concrete expectation in this re-reading of Wis is to establish whether or not the structures of the unit uncover elements for interpretation that contribute to an understanding of the ambiguity of death in the author's argument. The literary structures of Wis will provide a basis for an attentive reading of the whole unit with respect to the argumentation that the author is constructing.

This attentive reading, based on the literary structure, will employ methods akin to rhetorical criticism and to the relatively new method of "reader response criticism"[1]. The argument that the author constructs through the parallel structures of the units and through metaphorical imagery will be studied and followed with respect to the continuous responses the author expects from the reader. The complex argument that underlies the first six chapters of Wis will provide the widest context for understanding the author's employment of the images of death. Three studies will be integrated in the attentive re-reading of the text of Wis: a) the study of the literary structure, b) the study of the semantic range of pertinent phrases, c) the study of the dynamic of the author's argumentation.

The argument of this work will unfold in five chapters. The first will present critically an historical sketch of the attempts at structuring the various parts of the entire book of Wis. The importance of this chapter is to establish the weight of the author's literary technique to build arguments through parallel units and concentric structures. The second chapter moves specifically to the analysis of the literary structure of the first part of Wis (1–6).

---

[1] Both rhetorical and reader response criticism comprise variations of emphasis from one critic to another in each specialty. But each approach recognizes at least a relationship between the devices the author employs in a work and the interpretation on the part of the reader. If rhetorical criticism concentrates on the rhetorical resources available to the writer (W. BOOTH, *The Rhetoric of Fiction*, Chicago: 1970, see the preface), reader response criticism concentrates on the creative engagement of readers in their reaction to the presentation of an author (R. M. FOWLER, "Who Is 'the Reader' in Reader Response Criticism?" *Semeia* 31, 1985, 5-23). The attentive reading of Wis based on the literary structure will combine the study of the literary techniques the author employs in the work with a study of the dynamic of the argument that engages the reader to participate actively in the dramatic argument.

The third chapter will re-construct the argumentation of the author by following the employment of metaphorical language within the literary structures of the entire unit. In this chapter, the semantic range of words and phrases will be determined through comparisons with similar syntagmas in other related texts. This study of the author's argumentation will provide the context for clarifying the function the author makes of the idea of death.

An attentive reading of the concentric unit, 1:1–6:21, uncovers the author's sustained employment of the metaphorical image of a trial scene. The image remains metaphorical rather than dramatic in the strict sense of the term, because the sole speaker is the author. In other words, it is always the author who is speaking, even when the hypothetical speeches of the defendants are summarized.

The main elements of a trial scene are metaphorically brought into the author's exhortation: 1) the fact of an ultimate judgment; 2) an accusation against the wicked; 3) the wicked's defense and false counter-accusation; 4) the examination of the evidence: defence of the just, accusation against the wicked; 5) the confession of the wicked; 6) the reward of the just and conviction of the wicked; 7) a warning against incorrect judgment.

The fourth chapter will consist of a critical survey of the most representative explanations of the author's understanding of death in Wis. This critical survey necessarily involves a brief treatment of the Genesis creation accounts, in as much as these are alluded to within the author's development of the argument.

Finally the fifth chapter will elucidate the levels of meaning the author attributes to death as well as the reasons for the sustained ambiguity employed by the author.

CHAPTER ONE

AN HISTORICAL SURVEY:
THE STRUCTURE OF THE BOOK OF WISDOM

A - 1. Literary Structure

The outlining of the literary structure of a written composition uniquely permits the scholar to uncover and to follow the inner dynamic of the work itself. A literary composition created without the benefits of modern printing techniques required the use of external and internal stylistic features to guide the reader into the movement of the work. For the contemporary reader, various printing features that guide the actual reading of the text are commonplace, such as indentation, change of print styles, paragraph markers, page breaks, section indicators, chapters, etc.

The ancients were no less creative in devising ways and in constructing systems for the modulation of the actual reading of the composition[1]. Through a careful repetition of concrete words or even images, entire thematic sections could be clearly delimited. This technique of the inclusion, where a word or phrase introduces and closes a unit, is frequently employed in Hebrew poetry and is a favorite for the author of Wis. The referral back to a previous, opening verse may enclose all that transpires in a section through a concise phrase or image. In such a way, a section is enclosed within a literary unit by a repetition of words that express the theme. By paralleling phrases or lines, the author skillfully draws attention to comparisons, to contrasts, or even to developed nuances. Ancient texts, that is Hebrew, Greek and Roman, are prone to exemplify a constructed form.

---

[1] A. VANHOYE, *La structure littéraire de l'épître aux Hébreux*, Paris: 1963. In this fundamental work for explicating literary techniques, VANHOYE applies literary criteria to the text in order to clarify the organization of the Letter to the Hebrews. The method that VANHOYE employs will become a model for the study of Wis. For a brief summary statement of the principles VANHOYE developed see F. PERRENCHIO, "Struttura e analisi letteraria di Sapienza 1,1-15", *Sales* 37 (1975) 289-325. For a general summary of literary techniques employed by the ancients that become the subject for literary criticism see J.H. HAYES, C.R. HOLLADAY, *Biblical Exegesis*, chapter 5, "Literary Criticism: The Composition, Structure and Rhetorical style of the Text", pp. 67-77, Atlanta: 1982.

An aspect of the poetic genius of the authors of ancient texts is especially highlighted when such techniques are employed to aid the reader without the necessity of a direct and conscious reflection on the part of the reader. However, on a more critical level of reflection and reading of the text, the highlighting of the literary structure through literary analysis sheds further light on the inner dynamic of the composition and its content. Uncovering the literary structure of the composition allows for a clarification of the development of the ideas and themes expounded in the work.

The entire book of Wis will be the object of this general view of the literary structure of Wis, even though the following chapters will concentrate on the first six chapters of Wis where the image of death provides the critical theme for the author's argument. This general overview which includes the following sections of Wis will be useful in the final stages of the analysis where the author's understanding of death is verified precisely in the later sections of the book.

A further clarification may be in order as to how to read and follow the literary structures that will be analyzed in this work. The outlining of literary structures may become quite complex and consequently dry when read on the surface. Simplicity is a goal, but it is not always possible to achieve, especially when the structures become extensive. For the reader to overcome the possible dryness of viewing patterns and repetitions and to extract the greatest benefit in exploring the concrete literary structure, it will be important to follow and to verify the literary structure in the actual text of Wis.

A - 2.   Outlining the Book of Wisdom according to Theme

Prior to the rise of methods of literary criticism for determining the structure of narrative, dialogue and poetry, it was the theme and various topics of a literary work that constituted the main criteria for determining the organization of the units[2]. The relationship between a literary unit and its theme remains a primary criterion for assessing the limits of the unit[3].

---

[2] F. PERRENCHIO, "Struttura e analisi letteraria di Sapienza 1,1-15", *Sales* 37 (1975) pp. 289-291. It is interesting to note that even as early as the turn of this century, R. CORNELY recognized the weakness of uncovering the structure of Wis solely on grounds of the subject matter. But without the techniques of literary criticism, he finally concluded that the Book of Wisdom defies all attempts at structuring. "Quamobrem ex forma externa generalem divisionem desumere maluimus" (R. CORNELY, *Commentarius in librum Sapientiae*, Paris: 1910, p. 11).

[3] "The test of any plan is how well it matches the thought". A.G. WRIGHT, "The Structure of the Book of Wisdom", *Bib* 48 (1967) p. 166.

But an obvious limitation in using the topic as the sole criterion for delimiting a unit is the arbitrary or manifold manner in which topics can be arranged and organized[4].

BONAVENTURE's commentary on the Book of Wisdom from the 13th century provides an excellent example of the employment of the theme as the sole criterion for organizing the structure of the book[5]. BONAVENTURE divides the book into two exhortations. The first part (Wis 1–5) is termed "an exhortation for the practice of justice in a triple set of relationships"; 1-a) justice towards God (Wis 1), 1-b) justice towards the other (Wis 2–3), and 1-c) justice towards oneself, exemplified through a comparison of the states of the just and unjust (Wis 4–5).

In turn, each of these sections is further divided into units by the topic under discussion. 1-a) Justice towards God: 1) justice of the heart, 2) justice of speech, 3) justice of deeds to which one is instructed. 1-b) Justice towards the other: 1) justice drawn from a portrait of the unjust (Wis 2), 2) justice called forth from a portrait of the just (Wis 3). 1-c) Justice towards oneself: 1) the state of the unjust (Wis 4), 2) the state of the just (Wis 5).

The second part (Wis 6–19) is termed "an exhortation to wisdom adduced through a triple set of reasons"; 2-a) through the dangers of one's office (Wis 6), 2-b) through an instructive example (Wis 7–9), 2-c) through the many benefits and effects of wisdom (Wis 10–19). The last section which is rather long, consisting of ten chapters, is further divided. Wis 10 is entitled, "Wisdom promotes her wise friends"; Wis 11–19, "Wisdom punishes the adversaries", by light penalties (Wis 11–12) and by grave penalties leading to condemnation (Wis 13–19).

BONAVENTURE's presentation of the organization of the book according to its themes presupposes an initial decision to organize the themes in the contours of two exhortations. There is no explanation on the relationship between these two exhortations other than the simple assertion that wisdom and justice are related[6].

---

[4] On the methodological weakness of using the theme as the sole criterion for ascertaining the limits of a literary unit, particularly in the case of the Letter to the Hebrews, see A. VANHOYE, *La structure*, pp. 11-15.

[5] BONAVENTURE (?), *Commentarius in librum Sapientiae*, [Opera Omnia 1-10, ed. QUARACCHI, 1893] VI 139-171 (attributed to BONAVENTURE, circa 1270).

[6] BONAVENTURE, *Commentarius*. In the introductory remarks under "Divisio Generalis" BONAVENTURE summarizes the relationship between wisdom and justice that the first chapter of Wis presents. "Quoniam, sicut dictum est, principes et praelati, et per consequens omnes, provocantur in hoc libro ad studium et amorem sapientiae; sed quia non potest haberi sapientia sine iustitiae observantia...", p. 110. Similarly, when BONAVENTURE begins to comment on the second part, he simply mentions the existence of a change from the exhortation to justice to an exhortation to loving wisdom. "Postquam monuit principes et potentes ad iustitiam, hic incipit eos monere ad *sapientiam* inquirendam et

This presentation of the organization of Wis is intelligible. But it is not clear that such a division is primary in the author's organization of the composition. The theme alone of a work is not a sufficient category to display the organizing principle that the author or redactor used in its creation. Other criteria must be brought into play in order to root the organization of the work into a pattern or structure that does not solely depend on the theme that a critic has predetermined.

With the rise of source and redaction criticism, compositional and philological analyses were added to the set of criteria for determining the various literary units of a composition. Various scholars applied these criteria to Wis primarily to determine the integrity of the text and to determine authorship. This resulted in manifold presentations of the organization of the work.

C. L. W. GRIMM championed the integrity of Wis against EICHHORN[7]. Even with the added criteria of composition and philology, the theme remained the central issue for presenting the organization of the work. Along with other scholars, GRIMM recognized three sections within Wis[8]. The first part consists of Wis 1–5, which is an exhortation to wisdom. Wisdom leads to immortality; licentiousness and turning away from the Mosaic law lead to death. The second part consists of Wis 6–9, which is an exhortation to wisdom on grounds of her being and her intellectual and ethical effects. The third part consists of Wis 10–19, which is an exhortation to wisdom on grounds of her many blessings in Israel's ancient history.

W. WEBER took up the divisions of GRIMM precisely to highlight EICHHORN's claim that these sections stem from several different authors

---

amandam...", p. 144. There are no explanations provided for dividing the book into these two major sections of exhortation.

[7] C.L.W. GRIMM, *Das Buch der Weisheit*, Kurzegefasstes exegetisches Handbuch zu den Apokryphen des Alten Testaments VI, Leipzig: 1860. J.G. EICHHORN, *Einleitung in die Apokryphen des Alten Testaments*, Leipzig: 1803.

GRIMM refutes various arguments which EICHHORN proposed as evidence for diverse authorship (EICHORN, pp. 142-143) such as, the sudden change in theme and speaker in c. 11, the different causes of evil presented in the two halves of the book. In defense of the unity of the work, GRIMM notes that though the themes change, the image of wisdom remains in the background even throughout the second half of the book. The argument for diverse authorship based on two different explanations for the origin of evil can be explained by the parallel that the author draws between the licentious atheism depicted in the first half and the licentiousness of idol worship discussed in the second half (GRIMM, pp. 9-12).

[8] C.L.W. GRIMM, *Das Buch der Weisheit*, p. 4, n. 2. GRIMM agrees on the division of the book into three main sections with LORINUS, CORNELIUS A LAPIDE, TIRINIUS, CALONIUS, who in general describe the three sections in the following manner: I) Exhortation to strive for wisdom, Wis 1–6, II) Regarding the origins of wisdom, Wis 7–9, III) Regarding the works of wisdom, Wis 10–19.

because they manifest so recognizably diverse characteristics [9]. The structure of the book is analyzed from the point of view of proving diverse authorship. As with GRIMM, WEBER continues to employ the theme as the main criterion for delimiting the sections of the book. He then analyzes the point of view of the three main sections to show their differences [10]. From the content of these sections, he names the first section, "the eschatological book", the second, "the book of wisdom" and the third, "the book of God's method of punishing". He considered these separate books to have been complete in themselves prior to the final redaction. The second book had lost its ending, while the third had lost its introduction. In addition, within the third section, a fourth book is discernible, which WEBER defines as "the book of the idol makers" [11].

In turn, E. GÄRTNER relied upon WEBER's proposed division of Wis in order to pin down the specific qualities and characteristics of the respective authors of the book's major sections [12]. The division is only slightly modified from that of WEBER's regarding the last part of Wis. The criteria for division remain theme and vocabulary. The first part (1:1–5:24) is "the eschatological book"; the second (6:1–11:1) is "the book of wisdom proper"; a third part (13:1–15:19) GÄRTNER names "the treatment of idolatry"; and finally chapters 11:2–12:27, 16–19, are simply referred to as "the last section of Wisdom".

GÄRTNER employs this structure of Wis in an attempt to determine the characteristics of the diverse authors [13]. The greatest diversity, he observes, is noticeable between the first and second sections. The eschatological book represents thoroughly Jewish ideas and could very well have had its origins in Palestine [14]. The book of wisdom proper, on the other

---

[9] W. WEBER, "Die Composition der Weisheit Salomos", *ZWT* 47 (1904) 145-169.

[10] For instance, WEBER claims that the theme in the first five chapters has no bearing on the rest of the book. "... das in den ersten fünf Capiteln abgehandelte Thema hat aber wiederum nicht das Geringste mit dem Reste des Buches zu tun". W. WEBER, "Die Composition", p. 159.

[11] W. WEBER, "Die Composition", p. 169.

[12] E. GÄRTNER, *Komposition und Wortwahl des Buches der Weisheit*, (*Schriften der Lehranstalt für die Wissenschaft des Judentums*, II, 2-4; Berlin: 1912).

[13] The attempts to attribute various sections of the Book of Wisdom to diverse authorship have proven to be unconvincing. Though the theme and even certain vocabulary features do change in the work, there are similarities in structure, particularly in parallelism of various sections that make the work a coherent whole. At most, the sections could be attributed to the same author at various stages in life as both C. LARCHER and A.G. WRIGHT suggest. For a general discussion on the authorship and unity of the book see: C. LARCHER, *Le Livre de la Sagesse ou la Sagesse de Salomon*, Paris: 1983-85, pp. 125-139; D. WINSTON, *The Wisdom of Solomon*, Anchor Bible, vol. 43, New York: 1979, pp. 12-14; A.G. WRIGHT, "The Structure of the Book of Wisdom", *Bib* 48 (1967) 165-184.

[14] E. GÄRTNER, *Komposition*, p. 69-70.

hand, engages in polemics against mystery cults and is more likely to
have had its origins in Alexandria [15]. These observations, however, fail
to explain the presence of typically Greek stylistic constructions in the
first part of Wis (cf. Wis 1:14-15, 2:1-5, 5:9-14).

Even though P. HEINISCH, in his classical commentary on Wis, still
divides the various sections of the book according to theme, it is
particularly worth noting the presentation of the general divisions of the
text [16]. Careful attention to grammatical features and parallelism between sections enabled HEINISCH to focus with greater precision on the
changes of theme between units. The divisions presented in the commentary correspond in large part to the divisions that will be presented
with literary support by the literary critics.

The entire book of Wis is divided into three large sections:

1- 1:1–5:23	Wisdom is the source of temporal and eternal blessing	1:1-15 1:16–2:24 3:1–5:23
2- 6:1–9:18	The praise of wisdom	6:1-21 6:22–9:18
3- 10:1–19:22	The influence of wisdom in history	10:1–12:27 ⟋13:1-9 13:1–15:19⟨ 13:10–15:13 16:1–19:22 ⟍15:14-19

For the most part, HEINISCH explains the divisions of the units in
terms of changes in theme. On occasion, parallelism and grammatical
features are added for the clarification of the units' structures or ties to
other units. For instance, the first two sections are introduced with
parallel exhortations to rulers and kings [17]. Other instances of parallelism between various units are noted throughout the book, but these
observations are not integrated into the study as a principle of literary
organization. HEINISCH notes the parallelism between the two speeches of
the impious in Wis 2 and 5, but unfortunately this observation has no
bearing on the literary division of the units [18]. Similarly, HEINISCH
observes the parallelism between the two contrasts of the just/impious in
the first section and the Israelites/Egyptians in the third section [19].

---

[15] E. GÄRTNER, *Komposition*, p. 71-72.
[16] P. HEINISCH, *Das Buch der Weisheit*, Münster: 1912.
[17] P. HEINISCH, *Das Buch der Weisheit*, p. 111.
[18] "Ihre Rede ist das vollendete Gegenstück zu ihren Ausführungen" (P. HEINISCH,
Das Buch der Weisheit, p. 92).
[19] "Wie der Autor 3,1–5,23 das Los der Guten mit dem der Bösen verglichen hat, so
zieht er in diesem Teile eine Parallele zwischen dem Schicksal der Israeliten und dem der
Ägypter" (P. HEINISCH, *Das Buch der Weisheit*, p. 191).

As for the astute grammatical observations in the commentary, HEINISCH notes, in particular, the linking techniques the author employed to join one unit to another. For example, the author's use of the particles, οὖν and γάρ, is often shown to highlight a deliberate attempt to link succeeding units [20]. Verbal repetitions are noted to a lesser degree as a linking technique between units [21].

Although HEINISCH does not formally regard the literary techniques of the author of Wis as important criteria for the analysis of the organization of the text, the careful grammatical analysis that he employed to support the divisions according to theme already anticipates the strides that will be made by the literary critics.

At the turn of this century, several scholars turned their attention to literary techniques commonly used in Greek poetry and drama which could be uncovered in Wis [22]. These techniques would be analyzed with a view to uncovering strophic or metric patterns. L. MARIÈS, in an ingenious study [23], which built on the works of J.-K. ZENNER [24] and A. CONDAMIN [25], combined the study of Hebrew parallelism and Greek meter in Wis. This study resulted in the presentation of Wis 1-9 as three poems, organized in strophes and verses, which follow a numeric pattern. He notes the combination of Hebrew parallelism and Greek meter, particularly in the first part of the book [26].

---

[20] HEINISCH noted, particularly, how the author of Wis used particles to bind a small unit to a preceding discussion in order to allow for smoother transitions. "Die Partikel οὖν verbindet den Abschnitt mit dem vorhergehenden, zumal mit der Schilderung des Weltgerichts, und hier wiederum besonders mit 5,23d... " (P. HEINISCH, *Das Buch der Weisheit*, pp. 111-112). "Der Abschnitt 17-20 wird durch γάρ an das Vorhergehende angeschlossen" (p. 121, where HEINISCH is referring to 6:17-20).

[21] HEINISCH notes the continuity between cc. 9 and 10 through a repetition. "Die enge Verbindung von Kap. 10 mit Kap. 9 (vgl. 9:18: τῇ σοφίᾳ ἐσώθησαν) spricht dafür, daß die Weisheit, welche in diesem Teile die Guten beschirmt und die Bösen bestraft, die hypostatische Weisheit ist" (P. HEINISCH, *Das Buch der Weisheit*, p. 192).

[22] Early attempts to recognize the use of Greek meter in Wis have not met with a great deal of success. In his work, *Essai sur les origines de la philosophie judéo-alexandrine*, (Toulouse, 1890), H. BOIS identifies Greek metric patterns in a number of verses: Wis 4:15, two hexameters, 14:12,16, a trochaic trimeter, 17:11a, an iambic trimeter. H.St.J. THACKERAY, in an article, "Rhythm in the Book of Wisdom", *JTS* 6 (1905) 232-237, also identifies a frequent use of the final foot of hexameters, p. 235.

[23] L. MARIÈS, "Remarques sur la forme poétique du livre de la Sagesse (1:1–9:17)", *RB* 5 (1908) 251-257.

[24] J.-K. ZENNER, "Der erste Theil des Buches der Weisheit", *ZKT* 22 (1898) 417-431.

[25] A. CONDAMIN, *Le Livre de la Sagesse*, manuscript, 1907, quoted by L. MARIÈS, "Remarques", *RB* (1908) p. 251.

[26] L. MARIÈS, "Remarques", p. 251, "... le Livre de la Sagesse, bien qu'il ait été écrit en grec, a conservé d'une façon remarquable les formes de la poésie hébraïque, notamment le «parallélisme des membres»".

MARIÈS delimits three poems that are constructed in verses of
parallel members: a) a poem on immortality, 1:1–3:12, b) a poem on
divine judgment, 3:13–6:11, c) and a poem on wisdom 6:12–9:17. Each
poem consists of 8 strophes of various lengths. By a verse, MARIÈS
understands a unit of parallel members, usually two, but at times three
members. By a strophe, he understands a number of verses that form a
unit. His criteria for dividing a number of verses into a strophe are vague,
relying at times on theme, on symmetrical numerical patterns or on
repetitions[27]. The three poems would be read by two choruses which
alternate the first two strophes, and recite the third in unison. The three
poems each contain eight strophes (3 + 3 + 2) of various verse lengths
that display an interesting numerical pattern:

	1:1–3:12	3:13–6:11	6:12–9:17
	I II III	I II III	I II
Strophes:			
Poem on immortality:	6, 6, 9,	13, 13, 4,	7, 7, verses
Poem on divine judgment:	7, 7, 4,	13, 13, 9,	6, 6, verses
Poem on wisdom:	9, 9, 10,	18, 18, 8,	9, 9, verses

The first two poems are bound together in their chiastic structure
according to the verse length of the individual strophes, while the third
poem echoes the function of the third strophe, which was to be recited in
unison by the two choruses[28]. The numerical pattern of the strophes
reveals a deliberate balance in this first part of Wis[29].

As impressive as this study appears, there remain several lacunae in
the method employed by MARIÈS which gave rise to these results. The
organization of verses into strophes is achieved through artificial structuring and represents the most serious drawback of the work[30]. For
instance, MARIÈS eliminates verses 2:21 and 6:4-5. Elsewhere the division
follows no clear sense structure other than the number of verses that fits
the pattern (cf. 3:1-7,8-12, 4:11-12, 6:6-11).

---

[27] L. MARIÈS, "Remarques", p. 252.

[28] Whether or not the Book of Wisdom in whole or in part was formally meant to
be delivered orally is debatable. A.G. WRIGHT claims that the oratory style of the first part
is artificial. A.G. WRIGHT, "Wisdom", *The Jerome Biblical Commentary*, Englewood
Cliffs, NJ: 1968, pp.556-568.

[29] In a later work, MARIÈS studied the patterns of rhythm in the Book of Wisdom,
with specific studies of Wis 1:1-6a,6b-10, to show the integration of Hebrew parallelism
and Greek rhythm. L. MARIÈS, "Rythmes quantitatifs dans Le Livre de la Sagesse",
CRAI, 1935, pp. 104-117. The rhythm is based on the quantity of syllables in a stich,
varying from 5 to 7 feet in each stich. However, the use of Greek rhythmic patterns is
quite loose, in that little attention is given to such features as caesurae, hiatus or elisions.
For a critique of this study see C. LARCHER, *Le Livre de la Sagesse*, pp. 87-88.

[30] For a critique of MARIÈS' pattern see A.G. WRIGHT, "The Structure of the Book of
Wisdom", *Bib* 48 (1967) p. 166; C. LARCHER, *Le Livre de la Sagesse*, pp. 87-88.

However, this work had inaugurated a new approach in organizing the structure of Wis, namely the introduction of observable poetic criteria that can be brought to support the division of units according to their theme. It is not without a touch of irony that A.G. WRIGHT criticizes the poetic pattern of MARIÈS' hypothesis for its lack of thematic organization: "The test of any plan is how well it matches the thought", especially since the criterion of theme had been the exclusive means of uncovering the plan of Wis up to that particular time [31].

The numerical balance of the stichic structure of Wis continued to attract scholarly attention. P.W. SKEHAN tried to uncover the author's conscious and deliberate structure of stichic division [32]. A stich here is understood as a given line on a manuscript. Even though various manuscripts divide the lines differently so that the number of lines of Wis differs between 1000 and 1250, the margin of difference is small, much less than for other books in the OT [33]. If the number of stichs is fixed at 1120, then the half way mark in the text at stich 561 corresponds to chapter 11:1, which also marks the primary change in Wis. In this way, Wis contains a balance of two halves with equal numbers of stichs in each. Chapters 1–9 form the first part of the work with 500 stichs. Chapter 10, serves as a transition section to introduce the second part of the book and to make up for the remaining number of 60 stichs to form the balance.

A.G. WRIGHT studied numerical patterns in Wis based on verse structure rather than the line or stichic structure [34]. A verse is understood as a unity of stichs, which follow the pattern of parallelism in Hebrew poetry. For the most part, a verse consists of two stichs but may contain one or three, as is well attested in Hebrew poetry. The key for the progression in the numerical patterns of various units is the "Golden Mean Ratio" [35]. In this ratio the relation of one unit to a larger one stands in the same proportion as the larger unit to the sum of the two $[m/M = M/(m + M)]$. The quotient of the smaller number, divided by the larger, should come close to the number representing the Golden Mean 0.6180 [36].

---

[31] A.G. WRIGHT, "The Structure of the Book of Wisdom", *Bib* 48 (1967) p. 166.

[32] P.W. SKEHAN, "Text and Structure of the Book of Wisdom", *Traditio* 3 (1945).

[33] H.B. SWETE, *An Introduction to the O.T. in Greek*, Cambridge: 1902. For an outline of several tables which compare various stichic enumerations of the books of the O.T. see pp. 346-350.

[34] A.G. WRIGHT, "Numerical Patterns in the Book of Wisdom", *CBQ* 29 (1967) 524-538. WRIGHT had taken the cue to study numerical patterns based on verses rather than stichs from MARIÈS, p. 219.

[35] A.G. WRIGHT, "Numerical Patterns", p. 224.

[36] For a recent work on mathematics in Antiquity see O.A.W. DILKE, *Mathematics and Measurements*, British Museum, London: 1987.

For instance, Wis 1–6:21 = 138 verses; Wis 1–9:1 = 222 verses, Wis 11–19 (minus the digressions) = 138 verses. The two major sections together (1–9:1, 11–19) constitute 360 verses. These three numbers 138/222/360 belong to the pattern: 1,4,5,9,14,23,37,60, where the last three numbers are multiplied by 6. Chapter 10:1–11:1 is a transitional section containing 29 verses. This brings the number of verses of the first half of the book to 251. The digressions in the second half in 11:17–12:22 and in 13:1–15:17 contain 36 and 77 verses respectively. When these are added to the main second half, the total number of verses is 251.

1–6:21	=	138;	1–9:18	=	222;	11–19 (minus digressions)	=	138
			10–11:1			11:17–12:22	=	36
				=	29;	13:1–15:17	=	77
					251			251

Furthermore, the individual units of the first section are divided in a manner so as to create a concentric structure: a,b,c,b',a'. Having used a totally different system of counting the verses, WRIGHT has also arrived at a concentric structure of the first part, though, he did so in a slightly different manner from MARIÈS [37].

1:1-15	=	18 vv	a
1:16–2:24	=	30 vv	b
3:1–4:20	=	42 vv	c
5:1-23	=	30 vv	b'
6:1-21	=	18 vv	a'

In this way, both in the division of particular sections and in the whole, the author was trying to create a formal beauty based on units following a numerical proportion [38].

The evidence that WRIGHT has amassed to support this hypothesis is overwhelming: 21 examples of the Golden Mean ratio. Even though the verses had to be modified slightly from SWETE's versification of the text, the modifications are intelligible. At the least, these numerical patterns

---

[37] L. MARIÈS, "Remarques", p. 251. MARIÈS' division of the verses highlighted the chiastic structure according to the number of stichs of each of the three poems. WRIGHT's division focuses on the concentric structure according to the number of verses in the various units in 1:1–6:21.

[38] The author of Wis had a particular taste for completion which accounts for the number of inclusions employed in the text as well as a taste for proportion which accounts for the care at balancing sections with the ratio of the Golden Mean. "The author had a sense of and a desire for completion and hence repeated at the end of a section a key word from the beginning, and he had a sense of proportion and hence constructed his book on the basis of the Golden Mean" (A.G. WRIGHT, "Numerical Patterns", p. 231).

provide concrete evidence that the author of Wis has exercised great care in the construction and execution of this poetically artistic work [39].

A - 3. Outlining the Book of Wisdom according to its Literary Structure

J.M. REESE directed attention to the literary structure of the Book of Wisdom to find some order in the manifold divisions that had been offered for the main parts of the text [40]. R.H. PFEIFFER recorded 16 different plans for the book [41]. New interest in Wis was further galvanized by the publication of ZIEGLER's new, critical Greek edition of Wis [42], and by a study of the literary structure of the last nine chapters presented in an article by P. BEAUCHAMP [43]. REESE combines the study of the general plan of the book with the structure of individual sections using the literary device of inclusions for delimiting the units.

The main divisions of the book into four parts echo the divisions offered by W. WEBER and E. GÄRTNER. The thematic features of the parts are respected, but the literary device of the inclusion is used to uncover the structure of the units within the parts, particularly the first, "the eschatological book".

Part I	1:1–6:11 + 6:17-21	- the eschatological book
Part II	6:12-16 + 6:22–10:21	- the book of wisdom proper
Part III	11:16–15:19	- a digression in two parts
Part IV	11:1-15 + 16:1–19:22	- seven comparisons

---

[39] It remains true that the manipulation of numerical figures with specific units and with combinations of units to arrive at the Golden Mean Ratio at times may be forced. M. GILBERT critiques two particular combinations. It is unclear why sections 1-2:24 and 5-6:21 are combined except to arrive at the figures 48, 42, 48, 138. M. GILBERT, "Sagesse de Salomon (ou Livre de la Sagesse)", *DBS* 11 (1986) col. 89.

[40] J.M. REESE, "Plan and Structure in the Book of Wisdom", *CBQ* 27 (1965) 391-399.

[41] R.H. PFEIFFER, *History of the New Testament Times*, New York: 1949, pp. 321-322. All these divisions revolve around thematic considerations. PFEIFFER opts for the threefold division that is most common: cc. 1-5, 6-9, 10-19. An issue behind the interest of the structure is the question of the unity of the text, which refers back to the problems of unity raised by GRIMM, WEBER, GÄRTNER. "Whatever division is adopted, no part, in its present form could be separated from what precedes and follows and be regarded as a separate work. And this mutual cohesion of the parts is the chief obstacle to the attribution of the book to more than one author" (p. 323).

[42] J. ZIEGLER, *Sapientia Salomonis*, Septuaginta Vetus Testamentum Graecum, XII,1, Göttingen, 1962.

[43] P. BEAUCHAMP, "Le salut corporel des justes et la conclusion du livre de la Sagesse", *Bib* 45 (1964) 491-526.

Only parts I and IV are studied in some detail. Part I is organized as
a chiasm governed by both theme and key words. The first unit, 1:1-15, is
an exhortation to justice delimited by the inclusion in vv 1:1,15 of the
word, justice. This unit is parallel to the fifth unit, 6:1-11,17-21, delimited
by terms of royalty, kings (6:1) and reign (6:21), and which is an
exhortation to wisdom. Both units are exhortations directed to rulers.
The second unit, 1:16–2:24, is delimited by the phrase "of his part" (τῆς
ἐκείνου μερίδος) referring to the power of Hades and death (1:16, 2:24).
This unit is parallel to the fourth (5:2-23, no inclusion is mentioned), both
of which contain the monologue of the unjust. The central unit, 3:1-5:1, is
delimited by the reference to the just ones (3:1, 5:1), where a two-fold
picture of the fate of the just and the unjust is presented.

REESE presents the organization of Part IV as being governed by
seven sets of comparisons [44]. Each comparison revolves around an object
or event that God uses either to punish or to save. The inclusions that
delimit the various units are not studied in great detail or with precision,
but are presented as an objective means for locating the divisions of the
comparisons.

1) 11:4-14, thirst; 2) 16:1-4, torment; 3) 16:5-15, going upon/ go
forth, 4) 16:6–17:1, rain, hail; 5) 17:2–18:4, enclosed; 6) 18:5-25, de-
stroy/punish, experience; 7) 19:1-13, this final comparison has no
inclusion but contains seven compound words with the prefixes προ- and
προς-.[45]

---

[44] Each comparison includes within the unit a summary statement as to how God
uses an object to punish or reward: 11:5, (11:4-14); 16:2, (16:1-4); 16:10-11, (16:5-15);
16:24, (16:16–17:1); 17:2, (17:2–18:4); 18:8, (18:5-25); 19:4-5, (19:1-13). J.M. REESE,
"Plan", p. 395. These comparisons had been studied from the point of view of
exemplifying the genre of midrash by E. STEIN, "Ein jüdisch-hellenistischer Midrasch über
den Auszug aus Ägypten", *MGWJ* 78 (1934) 558-575. The comparisons within the
diptychs are twofold. Firstly, they express a causal relationship between sin and
punishment, which follows the principle enunciated in 11:16. Secondly, they draw a
contrasting relationship between the punishments against Egypt and the blessings of Israel
which follows the principle enunciated in 11:5 (cf. the outline of the twofold relationship
between sins and plagues and between plagues and blessings derived from the exodus
narrative, M. GILBERT, "Sagesse", *DBS* 11, col. 87).

[45] These series of comparisons are similar in form to the literary genre, syncrisis,
which forms a part of the epideictic genre in Aristotelian rhetoric. REESE mentions
Friedrich FOCKE, ("Synkrisis", *Hermes* 58 (1923) 327-368), as the first scholar to make
reference to this similarity which will ignite further interest for uncovering the literary
form of Wis (REESE, "Plan and Structure", p. 397). Differences between classical forms of
syncrisis and the comparisons in Wis would be quickly noted. Ordinarily, these
comparisons within the genre of syncrisis involve only two elements. I. HEINEMANN, in
"Synkrisis oder äußere Analogie", *TZ* 5 (1948) 241-252, drew a distinction between
internal and external comparisons. He termed the comparisons in Wis as "äußere
Analogie" because of the introduction of an external element in the comparison and
contrast between Egypt and Israel. BEAUCHAMP likewise had noted that in the case of Wis

REESE envisioned the second major digression on false worship (13:1-15:19) as a concentric structure with four parts and a central digression[46].

1) 13:1-9 criticism of nature worship
2) 13:10–14:9 worship of wooden idols
- 14:10–15:6 digression (inclusion with δράω)
3) 15:7-13 cult dealing with clay idols
4) 15:14-19 animal worship

Following the lead from BEAUCHAMP, REESE notes references in this part of the book back to the first section which function as "flashbacks"[47], used either as comparisons or contrasts. The image of "wandering in the desert" in 11:2 refers back to the speech of the impious in 5:7. Similarly there is the contrast between the Israelites being in the hands of the holy prophet (11:3) and the just one expecting to be freed from the hands of the impious (2:18).

Though this article merely touched upon the outline of the literary structure of Wis, its method of employing literary characteristics for determining the structure would continue to direct the subsequent study of the literary structure in Wis. It set a precedent by uncovering three techniques that the author of Wis applied in the work: a) the use of the

---

11-19 the comparisons introduce a third element, namely the activity of God (P. BEAUCHAMP, "Le salut corporel", p. 497).

[46] J.M. REESE, "Plan and Structure", pp. 392-94.
R. CORNELY had divided 13–15 into three major parts:
13:1-9   De praestantiorum creaturarum cultu
13:10–15:6 De cultu idolorum arte ab hominibus confectorum
15:7-19   De luteorum figmentorum et animalium cultu stulto ac funesto.
R. CORNELY, *Commentarius in librum Sapientiae*, Paris: 1910, pp. 458-512.
P. HEINISCH had noted the difficulty of disassociating 15:7-13, which deals with the potter kneading clay into practical utensils and into idols, from the preceding section. Noting literary ties among 13:1, 13:10 and 15:14, he divided the section into three parts:
13:1-9   Die Verehrung der Himmelskörper und der Naturkräfte
13:10–15:13 Der Bilderdienst
15:14-19   In ihren törichtem Wahn dienen die Heiden selbst den Göttern fremder Völker und beten Tiere an
P. HEINISCH, *Das Buch der Weisheit*, Münster: 1912, pp. 249-294.
[47] In a later work, REESE notes the flashback technique of the author of Wis particularly in the second half of the book, cc. 10–19. J.M. REESE, *Hellenistic Influence on the Book of Wisdom and its Consequences*, Rome: 1970, pp. 123-140. In chapter three of this same work, REESE identifies several units of Wis for the purpose of specifying the literary genre which they manifest. REESE organizes these units, according to their style, into four books: the Book of History (11:1-14, 16:1–19:22), the Book of Wisdom (6:12-16, 6:21–10:21), the Book of Eschatology 1:1–6:11, 6:17-20, and the Book of Divine Justice and Human Folly (11:15–15:19).

inclusion as an means of delimiting units, b) the use of parallelism in constructing concentric or parallel structures, c) the use of flashbacks to link various units.

A.G. WRIGHT was quick to employ these insights in a more detailed analysis of the literary structure of the entire book[48]. Using the additional criteria of inclusions, repetitions, and parallelism, WRIGHT presents an outline of the book's literary structure as well as an analysis of individual units. This analysis is consistent with his original scheme of division by verses.

In a short summary statement, WRIGHT presents the general results of the type of literary structures that the author of Wis utilized. Concentric symmetry is applied to three sections: cc. 1–6, 7–8, 13–15; parallel symmetry is used in chapter 9; and finally there is an arrangement which he terms "linear", in which an announced theme of a unit is developed by repetition, as in chapter 10 and in the midrash of Wis 11–19[49]. The main differences in structure from the study of REESE that WRIGHT postulates concern: a) the number of inclusions in the first section, b) the starting point of the last section (from 11:2 instead of 11:1), and c) the organization of the last section, not according to seven diptychs which correspond to the presentation of seven plagues, but rather according to five antithetical diptychs[50].

In general, WRIGHT accepts the concentric structure of the first part, 1:1–6:21, but adds a number of clarifying qualifications. The central section, 3:1–4:20, "hidden counsels of God", does not have an inclusion delimiting the entire unit. Rather, the central section consists of three units delimited by inclusions: a) 3:1-12, on suffering (ἄφρονον, 3:2,12); b) 3:13–4:6, on childlessness (κάρπος, 3:13, 4:5); c) 4:7-20, on early death (τίμιον, 4:8, ἄτιμον, 4:19).

The second part, 6:22–11:1, entitled, "the nature of wisdom and Solomon's request for her", contains four major sections. The first is an introduction (6:22-25). Solomon's speech (7:1–8:21) follows and is arranged concentrically:

---

[48] In two articles, WRIGHT studied the literary structure of parts of Wis and of the entire book. A.G. WRIGHT, "The Structure of Wisdom 11-19", *CBQ* 27 (1965) 28-34. A.G. WRIGHT, "The Structure of the Book of Wisdom", *Bib* 48 (1967) 165-184. It is the second article which is the most significant. In this analysis, WRIGHT built on the work of REESE, modifying it and enlarging the divisions of inclusions and chiastic structures. A model which WRIGHT followed in this study was the literary analysis done on the Letter to the Hebrews by A. VANHOYE. A. VANHOYE, *La structure littéraire de l'épître aux Hébreux*, Paris: 1963, 1975².

[49] A.G. WRIGHT, "Structure", p. 167.

[50] For WRIGHT's outline of the literary structure of Wis see A.G. WRIGHT, "The Structure of the Book of Wisdom", *Bib* 48 (1967) pp. 168-169.

a	7:1-6	8:17-21	a'
b	7:7-12	8:9-16	b'
c	7:13-22 [51]	8:2-8	c'
	d 7:22b–8:1		

The third section (9:1-18), which contains Solomon's prayer for wisdom, is WRIGHT's example of parallel symmetry:

address, petition, motive	9:1-5
general observation	9:6
address, petition, motive	9:7-12
general observation	9:13-18

The fourth section (10:1-11:1) is transitional in that it links the second part, which treats the nature of wisdom, with the final part, which treats God's fidelity to his people in the exodus. It was likely the last part of the book to be written [52]. WRIGHT's main argument for ending this section with 11:1 is thematic. The "holy prophet" refers to Moses precisely with the same instrumental role of salvation depicted in 10:16. Since, throughout 11–19, God acts directly to bring about salvation in the exodus, it would appear logical to place the verse as a conclusion to the section dealing with Israel's heroes. The play on words in 11:1-2 of εὐόδωσεν and διώδευσαν could function as link words between the two parts.

The third part of Wis, "God's fidelity to his people in the exodus" (11:2–19:22), unfolds through a series of five antithetical diptychs, some of which contain digressions that integrate theological reflections into the diptych (diptychs 2,3,5).

11:2-4 serves as an introduction, with 11:5 stating the primary theme of this last part. God employs the very things once used for punishing Egypt to save the Israelites in their need. The first diptych contrasts the plague of the Nile with the water from the rock in the desert (11:6-14). The second contrasts the plague of little animals with the gift of quails (11:15–16:14). This large section contains two main digressions: a) a digression on God's power and mercy, 11:17–12:22, b) a digression on false worship, 13:1–15:17, with a minor digression on the killing serpents in the desert, 16:5-14.

---

[51] Note the different divisions of 7:22 in the critical editions. RAHLF and the versions here follow the Vulgate division where v 22 begins the new section "ἔστιν γὰρ ἐν αὐτῇ". ZIEGLER begins v 22 with the previous stich, "ἡ γὰρ πάντων".

[52] A.G. WRIGHT, "Structure", p. 175.

The second large digression on false worship is organized in a concentric structure:

A) nature worship 13:1-9
B) idolatry

a	introduction	13:10	conclusion	15:14-1	a'
b	carpenter-wooden images	13:11–14:2	potter-clay images	15:7-13	b'
c	apostrophe	14:3-6	apostrophe	15:1-3	c'
	and transition	14:7-11	and transition	15:4-6	

d Origins of idolatry 14:12-31

The third diptych (16:16-29) contrasts the plague of storms with the rain of manna and includes a digression on creation (16:23-29). The fourth contrasts the plague of darkness with the pillar of fire (17:1–18:4). The fifth diptych (18:5–19:21) contrasts the death of the first-born with the exodus and includes two digressions on the plague of death in the desert (18:20-25) and on creation (19:6-21). The destruction of Pharaoh's army in the sea is presented as the completion of the tenth plague.

The two plagues that REESE had delimited as the third and seventh comparisons, which WRIGHT subsumes within his second and fifth diptychs, are the digression on the serpents in the desert, 16:5-14 [53], and the digression on the plague of death in the desert, 18:20-25.

The reason for postulating these five antithetical diptychs as the organizing units of this part, rather than the seven comparisons based on the plagues, is the stylistic introduction given to these five diptychs. The first four employ the preposition, ἀντί (11:6; 16:2; 16:20; 18:3), which functions as the hinge in each diptych. This hinge-word introduces the contrast which exemplifies the theme explicitly stated in 11:5. The fifth diptych does not employ the word, ἀντί, because, in this final diptych, instead of two contrasting events as in the previous, we have one event with two results. The tenth plague of Exod and the destruction of Pharaoh's army in the sea are bound together (cf. 18:5). Finally, verse 19:22 is taken as a succinct conclusion to the entire section.

In terms of presenting the literary structure of Wis, this dense article remains foundational. All the major sections of the work have been delimited through inclusions, repetitions, link words and parallelism. The division of the book into units according to theme is not merely dependent on the interpretation of the thematic units, but is supported through the stylistic and literary techniques employed and easily dis-

---

[53] A.G. WRIGHT, "Structure". Note the typographical error on pages 169 and 182-183 that may cause confusion. Instead of 16:16-29 read 16:15-29; cf. the reference to the same section on p. 177.

cernible in the text. However, just how these units relate to each other, and the internal structure of certain units in themselves will receive a great deal of attention and precision with the following studies.

M. GILBERT clarified the intricate concentric structure of Solomon's prayer in Wis 9 [54], which WRIGHT had classified as exemplifying parallel symmetry. The units parallel to one another in chapter 9 are the following:

$$
\begin{array}{ll}
\text{a 9:1-3} & \text{a' 18} \\
\text{b 4} & \text{b' 17aßb} \\
\text{c 5-6} & \text{c' 13-17a\alpha} \\
\text{d 7-8} & \text{d' 12} \\
\text{e 9} & \text{e' 10c-11} \\
& \text{f 10ab}
\end{array}
$$

Moreover, the unit c' is concentric within itself:

$$
\begin{array}{ll}
\text{a 13} & \text{a' 16c-17a\alpha} \\
\text{b 14} & \text{b' 16ab} \\
& \text{c 15}
\end{array}
$$

In the central unit, 9:10ab, stands the explicit request for God to send wisdom from the holy heavens and from God's holy throne. This request for God's wisdom on the part of Solomon is enclosed at both extremities by the recognition of the fundamental importance of God's wisdom for humanity. God has created humanity through wisdom (9:1) and it is through wisdom that humanity is saved (9:18).

The prayer of Solomon in Wis is elaborated and developed from the dream of Solomon in 1 Kgs 3:1-15 and the nocturnal vision of the Lord to Solomon in 2 Chr 1 [55]. Since GILBERT compared only the request for wisdom from the dream narrative in 1 Kgs 3:1-15 (vv 6-9) with the prayer for wisdom in Wis (c. 9), he did not note the concentric structure of the dream narrative as a whole. As a result, he did not recognize a structural relationship between Wis 9 and either of the pericopes of 1 Kgs or 2 Chr [56].

---

[54] M. GILBERT, "La structure de la prière de Salomon (Sg 9)", *Bib* 51 (1970) 301-331.

[55] GILBERT notes that the author of Wis has used both accounts in reconstructing the prayer of Solomon with a slight preference for 1 Kgs. "Au terme de cette analyse rapide, apparaît plus nettement le rapport entre Sg 9 et 1 R 3//2 Ch 1: Sg 9 tient de l'un et de l'autre" (M. GILBERT, "La structure (Sg 9)", *Bib* 51 (1970) p. 326). From Chronicles the explicit request for 'wisdom' is taken up as well as the use of the double request (1 Chr 1:9,10; Wis 9:4,10a). However, the difference in Wis is the emphasis on God's wisdom. From Kings the author integrates into the prayer the references to Solomon's humility and vulnerability (1 Kgs 3:7-8), which are expanded to include the vulnerability and fragility of all humanity (Wis 9:5-6,13-17).

[56] "...la division de 1 R 3 est bipartite... . Le schème que nous pensons avoir détecté

With this incontrovertible evidence of the concentric structure of Wis 9, it becomes lucidly apparent that the first half of Wis is constructed in units manifesting a concentric structure (Wis 1–6, 7–8, and 9). Wis 10 functions as a transitional section and does not manifest clear indications of either concentric or parallel structures.

In his doctoral thesis treating the second major digression against false worship, M. GILBERT analyzed in detail the literary structure of Wis 13–15 [57]. The concentric structure which REESE had hinted at, and which WRIGHT developed in more detail, is clarified with greater precision. The entire section, Wis 13-15, is divided into three parallel units, each dealing with a particular kind of idolatry [58].

1 - 13:1-9 philosophers incur slight blame
2 - 13:10–15:13 idolaters as well as their idols are severely condemned
3 - 15:14-19 the enemies of Israel who worship both idols and odious animals are most severely condemned.

The first unit is delimited by the inclusion, ἴσχυσαν, εἰδέναι (13:1b,9a). It is parallel to the second unit through the association between μάταιοι μέν (13:1) and ταλαίπωροι δέ (13:10) and to the third unit with πάντες δὲ ἀφρονέστατοι (15:14) [59]. The second unit is tightly

---

en Sg 9 est totalement différent", (M. GILBERT, "La structure (Sg 9)", p. 324). The relationship between Wis 9 and 1 Kgs 3 becomes even tighter, however, if one recognizes the concentric structure of Solomon's dream in 1 Kgs 3.

$$
\begin{array}{llll}
a & 3:4 & & a'\ 3:15b \\
& b\ 3:5 & & b'\ 3:15a \\
& \quad c\ 3:6 & & c'\ 3:14 \\
& \quad\quad d\ 3:7\text{-}8 & & d'\ 3:13 \\
& \quad\quad\quad e\ 3:9 & e'\ 3:11\text{-}12 \\
& \quad\quad\quad\quad f\ 3:10
\end{array}
$$

Compare this structure to the treatment of the chiastic structure of 1 Kgs 3 which H. KENIK presents (H. KENIK, *The Design for Kingship: The Deuteronomistic Narrative Technique in 1 Kings 3:4-15*, Chico, CA: 1983, pp. 41-56). In her study, KENIK presents the chiastic structure of the dream narrative as two sets of inclusions enclosing a central focus. Solomon's request and God's response are considered the central focus. She does not treat the central verse, "It pleased the Lord that Solomon had asked this" (3:10) with any importance and refers to it simply as a transitional phrase (p. 44). However, its centrality does correspond to a resolution of the tension produced with Solomon's requests. The Lord's pleasure confers value and importance to the content of Solomon's requests. It is precisely this feature of "pleasing the Lord" (καὶ ἤρεσεν ἐνώπιον κυρίου...), which also is taken up in Wis 9 in the use of the adjective, ἀρεστός 9:9,10,18. Solomon wishes to know what is pleasing to God, and wisdom will guarantee such knowledge.

[57] M. GILBERT, *La critique des dieux*, AnBib 53, Rome: 1973.
[58] M. GILBERT, *La critique des dieux*, p. 253.
[59] M. GILBERT, *La critique des dieux*, pp. 2, 253.

constructed concentrically, with the images of the carpenter and the potter constituting the outer inclusion. The third unit begins with an introduction (15:14), which qualifies and identifies the guilty and proceeds with two explanatory motifs, parallel to each other. The parallelism is designated by ὅτι καί (15:15a) and by καί (15:18a)[60]. The section is a critique of false worship which follows a crescendo from the less blameworthy, the philosophers, to the most foolish of all, the Egyptians with their animal worship.

The central concentric unit corresponds in large part to the concentric structure envisaged by WRIGHT, but again with clarifying precision[61].

  a 13:10-19 gold, silver, stone, wooden idols, - carpenter
  b 14:1-10 calling upon God, history of salvation, transition
    c 14:11-31 - punishment of idols
                - invention and result of idolatry
                - punishment of idolatry
  b' 15:1-6 calling upon God, history of salvation, transition
  a' 15:7-13 clay idols - potter

Just as the three units follow a quantitative order in terms of length (short, long, short), so too does the central unit follow the reverse quantitative order (long, short, long, short, long). An order of decreasing value of the material from which idols are formed can be discerned: gold, silver, clay. However, GILBERT does not consider the progression absolute because of the repetition of stone and wooden idols in the central unit (14:21).

In two separate articles, F. PERRENCHIO studied the minutiae of the literary units of the first two chapters within the context of 1–6:21[62]. These studies built on the results of the literary analyses by REESE and WRIGHT in which the concentric structure of the first six chapters was highlighted. In particular, PERRENCHIO notes the importance of determining the limits of each unit not simply by theme but by the author's use of literary techniques[63].

The concentric structure of the first six chapters, as projected by WRIGHT, is accepted in its general outline. But the structures of the units

---

[60] M. GILBERT, *La critique des dieux*, p. 225.

[61] M. GILBERT, *La critique des dieux*, p. 254.

[62] F. PERRENCHIO, "Struttura e analisi letteraria di Sapienza 1,1-15", *Sales* 37 (1975) 289-325; "Struttura e analisi letteraria di Sapienza 1,16–2,24 e 5,1-23", *Sales* 43 (1981) 3-43.

[63] F. PERRENCHIO, "Struttura Sapienza 1,1-15", pp. 289-292.

themselves are studied in greater detail to uncover both their internal structure and the relationship between the various units:

1:1-15
1-5   parenetic
6-10   doctrinal
11-15 parenetic

6:1-21
1-11   parenetic
12-20 doctrinal
21   parenetic

1:16–2:24
1:16   introduction
2:1-5   doctrinal / philosophy
2:6-21a   parenetic / praxis
2:21b-24 comment

5:1-23
1-2   introduction
3-8   narrative / praxis
9-14   doctrinal / philosophy
15-23   comment

3:1–4:20
a 3:1-9   the just   / narrative
b 3:10-12 the impious   / narrative
c 3:13-15 sterility + virtue / doctrinal
d 3:16-19 posterity + sin   / doctrinal
c' 4:1-2   sterility + virtue / doctrinal
d' 4:3-6   posterity + sin   / doctrinal
a' 4:7-15   the just   / narrative
b' 4:16-20 the impious   / narrative [64]

Even within the smaller units concentric or parallel structures are detectable. An interesting analysis is done on the concentric structure of the very first unit (1:1-5):

$$a = 1 \qquad\qquad a' = 5$$
$$b = 2 \qquad b' = 4$$
$$c = 3$$

Verses 1:2,4 compare and contrast in positive and negative terms divine action and human action:

divine action-positive
1:2 εὑρίσκεται
human action-positive
1:4 εἰς κακότεχνον ψυχήν

human action-negative
τοῖς μὴ πειράζουσιν αὐτόν
divine action-negative
οὐκ εἰσελεύσεται

Not all of the units and their structures which PERRENCHIO presents are equally convincing. This is particularly the case in the rather surprising break between 1:10 and 1:11. WRIGHT considered verses 6-11

---

[64] F. PERRENCHIO, "Struttura Sapienza 1,1-15", p. 307.

to be a unit based on the inclusion of the word, γλώσσης.[65]. PERRENCHIO offers several arguments for dividing the two verses into separate units. Verses 11-13 present a formal, external, concentric structure, based on the type of symmetry employed in each pair of stichs. 1:11ab is formulated in concentric symmetry, 1:11cd and 1:12 in parallel, and 1:13 is again formulated in concentric symmetry. There is a change between doctrinal and parenetic discourse. The words, γογγυσμῶν/γογγυσμόν, in 1:10b and 1:11a function as link words, joining the two units.

However, the symmetry of v 11 is too loose to build a convincing argument upon. The change between doctrinal and parenetic discourse is a matter of thematic division which is open to other formulations[66]. And the repetition of γογγυσμόν could equally well be an emphatic repetition that serves to bring the unit to a closure, rather than a link word that joins two separate units[67].

In the second article, PERRENCHIO compares the vocabulary of the parallel units of the speech of the impious[68]. More than 23 words occur in these two sections and not elsewhere in the first part. In addition to the general concentric structure of the first part, these two parallel sections of the speech of the impious are parallel concentrically[69].

a	2:1-5	- a'	5:8-13
b	2:6-11	- b'	5:6-7
c	2:12-20	- c'	5:4-5

The literary devices of concentric and parallel symmetry permeate the first section of Wis. The author has taken great care to build not only the larger units into parallel sections, but even the individual smaller

---

[65] A.G. WRIGHT, "Structure", p. 170.

[66] Cf. the critique of PERRENCHIO's division between verses 1:10 and 1:11 in P. BIZZETI, *Il Libro della Sapienza*, Brescia: 1984, pp. 51-53.

[67] It is important to note the various functions of repetitions in narrative, discourse or poetry in order not to confuse the precise nature of the repetition.

1   *emphatic repetition* - highlights a word or idea within one or more units
2   *inclusion* - a repetition of a word or image that introduces and closes a literary unit by theme
3   *linking repetitions* - repeat a word or phrase to maintain unity, or to compare and contrast (flash-backs, link words)
4   *epanalepsis*, where a phrase or word is repeated to conclude a sentence

When a repetition is noted, obviously the function of the repetition must be determined in order to assess its relationship to the particular unit. Otherwise, repetitions may falsely be attributed to a different function. For instance, if within a unit the same word is continuously repeated for emphasis, it is hardly likely that the occurrence of the repetition of itself is a sign of an inclusion, a flash-back or a link word.

[68] F. PERRENCHIO, "Struttura Sapienza 1,16-2,24 e 5,1-23", pp. 31-34.

[69] F. PERRENCHIO, "Struttura Sapienza 1,16-2,24 e 5,1-23", p. 35.

units, where pairs of stichs and cola are parallel; symmetry was a favorite technique for our author. For the interpretation of individual units and for the dynamic of the argument as a whole, the literary structures and techniques used by the author provide a valuable lens through which to perceive the unity of the argument.

In two dissertations, the literary structures of Wis were taken as a starting point for interpreting the text. U. OFFERHAUS studied the literary structures of the entire book in order to interpret the intention of the author in the various units[70]. P. BIZZETI studied the literary structures in order to determine the literary genre of the entire work[71]. In both cases, the overall structure presented by WRIGHT is accepted with partial changes and clarifications. The changes to the structure are not always totally convincing. But what is by now accepted as clear and indisputable in these works is the enormous aid that the literary structure of Wis presents for the interpretation of the text. In presenting the literary structure of Wis, which these two works cover, I will limit my scope to the literary analysis of the first part of Wis (Wis 1-6).

The division of the first part of Wis, which OFFERHAUS presents, departs in several details from the majority of previous analyses. For OFFERHAUS, the entire first section ends in 6:8 and contains three main parts[72].

$$
\begin{array}{ll}
\text{1:1-11} & \text{1:(12-15)16--3:12} \\
\text{1:(12-15)16--5:23} \quad\diagdown & \text{3:13--4:19} \\
\text{6:1-8} & \text{4:20--5:23}
\end{array}
$$

The chiastic structure of this first part (1-6:8), which previous scholars uncovered, is somewhat suppressed in the analysis of OFFERHAUS. Instead of the concentric structure of five units, he presents the central

---

[70] U. OFFERHAUS, *Komposition und Intention der Sapientia Salomonis*, Diss. Bonn: 1981.

"Die folgende Untersuchung ist so angelegt, daß sie nacheinander die drei Hauptteile der Sap.Sal. in der Abgrenzung von 1,1–6,8; 6,9–9,18 und 10,1–19,22 zum Gegenstand hat, und zwar so, daß sie in einem ersten, stärker analytisch orientierten Arbeitsgang die Komposition eines jeden Hauptteils erarbeitet und in einem weiteren, mehr synthetisch ausgerichteten Rückblick auf den jeweiligen Hauptteil die Kompositionsmittel, die Elemente der literarischen Rhetorik und die Funktion der einzelnen Teile innerhalb größerer Abschnitte und letztlich innerhalb des ganzen Buches beschreibt" (p. 28).

[71] "Secondo quanto indicato sopra, non si può risolvere il problema del genere letterario se non collegandolo a una attenta analisi del testo a livello di struttura letteraria" (P. BIZZETI, *Il Libro*, p.49).

[72] U. OFFERHAUS, *Komposition und Intention*, pp. 54-55.

section as containing a general parallel structure and an internal chiastic structure.

$$
\begin{array}{ll}
1{:}16{-}2{:}24 & -\ 4{:}20{-}5{:}14 \\
3{:}1{-}9 & -\ 5{:}15f \\
3{:}10{-}12 & -\ 5{:}17{-}23 \\[1em]
\text{a}\ \ 2{:}1{-}5 & -\ \text{a'}\ 5{:}9{-}13 \\
\text{b}\ \ 2{:}6{-}9(10f) & -\ \text{b'}\ 5{:}6{-}8 \\
\text{c}\ \ 2{:}(10f)12{-}20 & -\ \text{c'}\ 5{:}4\,^{73}.
\end{array}
$$

It was unfortunate that OFFERHAUS did not take into account the study of PERRENCHIO. To end the first part of the book at 6:8 overlooks the grammatical structure of the section encased in 6:1-21. The main reason for his postulating a division between the first two parts of the book at 6:8 is the change from indirect speech in the first section to direct speech in the second section[74]. However, the change to the first person, properly speaking, takes place only in 6:22 with the verb, ἀπαγγελῶ. This change to direct speech in the first person is simply prepared for by the possessive pronoun, μου, in 6:9,11. Not only is there the inclusion, βασιλεῖς-βασιλεύσετε, noted by WRIGHT, but the entire unit is logically held together through four instances of the adverb, οὖν (6:1a,9,11,21). Verse 6:9 also echoes 6:1 through the repetition of the verb μαθεῖν[75].

---

[73] Cf. this structure of the units 2:1-20 and 5:4-13 with that of PERRENCHIO (F. PERRENCHIO, "Struttura Sapienza 1,16–2,24 e 5,1-23", p. 35). Apparently, they had both uncovered this structure independently.

[74] "Das im Vergleich zum ersten Hauptteil überraschend Neue ist die Tatsache, daß der Verfasser im zweiten Hauptteil mit eigenen Worten und mit seiner Person hervortritt und sich als der König und Weisheitslehrer Salomo zu erkennen gibt. So ist es die Ich-Form, die den Hauptteil ab 6:9 beherrscht und die zur Ansetzung einer tiefen Zäsur genenüber dem ersten nötigt" (U. OFFERHAUS, *Komposition und Intention*, p. 71).

Another reason for deducing a change in style is the change from the threatening punishments which followed the opening and closing address to kings and rulers (1:1-5, 6:1-8) to a language of invitation, where positive attributes of wisdom are highlighted (6:9-11).

But the language of invitation based on the positive qualities of wisdom precisely offers the counterpoint to the threat of punishment within the concluding exhortation. The solicitation not to transgress is also present in verse 6:9, μὴ παραπέσητε, and positive qualities of wisdom and God are not altogether lacking in the opening exhortation, (cf. 1:1-2). It remains true that the general interest of the first section is to inspire justice and love of wisdom by presenting the negative results of folly, and the second part inspires justice and love of wisdom through the positive attributes of wisdom. But such a general difference is not sufficient to divide units purely on thematic grounds. The introduction of positive aspects of wisdom within the final exhortation prepares the reader for the second part, the eulogy of wisdom.

[75] F. PERRENCHIO, "Struttura, Sapienza 1,1-15", p. 292.

For BIZZETI, the main purpose of clarifying the literary structure of
the Book of Wisdom, in its single parts and in its entirety, was to
determine the literary genre[76]. This work presents us with the most
detailed analysis of the literary structure of the various units. Where
BIZZETI is in complete agreement with previous analyses of the literary
structure, as is the case for GILBERT's treatment of Wis 13–15, no detailed
study of the unit is presented and reference is simply made to the
accepted study. But this has still left most units to be subject matter for
analysis in the work[77].

BIZZETI's literary analysis of the first six chapters sheds new light on
certain procedures and techniques that the author of Wis employs in the
construction of the work. One important technique which BIZZETI
highlights is the author's penchant for linking sections together by means
of transitional units. This will be an important technique to comprehend,
for it explains, at least in part, some of the numerous difficulties that
scholars have had in delimiting the units, as well as the variety of
structures and divisions that have been proposed. A summary of
BIZZETI's division of the first part will permit us to locate rapidly the
transitional sections[78].

---

[76] In cc. 3 and 4, BIZZETI concludes that the genre which Wis follows corresponds, in
most aspects, with the epideictic style of the encomium which praises rather than exhorts
(P. BIZZETI, *Il Libro*).

[77] An unpublished manuscript representing the results of GILBERT's study of the
entire Book of Wisdom is employed throughout BIZZETI's study. This work can now be
consulted in its publication in *DBS*, "Sagesse de Salomon (ou Livre de la Sagesse)", Vol.
11, Paris: 1986, cols. 58-119.

[78] P. BIZZETI, *Il Libro*, p. 65.

```
A   1:1-5
    1:6-12

    1:13-16                                  1:13-15
B   2:1-20        2:17-20  ⎞ ⎞              1:16–2:1a ⎞
    2:21-24       2:21-24  ⎟ ⎟                        ⎟
                           ⎟ ⎟                        ⎟
    3:1-9         3:1-9    ⎟ /                        ⎟
    3:10-12       3:11     ⎟                          ⎟
    3:13-15                ⎞                          ⎟
    3:16-19       3:17     ⎟                          ⎟
C   4:1-2                  ⎟                          ⎟
    4:3-6                  ⎟                          ⎟
    4:7-16        4:18     /                          ⎟
    4:17-20       4:17-20  ⎞                          ⎟
                           ⎟ ⎞                        ⎟
    5:1-3         5:2b     ⎟ ⎟                        ⎟
B'  5:4-13        5:4-7    ⎟ ⎟                        ⎟
    5:14-23                / /                        ⎟

    6:1-11                                            ⎟
A'  6:12-16                                           ⎟
    6:17-21                                           ⎟
    6:22-25                                  6:22-25  /
```

Two transitional units that merit particular attention in this division of the text are: a) 6:22-25 and b) 1:12,13-16. This technique of linking various units is notably present also in the three middle units of the concentric structure, as is evident in the paradigm above.

a) 6:22-25

BIZZETI is the first to associate the unit, 6:22-25, with the preceding units. However, it should be noted that he is insistent on pointing out that the unit has the double function of concluding the first section and introducing the eulogy of wisdom in the second section[79]. As a dense, transitional unit, 6:22-25 picks up the thread of various images from the first part. To begin with, there is a parallel between 1:14 (σωτήριοι αἱ γενέσεις τοῦ κόσμου) and 6:24 (πλῆθος δὲ σοφῶν σωτηρία κόσμου). Only in these two cases does σωτηρία occur in connection with κόσμος. The term, φθόνος, denoting the adversary's envy in 2:24, is taken up in 6:23, the only such occurrences in the entire book. The term, μυστήρια, referring to the mysteries of God in 2:22, is parallel to 6:22. And finally the rare term, ἀφθαρσία, which is never used elsewhere in the LXX, occurs only at 2:23 and 6:19.

---

[79] "I vv. 6,22-25 dunque hanno una duplice funzione: chiudere la prima parte e aprire la seconda, in notevole continuità con la prima" (P. BIZZETI, Il Libro, p. 65).

BIZZETI unfortunately does not discuss the issue of the change of discourse to the first person. This is an important rhetorical technique for denoting a change in perspective. It outweighs, I believe, the echoing of previous terms and images in the unit for determining its proper relationship to other units. The unit operates well as the introduction to the second part of the book, while maintaining its transitional function by echoing terms from the first part.

b) 1:12,13-16

OFFERHAUS had already noted the linking characteristics of these verses [80], but BIZZETI clarifies their transitional function with greater precision. Though he accepts the general inclusion achieved in the parallel words, δικαιοσύνη, (1:1,15), he notes how verses 1:13-16 reveal interesting ties with 2:21-24. Verses 1:13-14 have parallel elements to 2:23-24: ὅτι ὁ θεός, ἐποίησεν, 1:13, 2:23; ἔκτισεν, 1:14, 2:23; κόσμος, 1:14, 2:24; and θάνατος, 1:12,13; 2:20,24. Both statements in 1:16–2:1a and 2:21-22 formulate the author's judgment on the impious and on their false reasoning. Verse 12 constitutes the link between 1-11 and 13-15. Verse 12 is bound to the unit 13-15 by the link words θάνατος and ὄλεθρος. The series of imperatives in 1-11 is completed in verse 12, where it reaches the significant number seven [81].

BIZZETI's analysis highlights the dynamic linking techniques that the author of Wis employs throughout the work. The various units are not rigidly cut pieces that fit a clearly defined puzzle [82]. The units flow into one another, building a momentum with a poetic sense that is particularly acute in the first half of the book. This dynamic structure, which is at the heart of the author's poetic sensibility to concentrate images in parallel fashion, must be tapped for a critical and synthetic appreciation of the theological import of the work [83]. The literary structure of the various units and of the work as a whole provide an objective literary context for

---

[80] U. OFFERHAUS, *Komposition*, p. 32.

[81] P. BIZZETI, *Il Libro*, pp. 52-53.

[82] Cf. BIZZETI's critique of PERRENCHIO's detailed analysis that tends to view the units as blocks in a puzzle, P. BIZZETI, *Il Libro*, p. 51, n. 7. Instead of conceiving the structure as rigid blocks, BIZZETI uncovers a structure that is pliable, dynamic and closely knit. "Infatti fin da queste prime righe appare chiaro che il nostro autore non ha compiuto alcune scelte univoche a proposito della struttura, ma con una geniale flessibilità e capacità di intreccio fa svolgere ad alcuni versetti una doppia funzione: di chiusa di un brano e di apertura su quello successivo" (p. 53).

[83] "Con queste brevi pagine, che mostrano il risvolto interpretativo dell'analisi strutturale, risalta già meglio l'importanza della medesima: la determinazione dei temi principali e delle concatenazioni non può essere lasciata *soltanto* alla sensibilità del lettore. La struttura emersa fornisce indizi oggettivi sia per comprendere l'unità del libro sia per scoprire i primari interessi teologici dell'autore" (P. BIZZETI, *Il Libro*, p. 111).

exploring with greater precision the theological nuances of particular images and ideas seminal in the work [84].

In response to his original question, BIZZETI proposes the epideictic genre of the encomium, following BEAUCHAMP [85] and GILBERT [86], as the literary form which best exemplifies the discourse of Wis. In this, BIZZETI differs from REESE who suggested the didactic method of the protreptic genre (J.M. REESE, *Hellenistic*). The three general forms of Aristotelian rhetoric are derived from the three essential forms of judgment: a) judging the past, the subject being the judge, forensic; b) judging the present, the subject being the spectator, epideictic; c) judging the future, the subject being the governor, deliberative. Protreptic discourse is didactic and persuasive, belonging to the method of deliberative discourse, whereas the encomium praises and entertains and belongs more to epideictic discourse. For BIZZETI, then, the genre of Wis is not essentially an exhortation but rather a praise of wisdom which, of course, even according to Aristotelian rhetoric, includes exhortative elements: [87]

> E così risalta come non sia il «futuro» il tempo del nostro libro. Quello dell'autore è un osanna, un canto, una lode, che sorge dall'attenta meditazione dei tempi della fine già operanti sotterraneamente nel presente (cap. 2-6), illuminata e sorretta dalla contemplazione delle grandi opere che la sapienza ha compiuto nella storia di salvezza. Il massimo consiglio che viene dato è in fondo quello di chiedere la sapienza (9,4.10.17) per godere di essa (P. BIZZETI, *Il Libro*, p. 157).

A - 4.   Conclusion: literary structure as a context for interpretation

This short history of the search for the structure of Wis permits us to clarify a few fundamental issues for the interpretation of this poetic work. The initial method (represented by the commentary attributed to

---

[84] For a summary analysis of Wisdom's literary structure see M. GILBERT, "Sagesse", *DBS* 11, cols. 65-77.

[85] P. BEAUCHAMP, *De libro Sapientiae Salomonis*, cursus in P.I.B., Rome: 1963, manuscript.

[86] M. GILBERT, "Sagesse", *DBS* 11, cols. 77-87.

[87] For a critique of BIZZETI's analysis of the literary genre of Wis, see D. WINSTON's review in *CBQ* 48 (1986) 525-527. WINSTON is essentially in agreement with the general tenor of epideictic discourse in Wis and its reflection of the encomium. However, because of our lack of extant sources which would provide examples of the theories regarding both protreptic and epideictic discourse, he concludes that the issue of Wisdom's genre necessarily must remain open. "It is thus extremely difficult to determine whether Wis is an epideictic composition with an admixture of protreptic, or essentially a protreptic with a considerable element of epideictic" (p. 527).

BONAVENTURE) of organizing the work according to perceived themes
endured until the rise of literary criticism. It offered a global perception
of the work, conceived as a unity of three major parts (1–5, 6–10, 11–19).
In its general outline, this original thematic structure of the work has
proven to be true, even under the scrutiny of literary analysis. However,
the literary analysis has not only clarified the delimitations of the larger
units, but has brought about a greater focus on the relationships between
the smaller units as well.

The organization of the work according to literary units does not
replace the criterion of theme. We have seen how inclusions, symmetry,
repetitions and grammatical features permit the scholar to clarify the
thematic interest of the author in a given unit. Moreover the relationship
between units, the development from one unit to another through
flashbacks, the re-echoing of images and ideas, all permit the literary
critic to follow the dynamic of the argument. In other words, the analysis
of the literary structure of Wis provides a method for uncovering the
theme of the units with greater precision and with an eye to highlighting
the dynamism embodied in the themes.

Analysis of the literary structure is indispensable in a work such as
Wis for uncovering the theological import of its specific terms and ideas.
Working within the movements of the literary structure provides fertile
ground for contacting the author's poetic sensibility. It is not enough to
study the meaning of death and life in this work in terms of philology or
in terms of comparison and contrast with OT and Hellenistic contexts.
The nuances, ambiguities and meaning of these rich references to life and
death in Wis must be understood, finally, in terms of the dynamic of the
work itself.

CHAPTER TWO

THE LITERARY STRUCTURE OF WIS 1–6:21

B - 1. Introduction: the poetic sensibility of the Wis author

The poetic artistry of Wis goes far beyond the employment of external verse features such as parallelism and figures of speech. But to specify more concretely the ramifications of the achievement of poetic art in Wis by the standards of literary criticism is not an easy task. Wis is a complex literary artifact. There is literally no other work quite like it in the Scriptures [1]. A few preliminary clarifications of the poetic style employed in Wis will render the terminology less ambiguous, while at the same time permitting greater precision in locating the particular functions of the work's poetic style.

Wis does not fit well into the dichotomy of prose and poetry. Its rhythm cannot be reduced to Greek metric patterns [2]. Nor is the concept of rhythmic prose applicable to the entire work, though it may describe the style of certain passages (Wis 8:19-21, 10:8-10 and the latter parts of the book) [3]. LARCHER explains the complexity of the style employed in the work by the author's varied cultural background. The author imitated the verse parallelism of Hebrew poetry and the prosodic style of Greek rhetoric in fashion at the time, which was similar to rhythmic prose employing cadence. Nonetheless, the overall impression remains rather that of a poetic work which includes passages of a freer verse style [4]. But

---

[1] J.M. REESE comments on the complexity of the style and contents of Wis that summarizes quite succinctly the reason for the difficulties interpreters face in their approach to the work. "Wis. is not a popular book. In fact, some commentators dismiss it as a sophisticated scholastic exercise of little contemporary value. Why did the author combine such a variety of topics and methods into a single writing? Wis. includes moral exhortations, philosophical reflection, apocalyptic threats and promises, an aretalogy of Lady Wisdom, a presentation of the Exodus miracles in the form of an elaborate syncrisis that contrasts God's dealings with his people and the pagans" (J.M. REESE, "Can Paul Ricoeur's Method Contribute to Interpreting the Book of Wisdom?", [*La Sagesse de l'Ancien Testament*, ed. M. GILBERT, BETL 51, Louvain-Gembloux: 1979] p. 389).

[2] C. LARCHER, *Le Livre de la Sagesse*, pp. 86-87.

[3] C. LARCHER, *Le Livre de la Sagesse*, p. 89.

[4] "Incontestablement, l'auteur a voulu composer une œuvre poétique, en imitant la poésie biblique et en hellénisant celle-ci. Il adopte, dès le début, la forme extérieure des

the effect of poetic mastery in Wis is enhanced through the internal technique of metaphorical language and not only through the external verse techniques of parallelism, rhythm, and flashbacks.

The distinctions and insights of R. JACOBSON and P. RICŒUR into the theory of literary functions are particularly illuminating for understanding the poetic function of images in Wis. The poetic function of imagery in Wis points to a device that goes beyond the dichotomy of prose and poetry to the use of metaphoric language.

In a famous closing article presented at a convention between linguists and literary critics, JACOBSON synthesized the functions of language within a literary work [5]. To the main constituents in the structure of discourse correspond a unique function of language:

                              context (REFERENTIAL)
                              message (POETIC)
        addresser (EMOTIVE)   addressee (CONATIVE)
                              contact (PHATIC)
                              code   (METALINGUAL)

The poetic function tends to focus on the message for its own sake. Though this function is necessarily present in all forms of verbal art, the density of its use is particular to poetic works. The poetic function promotes the 'palpability of signs', which deepens the fundamental dichotomy between signs and objects through ambiguity, but generates manifold possibilities [6].

P. RICŒUR qualifies and elaborates on JACOBSON's presentation of the poetic function in verbal art [7]. The poetic function in literary works does not abolish altogether the referent, that is the context and the world of the text. Rather, the suspension of the referential function of *ordinary language* in poetry is a negative condition for the liberation of another referential dimension of language. This suspension is effected by the

---

vers hébraïques et celle-ci réapparaît sans cesse dans les développements d'allure plus libre, apparentés dans une certaine mesure au style périodique, et que certains critiques traitent précisément comme de la prose" (C. LARCHER, *Le Livre de la Sagesse*, p. 90). Similarly, ALONSO SCHÖKEL, describes the artistry of the poetic achievement as a symbiosis of Hebrew and Alexandrian traditions. "La simbiosis de una tradición hebrea con una alejandrina engendra una obra original, a veces recargada y reiterativa, artificiosa, con alardes de artesenía estilística, rica en sorpresas y agudezas de ingenio" (L. ALONSO SCHÖKEL, *Ecclesiastes y Sabiduría*, Madrid: 1974, p. 75).

[5] R. JACOBSON, "Linguistics and Poetics", [*Style in Language*, ed. T.A. SEBEOK, Cambridge: 1960] 350-377.

[6] See R. JACOBSON, "Linguistics and Poetics", pp. 356-358. JACOBSON comments that ambiguity is a particular characteristic of poetry. "Ambiguity is an intrinsic, inalienable character of any self-focused message, briefly a corollary feature of poetry" (p. 370).

[7] P. RICŒUR, "Biblical Hermeneutics", *Semeia* 4 (1975) 29-145.

metaphorical process in poetry, which has the power of redefining reality. It is the use of metaphor in its contrasts, transformations and ambiguities that challenges readers to move from first level associations to second level associations of the projected world in the text [8].

The distinction between these two modes of referential language is grounded in two distinct ideas inherent in the notion of meaning: a) the sense, which is the ideal objective content of a term, b) the reference, which is the term's claim to truth [9]. "It is the function of poetic language to weaken the first order reference of ordinary language, in order to allow this second-order reference to come forth [10]." Poetic language does not purport to present to readers a-world-already-there, as does descriptive language. The world that is to be interpreted in a poetic text is a proposed world that readers might inhabit, where readers may project their own possibilities [11].

The further distinction that RICŒUR draws between rhetorical and poetic language on the one hand and poetic and religious language on the other also elucidates the issue of persuasion in Wis. Persuasion is the intention behind rhetorical language, whereas presentation is the intention behind poetic language. Religious language is a type of poetic language because it offers modes of redescribing life. However, the difference is in the total claim that religious language makes on its readers. Religious language insinuates what RICŒUR calls the 'still more' which intensifies every project in the discourse. With its limit-metaphors, religious language intensifies through paradox. "It prevents us from converting religious discourse into entirely political discourse, and forbids

---

[8] The idea of 'ordinary language' poses a difficulty for definition. This term of RICOEUR refers to the first level of meaning that words and terms communicate. Ordinary language would be analogous to JACOBSON's notion of metalanguage which is contrasted to poetic language (R. JACOBSON, "Linguistics and Poetics", p. 358), or to language exemplifying 'grammaticalness' a term coined by N. CHOMSKY and elaborated by S. SAPORTA ("The Application of Linguistics to the Study of Poetic Language", [*Style in Language*, ed. T.A. SEBEOK, Cambridge: 1960] p. 82).

[9] P. RICŒUR borrows this distinction of the two ideas inherent in 'meaning' from FREGE (Sinn, Bedeutung). P. RICŒUR, "Biblical Hermeneutics", *Semeia* 4 (1975) p. 81.

[10] P. RICŒUR, "Biblical Hermeneutics", *Semeia* 4 (1975) p. 84.

[11] P. RICŒUR, "Biblical Hermeneutics", *Semeia* 4 (1975) p. 80.

"In effect, as we have seen, the ordinary reference of language is abolished by the natural strategy of poetic discourse. But in the very measure that this first-order reference is abolished, another power of speaking (of) the world is liberated, although at another level of reality. This level is that which Husserlian phenomenology has designated as the *Lebenswelt* and which HEIDEGGER called 'being-in-the-world'. It is an eclipsing of the objective manipulable world, an illumining of the life world, of non-manipulable being-in-the-world, which seems to me to be the fundamental ontological import of poetic language" (ibid. p. 87).

its conversion into moral discourse (even if this morality is elevated to the dignity of proverbial wisdom)." [12]

This insight at least opens the possibility that the persuasive character of the discourse in Wis is not necessarily a sign of an exclusively rhetorical language, but concomitantly may be expressive of its religious character. This throws light on the controversy about Wisdom's genre as essentially containing a persuasive orientation (Protreptic) or as essentially containing an orientation of praise (Encomium). The religious discourse in Wis both praises the beauty of wisdom and exhorts the reader to embrace the world projected through wisdom with limit-metaphorical language. Both orientations of persuasion and of presentation are functional in religious language.

These insights and descriptions of poetic language allow for a three-fold clarification on the poetic achievement in Wis: A) The text exhibits a concentration of parallelism which brings the words and images of these sections closer together. Parallelism is a restriction which intensifies the relations between words and images making them interact and crisscross, thereby opening a wealth of potential references. B) The poetic function in artistic discourse relies on the use of metaphorical language to present a world before the reader. The images that emerge throughout the text in Wis evoke a reflection that goes beyond their surface value. This is the use of metaphorical language that, in RICŒUR's terminology, allows for a second-order reference. Ambiguity, paradox and juxtaposition are constantly playing in the text and constitute a subtle and intelligent dimension to the poetic discourse. C) Finally, the images that are chosen in Wisdom's discourse are not ordinary or commonplace. They are images that evoke a limit-response. In particular, the image of death which dominates the first section and surfaces again in the latter parts of Wis is an image that evokes reflection of one's total life within the parameters of the projected world of Wis.

By poetic discourse, then, is understood not simply the external restrictions of rhythm and verse structure. The inner restrictions of metaphorical language highlight the activity of the second level referent of emerging possibilities. Finally, the particular poetic language of Wis makes a claim on the reader's total vision of life and death, and in this is attested its religious discourse.

The high poetic quality of the first part of Wis was quickly recognized by scholars. This is evident from the historical analysis of the various approaches to the structure of Wis. Even despite subsequent discoveries of intricate parallel and concentric units in the second and third sections of the work, the original assessment of the poetic standard

---

[12] P. RICŒUR, "Biblical Hermeneutics", *Semeia* 4 (1975) p. 127.

of the first part stands. This section exhibits a poetic freshness of imagery, conciseness in comparisons, and tension in thought that evokes the dynamism of the argument in question. It was this 'poetic freshness' contained in the first part of the work, among other arguments, that led P.W. Skehan to postulate this section of Wis as the work of the author's prime [13].

Since the author of Wis exerted so much effort to formulate this first section with units characterized by parallel and concentric structures, it is only to be expected that an appreciation and an analysis of these forms may uncover with greater precision the dynamic of the argument. The following analysis of the literary structure of the single units and of the larger whole is not an exercise in geometrical literary patterns. The careful analysis of the literary structure of units is to be executed with the reasonable hope that these structures may provide a context for the interpretation of ambiguous terms and metaphorical images used throughout this poetic text.

The over-arching concentric structure of the first six chapters has been established from different viewpoints (eg. from the point of view of verse number, strophic number, and structure of literary units). Only U. Offerhaus down-plays the concentric structure in order to highlight the relationship between larger and smaller divisions [14]. This general consensus regarding the concentric structure of the first part of Wis points to a literary preference of the author of Wis. But it is not the only structure employed by the author in the formulation of the units. As P. Bizzeti is careful to point out, another preference, which is highly significant for the precise interpretation of the text, is that of weaving units together with sections that pick up the thread of thoughts and images from previous units, thereby linking units and thoughts together that might otherwise appear disparate. These two literary features of concentric structures and linking units dominate the first part of Wis to a high degree.

---

[13] P.W. Skehan, "Text and Structure of the Book of Wisdom", *Traditio* 3 (1945) p. 5. See also A.G. Wright, "The Structure of the Book of Wisdom", *Bib* 48 (1967) p. 165. Larcher offers a brief summary analysis on the syntax and vocabulary of Wis with a view to the characteristics of the author. He notes that the first part abounds in Hebrew parallelism but that as a result the Greek style suffers under syntax restrictions (eg. the monotonous succession of ὅτι, γάρ, καί in the first chapter). Syntax and vocabulary become more varied and complex in the third part. He accepts the same explanation for this change as that suggested by Skehan and Wright, namely that the author wrote different parts of the book at various stages. However, Larcher concludes the first section of Wis with c. 5 (C. Larcher, *Le Livre de la Sagesse*, pp. 100-109).

[14] U. Offerhaus, *Komposition und Intention der Sapientia Salomonis*, Diss. Bonn: 1981, pp. 54-55.

The procedure that I will follow for the preparation of the close analysis of the first 6 chapters is first of all to delimit the units with their sub-units using the criteria of literary criticism. Secondly, an over-view of the units in their relationship to one another will highlight the unity of the first part of Wis.

B - 2. Wis 1:1-15

This first unit which opens with a formal address to those who "judge the earth" (οἱ κρίνοντες τὴν γῆν) is marked off by an inclusion of the key-word, δικαιοσύνη (1:1, 1:15)[15], and supported perhaps by the repetition of γῆ in 1:14d. The exhortation to love justice dominates this first unit. Two prepositional phrases describe the manner in which the Lord is to be sought. These phrases are parallel to the idea of justice (ἐν ἀγαθότητι, ἐν ἁπλότητι καρδίας). Justice is identified with the Spirit of the Lord and with wisdom (ἅγιον πνεῦμα, 1:5; πνεῦμα σοφία, 1:6α; πνεῦμα κυρίου, 1:7)[16]. Antithetical terms to justice abound in the unit as well (eg. σκολιοὶ λογισμοί, 1:3; κακότεχνον ψυχήν, ἁμαρτίας, 1:4; δόλον, λογισμῶν ἀσυνέτων, ἀδικίας, 1:5). These antithetical terms provide negative reasons for embracing righteousness. At this point, the negative reasons for embracing righteousness dominate. The only two positive reasons are short but pithy: 1:6 (for wisdom is a spirit that loves people) and 1:15 (for righteousness is immortal).

Precisely in view of the concentrated antithetical terms to justice, three subunits can be delimited. Verses 1-5 contain a concentration of terms that revolve around those negative characteristics and intentions which resist the Spirit of God: crooked considerations, deceitful spirit, deceit, sinful body, foolish thought, injustice. Verses 6-11 contain a high concentration of terms regarding speaking and hearing. These terms are rooted in the terminology of court proceedings. The hidden intentions of the wicked will be revealed in an inquiry (blasphemer, lips, tongue, hearer, inquiry, a report of his words, a zealous ear, murmuring sound). And finally the third sub-unit, vv 12-15, contains the extreme negative reason for embracing righteousness. The choice of the wicked leads to death and destruction, but justice is immortal.

1:1-5

The first sub-unit is delimited by antithetical terms, δικαιοσύνη ἀδικία, 1:1,5. The tension between justice and injustice is a theme that

---

[15] J.M. REESE, "Plan", *CBQ* 27 (1965) p. 394; A.G. WRIGHT, "Structure", *Bib* 48 (1967) p. 166.
[16] D. WINSTON, *The Wisdom of Solomon*, New York: 1979, p. 100.

pervades the entire first section of the book. The antithetical inclusion established by the terms justice and injustice is indicative of the antithetical concentric structure of this unit[17]. In v 1 the rulers are urged to seek the Lord in goodness and in singleness of heart. In v 5 it is the Holy Spirit that flees from wickedness. Verses 2 and 4 continue the antithetical comparison begun with the inclusion. In v 2 the action of God is described with positive verbs, the action of humans with negative verbs. God is revealed to those who do not test him and to those who are not unbelieving. In v 4 the action of wisdom is described by means of negative verbs, whereas the state of humans by means of positive nouns. Wisdom will not enter a fraudulent mind, nor dwell in a body dominated by sin. Finally, in v 3 the contrast between God and wickedness is described in two stichs where the subject alternates. Devious thoughts depart from God; when tested, divine power exposes the foolish.

1:6-11

This unit plays on the vocabulary of court/trial terminology. Appropriately, the inclusion of γλῶσσῃ (1:6e,11b) introduces and concludes the warning against slanderous speech. Nothing spoken surreptitiously evades the Lord who hears all, for the spirit of the Lord pervades all. From the speech of the impious, an accurate account will be drawn of their innermost feelings and scheming[18]. The final stich of v 11 prepares the reader for the stark statements that follow the next sub-unit.

---

[17] PERRENCHIO was the first to propose the concentric nature of 1:1-5. His analysis was most effective regarding vv 2 and 4. For vv 1 and 5, PERRENCHIO relied on grammatical and structural affinities which are not altogether convincing due to their complexity. A clearer bond between 1 and 5 can be established precisely in the antithetical nature of the comparisons which is consistent with the contrast in vv 2 and 4 and in the central v 3. See F. PERRENCHIO, "Struttura e analisi letteraria di Sapienza 1,1-15", *Sales* 37 (1975) pp. 310-312.

[18] PERRENCHIO delimits this central sub-unit into vv 6-10, thereby ignoring the inclusion of γλῶσσῃ. His main reason for separating v 11 from v 10 is based on what he terms 'the parenetic' nature of vv 11-15 which begins in v 11 with the imperative, φυλάξασθε. Furthermore, passage between the two sub-units is achieved through the link-word, γογγυσμόν, 1:10b,11a. In this way the three sub-units are of more equal length, with the first and last exhibiting an exhortative nature, while the central is doctrinal. F. PERRENCHIO, "Struttura 1,1-15", *Sales* 37 (1975) pp. 314-319.

BIZZETI critiques this schematization based on parenetic and doctrinal categories as being a schematic imposition on the text. P. BIZZETI, *Il Libro*, p. 51, n. 7.

I would add to this critique the fact that the 'τοίνυν' in v 11 concludes the sub-unit which concentrates the terminology of speaking/hearing that abounds in v 11. Moreover, the exhortation in the third sub-unit, which parallels the first more adeptly by its contrast, begins in v 12: "Do not invite death" (μὴ ζηλοῦτε θάνατον, 1:12). This dissuasion which opens the third sub-unit is a counter-point to the explicit exhortation "seek the Lord" (ζητήσατε αὐτόν, 1:1).

The change, from the discourse using terms of speaking/hearing to the treatment of death, is prepared by 11c which links the two issues. "A lying mouth destroys the soul".

1:12-15

This third sub-unit introduces the most dramatic reason for seeking righteousness and avoiding injustice, namely death. The antithetical inclusion, which is achieved by means of θάνατος, ἀθάνατος (1:12,15), echoes in reverse order the antithetical inclusion of the first unit (δικαιοσύνη, ἀδικία). And just as there was a contrast in the opening sub-unit between wickedness and the activity of the Lord, so too is there a contrast in the final sub-unit between death and the will of God — immortality. God has nothing to do with death. He did not create it, nor does he delight in it.

The sub-unit abounds in synonyms for death that highlight the theme of destruction: ὄλεθρος (1:12b), which is parallel to θάνατος (1:12a) and repeated in 1:14c, ἀπώλεια (1:13b), ᾅδου βασίλειον (1:14d).

The final exhortation which begins this sub-unit is constructed in perfect parallel symmetry (1:12).

> Do not invite death   through the error of your life;
> Nor bring on destruction through the works of your hands.

This exhortation in negative terms complements the opening exhortation, which had been expressed in positive terms. And the conclusion, "for righteousness is immortal," completes the exhortation on a positive note [19].

---

[19] The unity of 1:1-15 has tentatively been called into question by both GILBERT and by BIZZETI because of their observation of the ties between 1:13-15 and 2:23-24. See M. GILBERT, "Sagesse", *DBS* 11, col. 66; P. BIZZETI, *Il Libro*, pp. 52-53. Their observation suggests that v 12, with its plural imperatives, could conclude the first unit, echoing v 1:1, while vv 13-15 could constitute an inclusion with 2:23-24, thereby delimiting the second unit. These two sections form a partial concentric structure based on their themes: A - action of God (1:13-15), B - judgment against the wicked (1:16-2:1a), B' - judgment against the wicked (2:21-22), A'- action of God (2:23-24) (P. BIZZETI, *Il Libro*, p. 53). The concentric structure is only partial because, in fact, 2:24 does not deal with the action of God, but rather is parallel to 1:16. However, neither insists that these ties determine the actual division of the units. They prefer to let stand the inclusions which were first offered by WRIGHT to delimit the first and second units (1:1-15, 1:16-2:24).

I offer two further reasons for not insisting on delimiting 1:13–2:24 as a unit. Firstly, the ὅτι clause which initiates v 13 provides an explanatory motive for not inviting death. With this sense, the clause is immediately bound to v 12:

> do not invite death... v 12
> (ὅτι) for God did not make death... v 13.

Secondly, the recurring terms in 2:23-24 which echo those of 1:13-15 do not necessarily call for an inclusion. These ties belong to the author's penchant for linking different units

Note on 1:15

Because of the textual complexities associated with this verse, special attention is required for verifying its position in the structure of the literary unit. Two difficulties have been noted with the verse, one textual, the other thematic.

a) The textual difficulty stems from the presence of a second stich in the Latin text: "iniustitia autem mortis est acquisitio". This sentence has been translated into Greek by C.L.W. Grimm, "ἀδικία δε θανάτου περιποίησις[20]". J. Ziegler, in his critical edition of Wis, lists 1:15b as a possible exception to the Vulgate's several instances of interpolation, thereby acknowledging a missing part in the Greek version of 1:15[21].

Two main arguments are used to support the authenticity of the Latin stich. The first argument notes that the accusative pronoun, αὐτόν, in 1:16 is rather distant from the noun, θάνατος, to which it presumably refers[22]. The noun, θανάτου, in 1:15b would conveniently supply a governing noun to the pronoun in 1:16. The second argument presumes that in continuity with the antithetical verse structures of the first chapter, the monostich of 1:15 requires an antithetical stich, which 1:15b of the Latin conveniently supplies. Neither of the two arguments is convincing. A Latin gloss explains better the presence of the additional stich in the Latin version[23]. The antithetical statement to the monostich is formulated in the following unit, 1:16–2:24.

---

together. The lines in question could in fact be broadened to comprise 1:12-16 and 2:21-24 (see U. Offerhaus, Komposition, pp. 30-32). The noun, πλάνη, is echoed by the cognate verb, ἐπλανήθησαν, in 2:21; the phrase, τῆς ἐκείνου μερίδος, in 1:16 is echoed in 2:24. In this light, both the first and second units conclude with a treatment on the source of death in contrast to the activity of God.

[20] C.L.W. Grimm, Das Buch der Weisheit, Kurzegefasstes exegetisches Handbuch zu den Apokryphen des Alten Testaments VI, Leipzig: 1860, pp. 63-64.

[21] J. Ziegler, Sapientia Salomonis (Septuaginta. Vetus Testamentum Graecum, XII, 1), Göttingen, 1962, ²1980, pp. 24,97.

[22] Larcher adds the observation that the pronoun in 1:16 could refer explicitly to the synonym for death, Hades, which also is masculine and which stands in closer proximity to the pronoun. C. Larcher, Le Livre de la Sagesse, pp. 206-207; so also J.M. Reese, "Plan and Structure", p. 394. Perrenchio admits the grammatical possibility for such an interpretation, but notes also a similar structure of three pronouns that refer to a distant composite noun, φιλάνθρωπον, in 1:6 (F. Perrenchio, "Struttura 1,1-15", Sales 37 (1975) p. 296, n. 13). The use of pronouns referring to distant nouns, therefore, could be a particular stylistic feature of our author.

[23] For summary statements regarding the arguments in defense of the authenticity of the monostich, see in particular U. Offerhaus, Komposition und Intention der Sapientia Salomonis, Diss. Bonn 1981, pp. 32-33, and C. Larcher, Le Livre de la Sagesse, pp. 205-206.

A recent attempt to defend the authenticity of the Latin stich on literary grounds was made by F. Perrenchio[24]. According to his analysis, the stichic structure of vv 11-15 requires that v 15 contain two stichs. Verses 11-13, which formally constitute a concentric structure, contain 8 stichs; v 14 contains 4 stichs, and, therefore, v 15 should have 2 stichs to achieve the pattern 8, 4, 2. However, this analysis is far from convincing. The concentric pattern of vv 11-13 is somewhat forced, to say the least. And finally, it is a rather dubious procedure to use the argument of pattern continuity in the case of textual anomalies. This is often the very argument used to support the proposition that the text has been emendated. W.J. Deane cited this very argument of completed parallelism as proof for the opposite thesis, namely that it is a Latin gloss[25].

b) On the other hand, a thematic difficulty of the monostich of v 1:15 has caused some scholars to call into question the authenticity of the single verse in the Greek text[26]. The reason given for support of this thesis is the supposed break in thought which v 1:15 brings about between 1:14 and 1:16[27]. However, it is not accurate to say that the monostich interrupts the wider argument of the first unit, 1:1-15. The immediate argument in the sub-unit, 1:12-15, revolves around the assertion that God has nothing to do with death and that the forces of the world are wholesome. Death is the result of the free choice of the wicked (v 1:12). In the wider argument of the entire unit, 1:1-15, the sub-unit cites death as the dramatic negative reason for loving righteousness. In light of these arguments, the monostich, 'for justice is immortal', ties together the negative motive for not being wicked with the opening imperative to love justice. This monostich, which concludes both the opening unit and the sub-unit, creates a dramatic pause in the argument for loving justice. Moreover, it is precisely this line which

---

[24] F. Perrenchio, "Struttura 1,1-15", *Sales* 37 (1975) p. 317-318.

[25] "This is probably a gloss added by one who wished to complete the parallelism and to give αὐτόν in v. 16 something to refer to" (W.J. Deane, *The Book of Wisdom*, Oxford: 1881, p. 116).

[26] The Authorized Version placed the monostich in parentheses. S. Holmes, considered it authentic but misplaced (originally it would have been situated between 2:22 and 2:23). S. Holmes, "The Wisdom of Solomon", in *The Apocrypha and Pseudepigrapha of the Old Testament in English*, ed. R.H. Charles, vol 1, London: 1913, p. 536.

[27] Goodrick agrees that there is a break in thought, but suggests that the Latin addition resolves the difficulty. The break in thought within the immediate context consists of the fact that the unit, 1:12-14, and the following section, 1:16–2:24, are more concerned with proving the result of death for the wicked rather than the reward of the just. A.T.S. Goodrick, *The Book of Wisdom*, London: 1913, p. 98.

defines the border of the first unit through the reference to δικαιοσύνη. The negative motive of death for choosing justice is to be elaborated closely by the author in the following unit.

B - 3. Wis 1:16–2:24

Thematically, this unit is easily delimited by its central section which provides an inner glance into the reasoning of the wicked. The speech of the wicked is encased by an introduction (1:16–2:1a) and by a conclusion (2:21-24), both of which contain the author's explanatory remarks regarding the false reasoning of the wicked. The opening statement of the unit echoes terms taken from the previous two sub-units. The wicked invite death through their deeds and their words: ταῖς χερσίν (1:16,12), τοῖς λόγοις ((1:16,9).

From a literary point of view, the theme of the unit is expressed through a double chiastic inclusion:

a   τῆς ἐκείνου μερίδος εἶναι (1:16d)
    b   λογισάμενοι οὐκ ὀρθῶς (2:1a)
    b' ταῦτα ἐλογίσαντο (2:21a)
a' τῆς ἐκείνου μερίδος ὄντες (2:24b)

The central inclusion introduces and concludes the theme of the false reasoning of the wicked, which links them to their fate.

b   εἶπον γὰρ ἐν ἑαυτοῖς λογισάμενοι οὐκ ὀρθῶς (2:1a)
b' ταῦτα ἐλογίσαντο, καὶ ἐπλανήθησαν (2:21a)

With the outer inclusion, the author hints at the ultimate fate of the wicked — death.

ὅτι ἄξιοί εἰσιν τῆς ἐκείνου μερίδος εἶναι (1:16d)
πειράζουσιν δὲ αὐτὸν οἱ τῆς ἐκείνου μερίδος ὄντες (2:24b)

Both endings of the first and second units conclude with a brief treatment of death, which is contrasted to the positive activity of God. In the first unit, death is treated as a negative motive for loving righteousness. In the second unit death is tersely presented as the chosen fate of the wicked. In this way, the sub-unit 2:21-24 has a double function of concluding the second unit and of paralleling the ending of the first unit, thereby achieving a direct link with the first unit.

2:1b-20

This central section of the second unit is delimited by the speech of the wicked in the first person[28]. Here the author has the wicked reveal their inner reasoning and projects. They present their reasons for their judgment on the futility of their lives. This judgment on the futility of life flows into and explains their project to exploit the brevity of their lives with power. Twenty-one instances of the pronouns, ἡμῶν/ἡμᾶς/ἡμῖν, and eighteen verbs in the first person plural chart the literary cohesiveness of this section.

2:1b-5

This sub-unit deals exclusively with the wicked's judgment on the futility of human life. Two inclusions introduce and focus this theme: τελευτῇ, τελευτῆς (2:1c,5b); ὁ βίος ἡμῶν (2:1b,4c). Both images of the human 'end' and the transience of human 'life' are placed in tension with one another. Moreover, the human condition is imagined and described with a phrase playing on the pronoun, ἡμῶν: ὁ βίος ἡμῶν, ῥισὶν ἡμῶν (2:2c), καρδίας ἡμῶν (2:2d), τὸ ὄνομα ἡμῶν (2:4a), τῶν ἔργων ἡμῶν (2:4b), ὁ καιρὸς ἡμῶν (2:5a), τῆς τελευτῆς ἡμῶν (2:5b).

2:6-20

The wicked's judgment on the futility of human life in the face of death is immediately followed by the projected praxis of the wicked. Grammatically, these verses are united by a series of imperatives and subjunctives through which the wicked exhort one another to exploit the short time they have at their disposal.

2:6-11

The first series of exhortations regards the relationship between the wicked and the world at large. An antithetical inclusion, achieved in χρησώμεθα, ἄχρηστον (2:6,11), focuses on the tension alluded to in the first part of their speech. The wicked are to 'make use' of whatever is available and enjoyable, and they are to exploit the weak because whatever is weak is 'useless'. The phrase, ἡ μερὶς ἡμῶν, (2:9c) is an ironic reference to the ultimate result of their praxis in that it echoes the

---

[28] PERRENCHIO includes in this central section the lines 2:1a and 2:21a which introduce and close the direct speech of the wicked. Both lines contain the verb, λογίζομαι. (F. PERRENCHIO, "Struttura 1,1-15", Sales 37 (1975) pp. 3-43.) But precisely because of their function to introduce and close the direct speech of the wicked, it would be more logical to include the lines respectively with the introduction (1:16–2:1a) and the closure (2:21-24) of the unit (with WRIGHT, BIZZETI, GILBERT).

author's judgment regarding the fate of the wicked (1:16, 2:24). It provides a break-point between their plan to enjoy the good things of creation (2:6-9) and their plan to oppress the weak: the poor, the widow and the elderly (2:10-11).

2:12-20

From v 12 onward the wicked single out the just person as their particular object of scorn and opposition. The verse is linked to the preceding section through the words, δίκαιον (2:10a,11a), and δύσχρηστος, ἄχρηστος (2:12a,11b). The tension between the just one and the wicked contains a dramatic progression. In vv 12-16, it is the wicked who consider the just one to oppose them and their life-style by his claim to be with God (2:13a,16d). In vv 17-20, it is the wicked who propose to oppose the just one right to the point of inflicting upon him a shameful death. This section contains an inclusion in οἱ λόγοι αὐτοῦ; ἐκ λόγων αὐτοῦ (2:17,20). The inclusion focuses the debate in the minds of the wicked on the disquieting claim of the just one who is considered to be a son of God (2:18).

This progressive opposition between the just one and the wicked is graphically highlighted through the author's play on pronouns in 2:12-20[29]. In 2:12, τὸν δίκαιον becomes the object under consideration. The just one is treated as an opposition to the wicked, who are referred to five times by the pronouns ἡμῶν, ἡμῖν. In 2:13-16, the tension between the just one and the wicked is depicted through the alternating use of pronouns referring to both the wicked and the just one, ἡμῶν, ἡμῖν, ἑαυτόν, αὐτοῦ, αὐτῷ. And finally in 2:17-20, eight instances of the pronoun, αὐτοῦ, αὐτόν, underscore the fact that the just one has become the passive object of oppression whereas the wicked are the active subjects who oppress.

B - 4. Wis 3–4:20

This central unit within the first part of Wis is unified by four diptychs which contain a series of contrasts the author establishes between the just and the wicked. In each diptych, the glory and peace of the just are treated first, while the fate and agony of the wicked are treated second. As has been duly noted by the literary critics, there is no inclusion to demark clearly the entire unit. The contrast within each diptych is indicated through an adversative δέ (3:10,16, 4:3,18). However, the parallelism of the four diptychs is sufficiently obvious to guarantee

---

[29] F. PERRENCHIO, "Struttura 1,1-15", Sales 37 (1975), p. 16.

the concise delimitation of the unit. Moreover, the relations and ties between the four diptychs (namely between the first and fourth and between the second and third) offer different possibilities for conceiving their structure. The various inclusions and word-repetitions within the unit display a woven chiastic unity.

3:1-12

The opening diptych contains the first volley aimed at dismantling the foolish reasoning of the wicked. Appropriately, an inclusion of ἀφρόνων, ἄφρονες (3:2,12) demarks the first diptych. The contrast between the just and the wicked falls heavily on the side of the just. Verses 3:1-9 contain twenty stichs, whereas 3:10-12 contain eight.

3:1-9

The presentation of the glory of the just is achieved through the explanation of a dramatic reversal of what on the surface appeared to have happened, namely that they have died. A play on the prepositional phrases governed by ἐν gives shape to the unity of this sub-unit and at the same time highlights the reversal of fortune.

ἐν χειρὶ θεοῦ	(3:1)
ἐν ὀφθαλμοῖς ἀφρόνων	(3:2)
ἐν εἰρήνῃ	(3:3)
ἐν ὄψει ἀνθρώπων	(3:4)
ἐν χωνευτηρίῳ	(3:6)
ἐν καιρῷ ἐπισκοπῆς αὐτῶν	(3:7a)
ἐν καλάμῃ	(3:7b)
ἐν ἀγάπῃ ... αὐτῷ	(3:9)

In the first part (3:1-5), two declarations claim that the just ones are in the hand of God and in peace despite appearances in the eyes of the foolish and in the sight of people. In the second part (3:6-9), the appearance of destruction is explained through the image of God testing the just as gold in a furnace. They will shine forth as sparks flashing in stubble, and they will remain with God in love.

3:10-12

Over and above the inclusion of ἄφρονος (3:2,12), the second half of the diptych is linked to the first half through the contrast between the hope of the just and that of the wicked (ἡ ἐλπὶς αὐτῶν, καὶ κενὴ ἡ ἐλπὶς αὐτῶν, 3:4b, 11b). For the just, their hope is the fullness of immortality. For the wicked, their hope is empty because of their disregard for the just and their opposition to the Lord. The final verse of the diptych introduces the terms, πονηρά, τέκνα, γένεσις, that will be taken up in the second and third diptychs, and which form a thematic unity (3:14b, 4:6b; 3:16, 4:1,6; 3:19).

3:13–4:6

This central sub-unit contains two parallel diptychs which center upon the significance of the apparent fruitfulness of the wicked and the apparent sterility of some who are just[30]. Through the contrasts, the author declares the reverse to be the case in each example. The primary inclusion, noted by WRIGHT, is achieved in the repetition of καρπόν, καρπός (3:13c,15, 4:5b). Other repetitions should be noted between 3:13-14 and 4:5-6 to indicate the strength of the inclusion; ἀνόμημα, ἀνόμων (3:14, 4:6), πονηρά, πονηρίας (3:14b, 4:6b). And finally, as GILBERT and BIZZETI noted, the two diptychs are further bound by the rare word ἀμίαντος, ἀμιάντων (3:13, 4:2d)[31].

The second diptych (3:13-19), which contrasts the blameless, sterile woman and the innocent eunuch with the children of adultery, contains parallel repetitions: κοίτην, κοίτης (3:13b,16b); the synonymous prepositional phrases: ἐν ἐπισκοπῇ ψυχῶν, ἐν ἡμέρᾳ διαγνώσεως (3:13c,18b). The third diptych which contrasts the virtuous who are childless with the brood of the wicked contains an antithetical inclusion in ἀτεκνία, τέκνα (4:1,6b). In this way the second and third diptychs form a unity through repeated terms, theme and an inclusion, while each diptych also expresses an internal organization based on parallel symmetry and an inclusion.

---

[30] It is possible to delimit each diptych as a separate unit, based on the adversative δέ which initiates the contrast for each diptych. PERRENCHIO, in his general outline of the first six chapters of Wis, goes so far as to treat each part of the diptych as a unit. But this is done without detailed analysis and more for the sake of showing the parallel of themes (F. PERRENCHIO, "Struttura 1,1-15", *Sales* 37 (1975) p. 307). BIZZETI treats each diptych as a unit and draws parallels between the first and the last, and the second and the third (P. BIZZETI, *Il Libro*, pp. 56-57). In this way, the four diptychs constitute a chiastic structure, a,b, b',a'. Both WRIGHT and GILBERT, while recognizing the organization of the unit according to four diptychs, delimit the entire unit into three sub-units based on the indices of inclusions and repetitions: 3:1-12, 3:13–4:6, 4:7-20 (A.G. WRIGHT, "Structure", *Bib* 48 (1967) 171; M. GILBERT, "Sagesse", *DBS* 11, cols. 66-67).

The main reason for insisting on the two central diptychs as a particular unity is the presence of obvious inclusions that delimit the two diptychs together, vv 3:13,14; vv 4:5,6. However, these inclusions which tie the two central diptychs together do not necessarily exclude a concomitant delimitation for each diptych. The parallelism of the two central diptychs is achieved through the use of synonyms, which is common in Hebrew poetry. The 'blameless sterile woman' (3:13) is parallel to 'childless with virtue' (4:1). The 'children of adultery' (3:16) is parallel to 'the brood of the ungodly' (4:3). It is best to speak of four diptychs in which the second and third are parallel to one another through a repetition of synonyms and united through inclusions.

[31] P. BIZZETI, *Il Libro*, p. 57.

4:7-20

The fourth diptych is more loosely organized than the previous three. The contrast is drawn specifically between a just person, who had been perfected in youth and died an early death, and the ultimate fate of the ungodly. There is no inclusion that enfolds the entire diptych. WRIGHT suggested τίμιον, ἄτιμον (4:8,19a) as a possible inclusion, but this antithetical repetition is hardly inclusive of the entire diptych. There is also a repetition of ἁμαρτωλῶν, ἁμαρτημάτων (4:10b,20).

Verse 16 is the central link around which the entire diptych turns [32]. This central verse draws the first half of the diptych to a close, through several repetitions of terms from the first verses, while at the same time it opens the second half by providing the change in subject and future tense.

The three terms, δίκαιος, τελευτῆσαι, γῆρας, in 4:7-8 are concentrated also in 4:16. The subject for the second half of the diptych is provided by ἀσεβεῖς (4:16). Whereas the first half is dominated by the past tense with verbs denoting the intervention of God to protect the just, in v 16, the first in a series of 15 verbs indicates the future judgment of the just over the wicked and the future demise of wickedness.

The unity of this diptych is achieved by the contrast between the past events experienced by the just in the first part of the diptych and the future experience of the just and the wicked at the time of judgment. The next unit focuses precisely on the judgment of the wicked through an anticipated reenactment of the future. The author provides an inner look, as it were, at the future reasoning of the wicked, thereby pronouncing an explanatory judgment of their first reasoning (2:1-20).

B - 5. Wis 5:1-23

This unit is separated from the previous series of diptychs through the declaratory, τότε, which underscores a new and specific time reference of future judgment being brought into the present argumentation [33]. But

---

[32] PERRENCHIO divides the fourth diptych at 4:15, and opens the contrasting half with v 16. The reason for this division is the change from a past to a future tense with κατακρινεῖ in 4:16 (F. PERRENCHIO, "Struttura 1,1-15", *Sales* 37 (1975) p. 307). However, there are strong indices to show that the verse cannot be divided from either half of the diptych. On the one hand, v 16 is tied to the first half because of the subject, δίκαιος (4:7,16), which governs the future tense, and because of the terms, γῆρας, τελεσθεῖσα. On the other hand, v 16 is tied to the second half of the diptych through the introduction of the future tense and through the naming of the subject, ἀσεβεῖς, for the remaining 14 occurrences of future tenses.

[33] As opposed to OFFERHAUS who considers 4:20-5:14 to be a unit (note the obvious typographical error in 4,20-4,14) and who, therefore, must disclaim τότε from indicating a

it flows in continuity with the last diptych, in particular, through the continuation of future tenses, which duplicates the procedure in 4:16 (future tense with δίκαιος as subject followed by the continuation of future tenses with the change of subject to the wicked).

An inclusion sets the frame of the unit: στήσεται, ἀντιστήσεται (5:1,23)[34]. It highlights the theme of confrontation between the just/God on the one hand and the wicked on the other. Internally, the unit is organized according to three sub-units: an introduction to the discourse of the oppressors (5:1-3), the discourse of the impious in the first person (5:4-13), and a conclusion which flows into an account of the glory of the righteous and the destruction of the wicked (5:14-23).

5:1-3

This brief introduction sets the context for the speech of the wicked who had oppressed the righteous and are thrown into confusion because of the change of fortune. There is a clever play on the words στήσεται, ἐκστήσονται (5:1,2b), an inclusion to indicate the change of fortune. The righteous one will stand with great strength; the oppressors will be in dismay at the paradoxical glory of the righteous. Verse 5:3, constructed in chiastic, repetitive symmetry (ABB'A': ἐροῦσιν, στενοχωρίαν, στενάξονται, ἐροῦσιν), sets the immediate context for the speech of the wicked[35].

5:4-13(14)

The speech of the oppressors in the first person expresses their painful examination of conscience in face of the just. A double inclusion is achieved in ἔσχομεν (5:4,13b) and in οὗτος, οὕτως (5:4,13a). They both point to the examination of accounts for the righteous one and for the oppressors[36]. At first it was they who had 'held' the just one in derision, but now it is they who 'hold' no sign of virtue.

The examination of conscience unfolds in three parts (5:4-5,6-8,9-13). The first part focuses on the just one whom they had oppressed (οὗτος referring to the subject δίκαιος in 5:1). Two parallel phrases give

---

new time reference (U. OFFERHAUS, *Komposition*, p.48). However, such a division of units overlooks the important inclusions indicated by WRIGHT and PERRENCHIO.

[34] This inclusion was first noted by WRIGHT and accepted by the major literary critics of Wis (A.G. WRIGHT, "Structure", *Bib* 48 (1967) pp. 168-169).

[35] Note that ZIEGLER differs from RAHLF by dropping the final καὶ ἐροῦσιν (S), considering it redundant. PERRENCHIO judges 5:3 to be part of the speech of the oppressors just as he attributes the lines 2:1a and 2:21a to be constitutive elements of the speech of the impious in c.2 rather than forming part of the introduction and conclusion (F. PERRENCHIO, «Struttura 1,1-15», *Sales* 37 (1975) p.307).

[36] P. BIZZETI, *Il Libro*, p.61.

structure to the section: τὸν βίον αὐτοῦ (5:4c) parallels ὁ κλῆρος αὐτοῦ (5:5b), and ἐλογισάμεθα (5:4c) parallels κατελογίσθη (5:5a). The reversal of fortune is ironically expressed through a double question introduced by πῶς.

The second section deals with the oppressors' explicit recognition of the error of their lifestyle. This recognition is highlighted by the inclusion ὁδοῦ ἀληθείας, ὁδὸν κυρίου (5:6a,7c). The section concludes with a question paralleling the question from the first section in v 5 [37].

The third section revolves around several images through which the oppressors elaborate the transience and fragility of their accumulated riches. Each of these images is introduced by ὡς: ὡς σκία, ὡς ἀγγελία, ὡς ναῦς, ὡς ὀρνέου, ὡς βέλους. These images are brought to a close in οὕτως καὶ ἡμεῖς (5:13a), where the oppressors relate their fruitless lives to these transient images [38]. We also find a concentration of four verbs with the prefix, δια (5:10ab,11ae) [39].

These three sections of the oppressors' speech parallel the sections in the speech of the wicked in c. 2, but in reverse order [40]. In c. 2 the speech of the wicked unfolds through three sections involving: a) their judgment on the transience of human life (2:1b-5), b) their resolution to exploit life and the weak to the utmost (2:6-11), c) their decision to oppress the just one whose words and example oppose their judgment and their decision (2:12-20). The speech of the oppressors in c. 5 begins precisely where the speech in c. 2 left the reader: a) the oppressors face the just one who is in fact a son of God (5:4-5), b) they recognize the fruitlessness of their lifestyle (5:6-8), and c) they repeat images depicting the transience of their values with the bitter realization that they have no virtue to show (5:9-13).

This reverse parallelism to c. 2 is also corroborated through the reverse order of the play on the pronouns in c. 5, οὗτος, αὐτοῦ / ἡμῖν, ἡμᾶς, ἡμεῖς, ἡμῶν. In c. 2, the pronouns for the first person gave way to

---

[37] OFFERHAUS agrees with this division but only on the basis of subject matter, without offering literary support (U. OFFERHAUS, *Komposition*, p. 49). BIZZETI and GILBERT attach 5:8 to 5:9-13. BIZZETI offers two indices for delimiting the unit 5:8-13 (P. BIZZETI, Il Libro, p. 61). Firstly, the series of nouns introduced with ὡς pervades the unit. Secondly, he cites the reptition of the pronoun ἡμεῖς (5:8,13) as an inclusion. The first argument has no force for including v 8 in the unit because the images introduced by ὡς only begin with v 9. The second argument dissolves when we realize that the repetition of the pronoun ἡμεῖς does not form an inclusion but, on the contrary, forms part of a larger pattern that encases the entire sub-unit 5:4-13. This sub-unit which contains the speech of the oppressors, shows a progression from αὐτοῦ to ἡμεῖς, which echoes the reverse parallel progression in Wis 2.

[38] PERRENCHIO and OFFERHAUS attach 5:14 to the speech of the oppressors, whereas WRIGHT, GILBERT and BIZZETI conclude the sub-unit at 5:13.

[39] P. BIZZETI, *Il Libro*, p. 61.

[40] U. OFFERHAUS, *Komposition*, p. 49; P. BIZZETI, *Il Libro*, p. 62.

those of the third person, just as in c. 5, the section regarding the just one begins with pronouns in the third person (4acd,5b), which give way to those in the first person (6bc,8ab,13ac) referring to the oppressors.

Verse 14 functions as a transitional verse which links the speech of the oppressors to the following section. It is not clear whether the verse belongs to the speech of the oppressors, who finally recognize explicitly their irreligion, or whether it is a concluding comment by the author. PERRENCHIO attributes the verse to the speech of the oppressors. Because of a lack of an explicit reference to first person speech, the verse reads more easily as a comment by the author. WRIGHT, GILBERT and BIZZETI have the last section of c. 5 begin with this verse[41].

As is often the case in Wis, these sections which are difficult to delimit have a double function: to bring one section to a close while opening another. The links between v 14 and the speech of the oppressors are very clearly defined. The term, ἀσεβοῦς (5:14), complements οἱ ἄφρονες (5:4). Both terms are previously used to name the oppressors of the just one (3:2,10). Furthermore, the very stylistic features that unite 5:9-13, namely the structure, ὡς + noun, as well as the use of verbs with the prefix, δια (4X), are continued in 5:14 (2X). Through these stylistic features, the author clearly continues the judgment against the irreligious in the very style that they have pronounced against themselves. Before turning to the contrasting situation of the just in the end times (5:15-23), the author pronounces judgment against the oppressors.

5:(14)15-23

Verse 14 is linked to the following section by the inclusion, λαίλαπος, ὡς λαῖλαψ (5:14,23), and by the contrast it establishes to the situation of the just (5:15-16) which introduces the images of an apocalyptic judgment (5:17-23)[42]. The inclusion focuses on the theme of a cosmic destruction of evil. The just will live forever; lawlessness will be destroyed.

The description of the apocalyptic judgment unfolds in two stages: a) the preparation, where God and the cosmos are armed (5:17-20), b) the images of destruction through cosmic terms (5:21-23). The first part of the description is delimited through the possible inclusion of the synonyms τὴν κτίσιν, ὁ κόσμος (5:17,20b). Both God and the universe are armed to do battle. Terms referring to armaments are linked to virtues as in Isa 59:17 (LXX).

The second part of the description is delimited through the stylized phrase, καὶ ὡς (5:21b,23b), indicating the manner of destruction. In this

---

[41] P. BIZZETI, Il Libro, p. 61.
[42] M. GILBERT, «Sagesse», DBS 11, col. 67.

concluding section, various terms representing the four elements of nature are named as carrying out divine justice: βολίδες ἀστραπῶν, χάλαζαι, ὕδωρ θαλάσσης, ποταμοί, πνεῦμα δυνάμεως, λαῖλαψ (earth is mentioned only as the locus of destruction).

The final ἀντιστήσεται (5:23) recalls the στήσεται from 5:1 where the just is introduced as one who will stand with great confidence in face of the oppressors. In the closing part of the inclusion it is the Spirit of the Almighty (a mighty wind) which will stand to oppose lawlessness [43]. With the apocalyptic conclusion, which finally resolves the tension between the wicked and the just, the author turns again to the rulers of the earth. The resolution in favor of the just provides a dramatic quality and intensity for the following appeal to learn justice and wisdom.

B - 6. Wis 6:1-21

The exhortation to kings and judges, which concludes the first part of Wis, recalls the opening address to rulers. The unit is intricately woven with repetitions to form a whole. It is also bound to the previous unit through the immediate link words γῆν, γῆς (5:23c, 6:1b) and to the following unit with the link words σοφίαν, σοφία (6:21b,22a). This unit has been subjected to multiple theories of delimitation, particularly with respect to the demarcation between the first and second parts of the Book of Wis. A discussion of these theories also will shed light on the intricately woven nature of the unit which prepares the reader for the eulogy of wisdom.

There are two major unifying factors that define the limits of the unit. Firstly, we find the inclusion achieved in βασιλεῖς, βασιλεύσητε (6:1,21b) [44]. Secondly, the adverb, οὖν, is used four times in conjunction

---

[43] PERRENCHIO presents several arguments for interpreting πνεῦμα δυνάμεως (5:23) by 'the Spirit of the Almighty' rather than by 'a mighty wind', although, since God and the cosmos in unison are battling against evil, both interpretations are possible. The immediate context (vv 21,22) would favor an interpretation of wind, in continuity with cosmic forces. However, the only other use of the phrase, πνεῦμα δυνάμεως, in 11:20 clearly refers to the divine sphere. Moreover, the parallelism between the verb, ἀντιστήσεται (6:23), and the verb, ἀνθεστηκότων (2:18) would be complemented with an interpretation of πνεῦμα as a divine sphere, thereby contrasting the oppressors with God. "... ma proprio perché il lottatore principale è Dio, appare un po' strano che della sua azione non ci sia alcun cenno diretto" (F. PERRENCHIO, "Struttura 1,16–2,24 e 5,1-23", *Sales* 43 [1981] pp. 31-32).

[44] This inclusion was noted first by J.M. REESE (terms of royalty, kings and reign, J.M. REESE, Plan, *CBQ* 27 [1965] p. 395-396) and accepted by WRIGHT and GILBERT.

with imperatives at the beginning, center and end of the unit to highlight
the concluding function of the exhortation (6:1,9a,11,21)[45].

6:1   ἀκούσατε οὖν, σύνετε
      μάθετε, ἐνωτίσασθε

6:9   πρὸς ὑμᾶς οὖν
      ἵνα μάθετε, μὴ παραπέσητε
6:11 ἐπιθυμήσατε οὖν
      ποθήσατε

6:21 εἰ οὖν ἥδεσθε
      τιμήσατε σοφίαν

According to these concentrations of imperatives with οὖν, the unit
unfolds in three parts: a) 6:1-8 focuses on the theme of judgment on those
in power (inclusion: κρατοῦντες, κράτησις, κραταιοῖς 6:2,3,8); b) 6:9-11
serves as a linchpin between the two extreme sections of the unit
(inclusion: οἱ λόγοι μοῦ, τῶν λόγων μοῦ,6:9,11); c) 6:12-21 concentrates
on the qualities of wisdom as the object of the exhortation (inclusion in
σοφία, σοφίαν, 6:12,21b).

The link section 6:9-11 is tightly organized through the two-fold
repetition of οὖν and λόγοι μοῦ. However, it is linked to both extreme
sections in such a manner that attributing it to either one does not do
justice to the unity of the entire unit[46]. It is linked to the first section
through the repetition of the verb, μανθάνω (6:1b). It is linked to the
following section through the repetition of σοφία (6:9,12,21, particularly
through μάθετε σοφίαν, τιμήσατε σοφίαν 6:9,21) and through the
repetition of τύραννοι, (6:9,21), which we read for the first time in the
first part of Wis (it occurs next in 8:15)[47].

The final section of the unit is united by virtue of the inclusion in
σοφία (6:12,21) and by the repetition of the pronouns referring to
wisdom. It evolves in two parts: a) the qualities of wisdom (6:12-16); b)
the sorites that explains how wisdom leads to a kingdom (6:17-20).
Verse 21 concludes the entire unit with repetitions to each preceding

---

[45] M. GILBERT, "Sagesse", *DBS* 11, col. 68.

[46] PERRENCHIO and GILBERT divide the unit between 6:11 and 6:12. PERRENCHIO draws
a thematic distinction between the two sections (6:1-11, parenetic and 6:12-20, dogmatic)
by separating v 21 from the second section (F. PERRENCHIO, "Struttura 1,1-15", *Sales* 37
[1975] p. 293). But in light of the inclusion σοφία, σοφίαν (6:12,21), this is not justifiable.
GILBERT attaches 9-11 to 1-8 on the sole basis of the repeated verb μανθάνω (M. GILBERT,
"Sagesse", *DBS* 11, col. 68).

[47] BIZZETI divides the unit according to the smaller sub-units, based on inclusions
and repetitions (1-8, 9-11, 12-16, 17-20, 21), but without noting the linking function of
9-11 (P. BIZZETI, *Il Libro*, p. 63).

section of the unit, οὖν, τύραννοι, σοφίαν, βασιλεύσητε. The section
which presents the qualities of wisdom is delimited by the grammatical
sequence of two stichs beginning with καί for the two extreme verses
(12,16) and by the possible inclusion of the homophones εὐχερῶς,
εὐμενῶς (6:12b,16b)[48]. The sorites (6:17-20), which usually consists of a
six-part chain syllogism concluding with a surprise affirmation, is easily
delimited by the inclusion in ἐπιθυμία (6:17,20).

As I mentioned above, scholars have differed considerably on the
location of the actual conclusion of the first part of the Book of Wis and
the beginning of the second. By now this should be clearly intelligible as
due to the author's penchant to link units together through transitional
units. A discussion of these positions will provide further clarifications
regarding this concluding unit and the introduction to the eulogy of
wisdom (6:22-25).

B - 7.   The Division Between the First Two Parts of Wis

Prior to the application of literary criticism to Wis, it was common
to end the first part of the book with c. 5. The exhortation in c. 6 was
seen as the introduction to the eulogy of wisdom which dominates the
second part (eg. BONAVENTURE, HEINISCH, ALONSO SCHÖKEL, LARCHER).
But with the uncovering of the concentric structure of the first six
chapters by REESE, some part of c. 6 has usually been attributed to the
first part of the book by subsequent scholars. REESE himself had the
second part of the book begin with 6:12, where the first detailed
description of personified wisdom takes place[49]. But this division is
perceptible purely on thematic grounds and through a rearrangement of
the text. With the inclusion that WRIGHT established in βασιλεῖς,
βασιλεύσητε (6:1,21) and accepting the textual sequence of verses, the
place of the conclusion was extended to v 21. This concluding unit
(6:1-21) was analyzed with even greater precision by PERRENCHIO and
GILBERT and is the delimitation followed in this work.

Two differing divisions merit special attention precisely because of
the literary grounds they bring to bear on their positions. OFFERHAUS
ends the first part of the book with 6:8. BIZZETI considers 6:22-25 a
transitional section but collocates it with the first part.

---

[48] M. GILBERT, "Sagesse", *DBS* 11, col. 68.
[49] REESE attributed different sections of c. 6 to both the first and second part of Wis
through a re-arrangement of the text. The sorites in 6:17-21 concludes the first part of
Wis, whereas the section dealing with the first detailed description of wisdom opens the
second part. J.M. REESE, "Plan", *CBQ* 27 (1965) pp. 392-396.

The two main arguments which OFFERHAUS brings forward for the major caesura at 6:8 are: a) the change in theme from negative reasons to the positive attributes of wisdom as a motive for the exhortation; b) the change to first person speech [50].

The first argument is primarily thematic, but even from the thematic point of view this argument is questionable insofar as providing grounds for a major literary caesura. The contrast which the author draws between the just and the wicked in the four diptychs has constantly held in tension positive and negative aspects. In the concluding unit to the first part of Wis, therefore, it is not surprising to find a contrast in the motives for embracing wisdom, through fear of divine judgment and through love of wisdom's positive attributes. The latter attributes provide a link and a transitional basis for the eulogy of wisdom which follows. The positive motives for embracing justice and wisdom are not altogether lacking in the first unit (1:1-15, cf. vv 6a,15).

The second argument of OFFERHAUS appeals to the literary feature of a change in speech which, supposedly, is inaugurated with the two phrases, οἱ λόγοι μου, τῶν λόγων μου (6:9,11). However, there is not a single verb in the first person in 6:1-21. The change in speech which dominates the second part of Wis is simply prepared by the two phrases where the speaker refers to 'my words'. It is only with 6:22 that the actual change of speech takes place in concentrated form with six verbs [51].

OFFERHAUS's observations do point to a significant insight regarding the first and second parts of Wis. The primary motive in the exhortation to justice in the first part is negative, the fear of judgment and death. This is particularly true in the parallel sections A - A' (1:1-15, 6:1-21) [52]. This negativity stands in contrast to the eulogy of wisdom in the second part of Wis, which extols the benefits of wisdom for humanity.

BIZZETI equally appeals to literary grounds for attaching 6:22-25 to the first part of Wis [53]. First of all, there are verbal and syntactical links to the preceding unit, 6:1-21. Βασιλεύς (6:24) continues the royal terms in 6:1,20,21. The exhortation in v 25 recalls the triple exhortation in 6:1-2, 9-11, 21. These two repetitions, however, deserve qualifications.

Firstly, it is the plural verb form, βασιλεύσητε (6:21), which more clearly constitutes the inclusion to the plural noun, βασιλεῖς (6:1). The phrase, 'a wise king is the stability of his people' (6:24b), already

---

[50] U. OFFERHAUS, *Komposition*, pp. 52-53.

[51] Cf. F. PERRENCHIO, "Struttura 1,1-15", *Sales* 37 (1975) pp. 292-294.

[52] GILBERT also draws attention to the aspect of judgment which binds the unit 6:1-21 to the opening unit. This is highlighted through the repetition of the rare word ἐξέτασις (1:9) in its verbal form ἐξετάσει (6:3). M. GILBERT, "Sagesse", *DBS* 11, col. 68.

[53] "I vv. 6,22-25 dunque hanno una duplice funzione: chiudere la prima parte e aprire la seconda, in notevole continuità con la prima" (P. BIZZETI, *Il Libro*, p. 65).

anticipates the wisdom of Solomon which the following chapters divulge. Secondly, the exhortation in 6:25 lacks the adverb, οὖν, which indicates the concluding nature of each specific exhortation in 6:1-21. For these reasons, it is preferable to view these repetitions as linking techniques between the two units rather than as an indication of unit demarcations.

In the second place, over and above these links to the immediately preceding sub-units, Bizzeti observes several important verbal links which exist between 6:22-25 and the first part of Wis, primarily the sub-units 1:13-15 and 2:21-24: σωτήριοι αἱ γενέσεις τοῦ κόσμου (1:14); πλῆθος δὲ σοφῶν σωτηρία κόσμου (6:24); φθόνῳ (2:24, 6:23), μυστήρια (2:22, 6:22)[54].

The question remains, however, whether or not such verbal links alone provide sufficient grounds for collocating the unit to the first part. Verbal repetitions exist across the entire spectrum of the Book of Wis. They constitute a linking technique between various units rather than providing unequivocal signs of unit delimitations. Together with inclusions or other syntactic similarities, verbal repetitions often confirm the limits of a smaller unit through their concentration within clearly defined parameters.

The difficulty with collocating 6:22-25 to the first part is the change to direct speech in the first person in 6:22. This change to the first person, affirmed in the six verbs within four verses, lies in immediate continuity with the speech of the unnamed Solomon, εἰμὶ μὲν κἀγώ (7:1), which continues with verbal forms in the first person. This change to the first person is a major shift in perspective, one in which the narrator's experience of wisdom becomes the focal point.

This syntactical change is bolstered by the announcement of themes which Wis 7–9 treats[55]. If the unit, 6:22-25, shows verbal links to the first part, even more so does it show contact with the following units. On the one hand, the verbal links to the first part, which Bizzeti rightly highlights, do not touch upon the main thematic points of the first part: the exhortation to justice, the folly of injustice, the immortality of the just. On the other hand, the verbal links between 6:22-25 and the following sections touch precisely on the main themes of the second part of Wis, the person of Solomon, the origins of wisdom, the benefits of wisdom.

The unit 6:22-25 is bound to the succeeding unit through an important series of repetitions. The repetitions are emphatic precisely because they touch on the themes that are expounded through the units

---

[54] Bizzeti also quotes the repetition of ἀφθαρσία (2:23, 6:19), but this is not to the point, for this repetition is not part of 6:22-25 (P. Bizzeti, Il Libro, p. 64).

[55] The unit, 6:22-25, has been understood as the introduction to the following concentric units of Wis 7–8 precisely because of the announcement of theme by Wright, Perrenchio, Gilbert, (see M. Gilbert, "Sagesse", DBS 11, cols. 69-70).

in Wis 7–8. PERRENCHIO goes so far as to consider the repetitions of the key words, σοφία, ἀποκρύψω, ἐμφανές in 6:22 and 7:21-22 as an inclusion [56]. These verses highlight the theme of the revelation of God's wisdom. Moreover, the very question that 6:22 poses is presented as the project for what Solomon will reveal in the following speech. "What wisdom is and how she came to be, I will announce."

In conclusion, 6:22-25 appropriately constitutes the introduction to the concentric units of Wis 7–9. This introduction manifests links with the preceding units which confirm the author's ability to weave literary units into a flowing unity. These links are also forcefully present throughout the concentric units of the first six chapters. The dynamic of the argument in the first part of Wis cannot be sufficiently clarified without reference to the interconnection of the concentric units themselves.

B-8. The Literary Unity of Wis 1–6

The literary unity of the first part of Wis is achieved through the concentric structure of the major units and through their employment of repetitive and antithetical images. The technique of concentric structuralization links the extreme units in parallel fashion, manifesting a direction towards the center, whereas the technique of repetitive images links the units together in linear fashion. Both techniques are employed by the author of Wis, culminating in a dense and complex poetic achievement.

B-9. The Concentric Structure of Wis 1–6

A (1:1-15) = (6:1-21) A'

The clearest sign of parallelism between the opening and concluding units appears in the very first verses of each unit (1:1, 6:1). Three imperatives, in the first verse of both units, open the exhortation directed to the rulers of the earth. Imperatives are also used in the closing sections

---

[56] F. PERRENCHIO, "Struttura 1,1-15", *Sales* 37 (1975) p. 292. A difficulty in considering 6:22 and 7:21-22 as an inclusion is the rupture that such an inclusion would cause in the concentric structure that is achieved in Wis 7–8. Not every repetition of a phrase and series of terms need be considered an inclusion that delimits a unit. The concentric structure of Wis 7–8, that is grounded in a series of inclusions that match the respective themes of the individual units, is sufficiently clear to postulate the repetitions in 6:22 and 7:21-22 as linking repetitions used for the purpose of emphasis.

of each unit [57]. The two units are thereby paralleled to one another through an exhortation directed to the rulers of the earth. In the first unit, the rulers are entitled "οἱ κρίνοντες τὴν γῆν"; in the last unit, they are called "βασιλεῖς" and "δικασταὶ περάτων γῆς". In both cases, ἡ γῆ, establishes the common ground of universality.

Three verbs employed in the opening verses (1:1-2) within the context of the exhortation to love justice and to seek the Lord are repeated in the exposition of wisdom in the last unit (6:12): ἀγαπάω, ζητέω, εὑρίσκομαι. Through these repetitions a parallelism is drawn between the opening exhortation which is more general (to love justice, to seek the Lord) and the specific exhortation to learn wisdom in the last unit which prepares for the eulogy of wisdom (6:22–11:1). Whereas in the first unit the object of the exhortation is varied (justice, the Lord, the Spirit of the Lord, wisdom), in the final unit the object is exclusively wisdom.

Finally, the rare word, ἐξέτασις (1:9), and its cognate verb, ἐξετάσει (6:3), heighten the paralleled idea of judgment in both units [58].

B (1:16–2:24) = (5:1-23) B'

These two units parallel each other primarily through the speech of the impious. The author has the enemy of the just speak for themselves regarding their life-project (Wis 2) and regarding their recognition of error (Wis 5). Both units prepare the direct speech of the impious through a brief introduction (1:16–2:1a; 5:1-3) and the units close with the author's reflection and conclusion upon their reasoning (2:21-24, 5:14-23).

The two speeches of the impious parallel one another in concentric fashion [59].

a	2:1b-5	–		5:9-13	a'
	b	2:6-11	–	5:6-8	b'
		c	2:12-20	– 5:4-5	c'

---

[57] 1:1, ἀγαπήσατε, φρονήσατε, ζητήσατε 6:1, ἀκούσατε, σύνετε, μάθετε. Verse 6:2 continues the opening exhortation with another imperative, ἐνωτίσασθε. The concluding imperatives in the first unit are constituted by φυλάξασθε, φείσασθε, μὴ ζηλοῦτε, μηδὲ ἐπισπᾶσθε (1:11-12); in the closing unit by τιμήσατε (6:21). In the last unit, there are the additional imperatives in v 11, ἐπιθυμήσατε, ποθήσατε. There is a final imperative directed to the kings in 6:25, παιδεύεσθε, which links the following eulogy of wisdom to the exhortation of the first part of Wis. Note that each imperative is expressed through a different verb.

[58] M. GILBERT, "Sagesse", DBS 11, col. 68.

[59] This concentric structure of the speeches of the impious has been recognized in varying degrees by PERRENCHIO, OFFERHAUS and BIZZETI. F. PERRENCHIO, "Struttura, 1,16–2,24 e 5,1-23", Sales 43 (1981) pp. 33-35; U. OFFERHAUS, Komposition, pp. 54-55; P. BIZZETI, Il Libro, pp. 62-63. The concentric structure of the two parallel units is recognized

a) their judgement regarding the transience of life (2:1b-5, 5:9-13); several poetic images referring to the human body and to nature are employed to describe the transience of life; terms repeated in the sections are: ἀήρ (2:3, 5:11,12), ἴχνος (2:4, 5:10), πάροδος, δίοδον (2:5, 5:12), ἀναλύω (2:1, 5:12), παρέρχομαι (2:4, 5:9);

b) their stance towards life of exploitation and their recognition of its fruitlessness (2:6-11, 5:6-8): μὴ παροδευσάτω, διωδεύσαμεν (2:7, 5:7), πλησθῶμεν, ἐνεπλήσθημεν (2:7, 5:7);

c) their decision to oppose the just one to the point of death and their recognition of the surprising glory of the just one (2:12-20, 5:4-5):

ὁ βίος αὐτοῦ, τὸν βίον αὐτοῦ (2:15, 5:4),
ὀνειδίζει, ὀνειδισμοῦ (2:12, 5:4),
υἱὸς θεοῦ, ἐν υἱοῖς θεοῦ (2:18, 5:5),
ἐλογίσθημεν, ἐλογισάμεθα (2:16, 5:4).

In addition to these terms, which constitute the parallelism between the various components of the units, other words are repeated that bind together the speeches of the impious as a whole [60]. ἥλιος (2:4, 5:6), σκιά (2:5, 5:9), ὁδός (2:16, 5:6,7), τελευτή (2:1,5, 5:4), κλῆρος (2:9, 5:5).

Finally, other terms are repeated in the introductions and conclusions to the speeches of the impious. The concluding comment of the author in the first speech (ἐπλανήθησαν, 2:21) is taken up in the oppressors' recognition of the error of their lifestyle (ἄρα ἐπλανήθημεν, 5:6). Creation, which the impious decide to exploit in the first speech (χρησώμεθα τῇ κτίσει, 2:6) returns with a vengeance on the side of the just in the concluding section of the second speech (ὁπλοποιήσει τὴν κτίσιν, 5:17). The impious oppressed the just with the deriding challenge to see whether their claim was true that God would save the just one

---

by these authors even with the slight differences they share in the delimitations of the sub-units.

PERRENCHIO: a 2:1-5   - a' 5:8-13
                   b 2:6-11   - b' 5:6-7
                   c 2:12-20   - c' 5:4-5

OFFERHAUS: a 2:1-5   - a' 5:9-13
                   b 2:6-9(10f)   - b' 5:6-8
                   c 2:(10f)12-20   - c' 5:4f

BIZZETI (GILBERT): a 2:1b-5   - a' 5:8-13
                   b 2:6-9   - b' 5:6-7
                   c 2:10-20   - c' 5:4-5

[60] For a detailed analysis of all the repeated words in the speeches of the impious and their frequency in the entire work of Wis, consult F. PERRENCHIO, "Struttura, 1,16–2,24 e 5,1-23", Sales 43 (1981) pp. 33-34.

from the hands of oppressors (ἐκ χειρὸς ἀνθεστηκότων, 2:18). It is the just ones, in the end, who will receive from the hand of the Lord a diadem (ἐκ χειρὸς κυρίου, 5:16). In the conclusion to the first speech, the impious did not hope for the wages of holiness (οὐδὲ μισθὸν ἤλπισαν ὁσιότητος, 2:22). Three words from this single stich are taken up in the concluding part of the second speech. 1) The hope of the ungodly at the end is compared to chaff taken by the wind (ἐλπὶς ἀσεβοῦς ὡς φερόμενος χνοῦς ὑπὸ ἀνέμου, 5:14). 2) But the wages of the just are in the Lord (ὁ μισθὸς αὐτῶν, 5:15). 3) The Lord will take holiness as an invincible shield (ὁσιότητα, 5:19).

All of these repetitions between the two units manifest a concerted effort on the part of the author to establish a correlation between the two speeches of the impious.

C 3:1–4:20

By virtue of its centrality, the central unit has no parallel unit. Already within itself the unit manifests a chiastic structure based on the parallelism between the first and last diptych and the parallelism between the second and third. The links that it manifests with the other units points to the the linear development of the various units.

B-10. The Linear Links of Wis 1–6

The analysis of the unit delimitations focused on the literary techniques of inclusions and repetitions within the units. The analysis of the concentric structure highlighted the technique of linking major units into a specific pattern through thematic and vocabulary repetition. Without the analysis of the linear, linking techniques that the author employs, the literary analysis would be incomplete. It is this technique of linking the units by means of a linear, progressive development of images that adds a dynamic quality and perspective to the first six chapters. The progression of thought is already perceivable in the concentric structure of the units. The linear progression of images from unit to unit highlights the dynamic movement of the argument. It is here that the author employs poetic sensibility to the utmost, whereby nuances are added to the argument through the adaptation of images through repetition or antithesis.

A 1:1-15 - 1:16–2:24 B

The first two units regarding the exhortation to justice and the speech of the impious are bound together by the endings of both units which deal with the topic of death. The exhortation to justice concludes with the climactic motive of avoiding death. The assertion is made by the author that God has nothing to do with death and that it is not part of creation (1:13-14). In the conclusion of the speech of the wicked, the author recalls how God made humanity for eternity and that death entered the world through the envy of the devil (2:23-24).

Verbal links between the two conclusions (1:11-15, 2:21-24) are numerous[61].

θάνατον, θάνατος (1:12,13, 2:24),
θεός, θεοῦ (1:13, 2:22,23),
ἐν πλάνῃ ζωῆς ὑμῶν, ἐπλανήθησαν (1:12, 2:21),
ἔκτισεν (1:14, 2:23),
κόσμου, κόσμον (1:14, 2:24).

Moreover, v 1:16 which opens the second unit is linked to both the previous unit through χειρῶν, χερσίν (1:12,16), λόγων, λόγοις (1:9,16) and to the conclusion of the second unit through τῆς ἐκείνου μερίδος (1:16, 2:24). The object for v 16, θάνατος, is taken from the conclusion to the first unit (v 13). It is the underlying subject matter of the false reasoning of the impious (2:1-5). Through these ties between the first and second units, the shift from the exhortation to the speech of the impious is achieved smoothly.

B 1:16–2:20 - 3:1–4:20 C

The four diptychs in the central unit of Wis 1-6 take up various terms from the reasoning and projects explained in the speech of the impious. These terms are repeated with a touch of irony or with dramatic effect in order to dramatize the radical turn-about of events between the just and the wicked.

In the opening diptych, the radical turn-about is emphasized through a backward glance at the challenge of the impious. The wicked wanted to see whether or not God would save the just from the hands of the adversaries (ἐκ χειρὸς ἀνθεστηκότων, 2:18); in fact, the just are in the hand of God (ἐν χειρὶ θεοῦ, 3:1). The wicked planned to inflict torture on the just (βασάνῳ, 2:19); but no torture will touch them (βάσανος, 3:1). The wicked are worthy of the devil's part (ἄξιοι, 1:16); the just have been found to be worthy of the Lord (ἀξίους, 3:5). The wicked derided the claim of the just that there would be an accounting (ἐπισκοπή, 2:20); at the time of accounting (ἐν καιρῷ ἐπισκοπῆς, 3:7), the just will shine forth (also 4:15). The wicked compared their lives to the transiency of a spark

---

[61] As we had seen in the first chapter treating these sections, the verbal and thematic links between 1:13-16 and 2:23-24, noted by BIZZETI and GILBERT, gave cause to a question

(σπινθήρ, 2:2); but the just will be dynamic like sparks (σπινθῆρες, 3:7) flashing through stubble [62].

Even the remaining diptychs refer to various terms in the speech of the impious to add a touch of irony to the exaggerated claims and projects of the wicked. They exhorted the exploitation of life with the image of crowning their heads with crowns of rosebuds (στεψώμεθα, 2:8); but it is virtue which marches through the ages carrying the crown of victory (στεφανηφοροῦσα, 4:2). The wicked considered wealth and power to be their lot (κλῆρος, 2:9), but it is the just who have their lot (3:14) in the temple of the Lord. The wicked had judged life to be valueless because their name and their deeds would not be remembered (οὐθεὶς μνημονεύσει, 2:4); in fact there is immortality in the memory of virtue (ἐν μνήμῃ αὐτῆς, 4:1), but the memory of the wicked will be destroyed (ἡ μνήμη αὐτῶν, 4:19). The wicked wanted to see (ἴδωμεν, 2:17) whether the just would be saved; indeed, they will see the end of the wise and be filled with contempt (ὄψονται, 4:17,18).

C 3:1–4:20 - 5:1-23 B'

The unit containing the second speech of the impious not only is parallel to their first speech in Wis 2, but it also contains significant expressions that refer to the immediately preceding unit.

— The central unit highlighted the contrast between the hope of the just and the empty hope of the wicked (ἡ ἐλπὶς αὐτῶν ἀθανασίας, κενὴ ἡ ἐλπὶς αὐτῶν, 3:4,11). This judgment is emphasized in the comment of the author after the second speech of the oppressors (ὅτι ἐλπὶς ἀσεβοῦς ὡς φερόμενος χνοῦς, 5:14).

— The Lord will simply laugh at the contempt the wicked bear for the just one (ἐκγελάσεται, 4:18). In their astonishment, the oppressors realize they had considered the just one whom they now see in glory 'a subject of laughter' (εἰς γέλωτα, 5:4).

— The possession of virtue (μετὰ ἀρετῆς, 4:1) brings immortality. At the time of judgment, the wicked confess that they have no sign of virtue to show (καὶ ἀρετῆς μὲν σημεῖον οὐδὲν ἔσχομεν, 5:13).

Another pair of 'flashbacks' refers to statements in the preceding unit of diptychs in continuity with the first speech of the impious.

---

mark regarding the delimitation of the first two units as envisaged by WRIGHT. However, these verbal links need not indicate an inclusion. They signify a parallelism between the endings of the first two units.

[62] ALONSO SCHÖKEL, drew attention to the referral back to the speech of the impious in the declaration of glory for the just. He notes several verbal or synonymous repetitions of Wis 2 in Wis 3. L. ALONSO SCHÖKEL, *Ecclesiastes y Sabiduria*, Madrid: 1974, pp. 97-98. See also P. BIZZETI, *Il Libro*, p. 55.

— The play on the verb, to see, is brought to a close. At the end, the wicked, seeing the just one in glory (ἰδόντες, 5:2), will be shaken with great fear. This 'seeing' of the wicked picks up the thread of 'seeing' from the central unit (4:14,17,18), and is the final, clinching response of the author to the challenge launched by the wicked in c. 2 (ἴδωμεν εἰ οἱ λόγοι αὐτοῦ ἀληθεῖς, 2: 17) [63].

— Similarly, the play on a word for death, τελευτή, is brought to a conclusion, never more to appear in the book. In the final speech, the oppressors remember how they had considered the end of the just one, whom they condemned to a shameful death, to be worthless (τὴν τελευτὴν αὐτοῦ ἄτιμον, 5:4). This reference to the end of the just recalls the reasoning of the wicked on their own lives when they decided there was no healing for their 'end' (οὐκ ἔστιν ἴασις ἐν τελευτῇ ἀνθρώπου, 2:1). In the central unit, the author declares that the wicked will see the end of the wise and not understand (τελευτὴν σοφοῦ, 4:17).

— The final judgment presented at the end of Wis 5 attributes a crucial role to the cosmos which will fight alongside the Lord against iniquity (συνεκπολεμήσει δὲ αὐτῷ ὁ κόσμος, 5:20). This reference to κόσμος picks up the assertion from the first unit that the forces of the cosmos are wholesome (σωτήριοι αἱ γενέσεις τοῦ κόσμου, 1:14).

The last sub-unit of Wis 5 (5:15-23) contains a pattern which reproduces the opening of the central unit (3:1-12). Both of the sub-units follow immediately upon the speech of the impious. They state the glorious situation of the just and the miserable end of the wicked. The verbal links appear in both parts of the contrast.

3:1	δικαίων δὲ ψυχαὶ ἐν χειρὶ θεοῦ
5:15	δίκαιοι δὲ εἰς τὸν αἰῶνα ζῶσιν
3:10b	καὶ ἐν κυρίῳ ὁ μισθὸς αὐτῶν
	καὶ τοῦ κυρίου ἀποστάντες
5:23	ἀντιστήσεται αὐτοῖς πνεῦμα δυνάμεως

This similarity between the two units that follow the speeches of the wicked point to a simple emphasis the author establishes. The wicked do not have the last word. Rather it is the just who are praised by the author after the wicked have presented their case (Wis 2) and their confession (Wis 5).

---

[63] The time sequence is followed perfectly in the author's use of the verb, to see: "let us see if his words are true" (2:17), "seeing (the death of the just) they did not understand" (4:14), "they will see the end of the wise" (4:17,18), "seeing the just one in glory they will tremble" (5:2).

A' 6:1-21

The final unit, which contains the exhortation to honor wisdom, not only parallels the opening exhortation but also picks up the threads referring to wisdom throughout the previous units. This is primarily achieved through the use of the sorites which links various attributes to the desire for wisdom (παιδείας, ἀγάπη, νόμων, ἀφθαρσία, βασιλείαν/ βασιλεύσητε, 6:17-21).

The actual object of the final exhortation in Wis 6 remains open until v 9 where we find the explicit object, 'ἵνα μάθητε σοφίαν'. Wisdom becomes the subject of discussion for the remainder of the unit, which closes with the exhortation, 'τιμήσατε σοφίαν' (6:21). This concentration of the subject, σοφία, in the final exhortation prepares the reader for the following eulogy of wisdom and picks up the references to wisdom from the previous units (1:4,6, 3:11, 4:17). The term for wisdom is absent in both units containing the speeches of the impious! This absence heightens the contrast between the wicked who are foolish and the just who are wise.

The sorites contains a dense concentration of terms employed in the previous units:

— ἀγάπη (6:17,18): refers to the opening exhortation, ἀγαπήσατε δικαιοσύνην (1:1); the believers will remain in the love of the Lord (ἐν ἀγάπῃ 3:9); there was one loved by God (ἠγαπήθη, 4:10, intimating Enoch, Gen 5:24); and wisdom is quickly recognized by those who love her (ἀγαπώντων αὐτήν, 6:12).

— παιδεία (6:17ab): discipline is a quality of the Holy Spirit (πνεῦμα παιδείας,1:5); the wicked criticize the just for recalling the sins of their youth (ἁμαρτήματα παιδείας ἡμῶν, 2:12); the just were disciplined for a short while and, therefore, they will receive a great reward (ὀλίγα παιδευθέντες, 3:5); the ungodly despised both wisdom and discipline (σοφίαν γὰρ καὶ παιδείαν, 3:11); the final exhortation encourages learning for the sake of being disciplined (παιδευθήσεσθε, 6:11).

— νόμων (6:18): contrasts with the claim of the unjust that might is their law (ἡ ἰσχὺς νόμος, 2:11), the just one accuses them of their sins against the law (ἁμαρτήματα νόμου, 2:12); the kings are warned of the judgment if they do not keep the law (οὐδὲ ἐφυλάξατε νόμον, 6:4).

— ἀφθαρσία (6:18, 19): picks up the declaration of the author that God had made humanity for immortality (ἐπ' ἀφθαρσίᾳ, 2:23).

— βασιλείαν, βασιλεύσητε (6:20, 21). The concentration of terms referring to royalty provides a backdrop for the eulogy of wisdom by the anonymous speaker, Solomon. These terms of royalty in the sorites pick up the declaration of the author that the kingdom of Hades is not on the earth (οὔτε ᾅδου βασίλειον ἐπὶ γῆς, 1:14). The Lord will rule over the just forever (βασιλεύσει αὐτῶν κύριος, 3:8). The just will receive the kingship of splendor (τὸ βασίλειον τῆς εὐπρεπείας, 5:16).

Apart from the sorites, two rare phrases from the preceding units are also picked up in the final exhortation.

— τοὺς ἀξίους αὐτῆς (6:16), those who are worthy of wisdom will be sought out by her. On the one hand, this assertion is diametrically in contrast to the earlier assertion claiming that those who are worthy of death belong under its sphere (ὅτι ἄξιοί εἰσιν τῆς ἐκείνου μερίδος εἶναι, 1:16). On the other hand, it recalls the image of the just who have been found worthy of God (καὶ εὗρεν αὐτοὺς ἀξίους ἑαυτοῦ, 3:5).

This linear development of images, whereby later units pick up the threads of arguments from previous units for the sake of dramatizing or drawing nuances, continues throughout Wis. The speeches of the impious with the author's comments on them find a parallel in the critique of nature, idol, and animal worship in the final part of the book. Similarly, the diptychs in the central unit, which contrast the virtuous with the impious, find a parallel in the contrasts between the plagues against the Egyptians and the blessings for the Israelites. The final judgment (5:15-23), which is a focal point in the author's resolution of the challenge of the impious, is echoed in the conclusion of the book where the cosmos itself is transformed to aid those on the side of the Lord.

The following outline of the concentric and linear development of the first part of Wis illustrates the various ties that exist between the various units. The far left of the diagram indicates the concentric structure of the main units, according to the theme of each unit delimited by their inclusions. The central part of the diagram highlights the structures of the various sub-units, also with indications of the main inclusions and repetitions of key words. The far right of the diagram points to the main linear links achieved through the repetition of key words throughout the structure.

Wisdom 1:1–6:21

UNITS	Inclusions Characteristics	SUB-UNITS	Inclusions Characteristics	LINEAR LINKS
A 1:1-15	δικαιοσύνη (1:1,15) – exhortation to justice in the Lord..	1:1-5 1:6-11 1:12-15	δικαιοσύνη, ἀδικία (1:1,5) – antithetical concentric structure – a, b, c, b', a' γλώσση (1:6e,11b) – vocabulary of speech/court-case θάνατος, ἀθάνατος (1:12,15) synonyms for death	θάνατος 1:12,13; 2:24 θέος 1:13; 2:22-23
B 1:16–2:24	τῆς ἐκείνου μερίδος (1:16d, 2:24b) (2:9c) λογισάμενοι, λογίσαντο (2:1a,21a) – speech of the impious	1:16–2:1a 2:1b-5 2:6-11 2:12-20 2:21-24	– Introduction χερσίν, λόγοις τελευτή, τελευτῆς (2:1c,5b) a ὁ βίος ἡμῶν (2:1b,4c) – tension between life and "end" χρησώμεθα, ἄχρηστον (2:6,11) b – call to exploit nature and the weak – the project to oppress – progression c – the alternation of ἡμῶν/αὐτόν – Conclusion	πλάνη 1:12 ἐπλανήθησαν 2:21 ἔκτισεν 1:14; 2:23 κόσμος 1:14; 2:24
C 3:1–4:20	– Four diptychs, each contrasting the just with the wicked – adversative δέ indicates each contrast	3:1-12 3:13-19 4:1-6 4:7-20	ἀφρόνων, ἄφρονες (3:2,12) – prepositional phrases with ἐν ἐν ἐπισκοπῇ (3:13c) ἐν ἡμέρᾳ διαγνώσεος (3:18b) — καρπός κοίτην, κοίτης (3:13b, 16b) 3:13,15 4:5 ἀτεκνία, τέκνα (4:1,6b) δίκαιος, τελευτῆσαι, γῆρας = past in 4:7-8 = 4:16 ἀσεβεῖς = subject (4:16) in 4:17-20 = future	δίκαιοι 3:1; 5:15 κύριος 3:10; 5:15
B' 5:1-23	στήσεται, ἀντιστήσεται (5:1,23) – speech of the impious	5:1-3 5:4-13(14) 5:(14)15-23	– Introduction στήσεται, ἐκστήσονται (5:1,2b) ἔσχομεν (5:4,13b) c'5:4-6 οὗτος, οὕτως (5:4,13a) b'5:7-8 – confession of guilt a'5:9-13 λαίλαπος, ὡς λαῖλαψ (5:14,23) – glory of just, final victory	

A' 6:1-21	βασιλεῖς, βασιλεύσητε
	(6:1,21b)
	– exhortation to wisdom
		6:1-8
		
		6:9-11
		
		6:12-21
			κρατοῦντες, κράτησις, κραταιοῖς,
			(6:2,3,8)
			οἱ λόγοι μοῦ, τῶν λόγων μοῦ, 6:9,11
			– qualitires of wisdom
			σοφία, σοφίαν, 6:12,21b
			– sorites = wisdom leads to a kingdom
				σοφία – 1:4,6
				         – 3:11
				         – 4:17
				ἀγάπη – 1:1; 3:9
				         – 4:10
				παιδεία – 1:1
				         – 3:5,11
				νόμος – 2:11,12
				ἀφθαρσία – 2:23
				βασιλεία – 1:14
				         – 3:8; 5:16
				ἄξιος – 1:16; 3:5

Chapter Three

THE DYNAMIC OF THE ARGUMENT IN WIS 1–6

C-1. A Preliminary Qualification: can a concentric structure be dynamic?

The first six chapters of Wis clearly are ordered according to a deliberate concentric structure where various enclosed units parallel one another. The structure itself highlights the relationship of the units with their themes to one another. But the parallel units do not simply mirror one another. Although the verbal and thematic similarities are meant to catch the reader's attention in the flow of the presentation, there are differences that become equally evident in the repetitions. These differences between the parallel units give room for development and momentum within a concentric structure.

Moreover, the progression and juxtaposition of images and concepts in the concentrically constructed discourse convey the tension and the momentum that builds up in the central argument of the section. In this way, a concentric structure need not express its themes in a static manner. In the discourse, between the theme announced at the beginning and repeated at the end of the section, the reader is led through a dramatic argument. Like a moving spiral, the concentric structure of Wis 1–6 is a vehicle which conveys a progression of thought by means of a growing momentum.

Several phrases, images and even individual words are charged with emotion and ambiguity. The overall dynamic of the argument in the discourse is the context where the ambiguity of terms may be understood with greater clarity as being deliberate.

C-2. The Opening Exhortation (Wis 1:1-15): setting out the ramifications of the discourse

The address to the rulers of the earth combines two specific exhortations in the opening of the discourse: to love justice and to seek the Lord. Loving justice is the first objective in the exhortation. But,

immediately in the first verse, seeking the Lord is placed parallel to the
love of justice. Furthermore, Wisdom (v 4) and the Holy Spirit (v 5) are
presented as qualifications of the subject, the Lord. These subjects are
deliberately connected to one another.

At once, these positive terms of the exhortation, justice, the Lord,
Wisdom, the Holy Spirit are placed in juxtaposition to the negative terms,
injustice (v 5), crooked thoughts (v 3), a deceitful mind (v 4). The effect of
this juxtaposition is a heightening of tension and conflict. To achieve the
love of justice and union with God requires the renunciation of
wickedness. The locus of conflict resides in the human person, who is
exhorted to do justice and refrain from wickedness. The antithetical
inclusion of justice/injustice (vv 1,5) and the alternation of positive
subject/negative verb (vv 2,4) give a formal stylistic support to the tension
which the juxtaposition of opposites thematically presents.

With the employment of a particular aspect of juridical terminology
in 1:6-11, namely false speech, the tension introduced in the opening unit
takes on a new and more precise direction[1]. The conflict between
wickedness and justice is moved into the juridical arena of a trial where
effective judgment against wickedness is paramount. Terminology which
reflects the background image of a trial is introduced in a bipolar
structure: the wicked, who are under the accusation of false, slanderous
speech, and an all-knowing judge. As of yet, the victim of the false speech
does not enter into the discourse. The conflict is maintained between false
accusers or slanderers, on the one hand, and God, whose wisdom and
spirit champion justice, on the other.

The wicked under accusation are described as blasphemers[2]; they
have hidden thoughts and plans, they celebrate injustice, they slander.

---

[1] For a detailed overview of the vast forensic terminology in both poetic and prosaic
texts of the Hebrew bible, see P. Bovati, *Ristabilire la giustizia*, AnBib 110, Rome: 1986.
Regarding the terminology and imagery related to false accusation and to false witnesses,
see pp. 257-260.

The imagery used to dramatize the false accusations of the enemy often highlight the
power of the spoken word through metonymy. Through the use of metonymy, a particular
aspect of human speech (such as the mouth, tongue, lips), in conjunction with negative
terms (such as evil, lying, wicked), presents the process of false accusation with its obvious
reliance on the power of speech (Ps 139(140):3,4,10,12, Prov 16:27-30, 18:6-8, 26:20-28).

[2] The term, βλάσφημος, in its ordinary Greek usage, refers to damaging speech. It
need not refer to the invoking of the name of God as in cursing. The damaging effects of
the false speech of the wicked occur in the social context, namely injustice with regards to
others, as the other terms such as ἀδικίας (1:5c), καταλαλῖας (1:11b), καταψευδόμενον
(1:11d) indicate. It is concretely the aspect of injustice in wickedness which creates such
tension between God and the wicked. So, although the conflict presented in the unit is
definitely between wickedness and God, this does not mean that the particular feature of
wickedness, which is juxtaposed to the divine, is a blasphemous cursing of the divine,
devoid of social implications. See C. Larcher, *Le Livre de la Sagesse*, p 180.

The particular nuance highlighted in this description of the wicked is false speech. The wickedness that they exercise is achieved through their faculty of reason externalized in speech. The accusatory attacks of the wicked are presented through metonymy, wherein a particular bodily aspect of speech is employed to represent the verbal function. With such images as blasphemous lips (v 6), God being a hearer of tongues (v 6) the utterances of the wicked (v 8), and a lying mouth (v 11), emphasis is placed on the damaging effect of slander perpetrated through the false speech of the wicked.

This use of metonymy where a part of the body represents a human activity, of course, is wider than the narrower context of forensic terminology. For instance, in various psalms of lament, the violence threatening the psalmist is often enough described through metonymic images which parallel verbal speech with weapons of war or attacking animals (cf. Pss 21(22):12-13, 16-18, 20-21; 54(55):20-21; 56(57):4; 57(58): 3-6). However, several phrases in the sub-unit, 1:6-11, clearly define the context with juridical overtones.

The images describing the activity of wisdom and God in relation to the spoken word of the wicked is unambiguously juridical. Wisdom will not acquit the blasphemer (οὐκ ἀθῳώσει 1:6b)[3], cf. 3 Kgdms 2:9 where ἀθῳοῦν translates the Hebrew נקה (אל־תנקיהו), which, in the Piel, conveys the meaning 'to exempt from punishment'. God is a witness (μάρτυς, 1:6c, cf. Job 16:20). The parallel term to μάρτυς, namely ἐπίσκοπος in 1:6d, carries the connotation of an official task to judge[4]. Justice is personified

---

[3] The particular nuance of the phrase, φιλάνθρωπον γὰρ πνεῦμα σοφία (1:6a) is not easy to assess in light of the following stich. There are two possible meanings for the adjective, φιλάνθρωπος, a) one who loves mankind (etymological), b) one who is benevolent. The first meaning expresses the quality of solidarity between human beings who share similar situations and interests; the second conveys a quality of affection and generosity. A. PELLETIER is critical of applying the first meaning to our verse because he claims that such an etymological use of the adjective was reintroduced only with the NT (Titus 3:4). The ordinary use of the adjective, particularly in Alexandria, refers either to a common attitude of kindness, as evident in letters, or to the attitude of generosity and moderation characteristic of a king or judge who does not rigidly apply the letter of the law. A. PELLETIER, "Ce n'est pas la Sagesse mais le Dieu sauveur qui aime l'humanité", RB 87 (1980) 397-403. However, it is the first nuance based on the word's etymological meaning of 'lover of mankind' that fits the context best (C. LARCHER, Le Livre de la Sagesse, p. 179). It is wisdom's solidarity with mankind that will not allow her to acquit the blasphemer of the destructive results of his lips.

[4] ἐπίσκοπος has various meanings ordinarily conveying an official capacity which the root meaning indicates, one who oversees, such as an officer, a guardian (cf. 4 Kgdms 11:15, Isa 60:17). In v 6d, ἐπίσκοπος is a term attributed to God parallel to μάρτυς. God is at once the witness of inner thoughts and the judge of hearts. A clear example of the noun ἐπίσκοπος referring to God with the official capacity of judge occurs in Job 20:29:

This is the wicked man's portion from God,
the property granted to him by the judge.

as an accuser (ἐλέγχουσα, 1:8) [5]. A report of the words of the wicked will reach the Lord, (λόγων δὲ αὐτοῦ ἀκοή, 1:9), cf. Exod 23:1, 1 Sam 2:24, 2 Sam 13:30. The report will constitute a conviction (ἔλεγχος, 1:9) of their lawlessness, cf. Job 23:4, John 16:8, 1 Cor 14:24.

Because of this juridical context, the metonyms characterizing the speech of the wicked should be understood to convey the particular social contravention which is perpetrated through verbal declarations. This interpretation receives corroboration in the following section of the discourse, which treats the false reasoning of the wicked 2:1-20. Ultimately, the wicked plan to put the just one through a test of insult and death (2:19-20) to verify whether his declarations are true. This initial attack against slander prepares the reader to be highly critical of the positions that eventually will be set forth by the wicked. ARISTOTLE noted the rhetorical importance of attacking slander in the exordia of deliberative oratory in order to undermine the positions of the opposition or the accuser [6].

It is the relationship between the devious thoughts of the wicked and their destructive slander mediated through false speech that constitutes the particularity of their wickedness. In false accusation, the violence of the spoken word is accentuated by the defenselessness of the victim. It is necessary for a witness to arise and refute the false testimony of the accusers.

For the author, the ultimate judge is none other than the Lord, who precisely in the capacity of a witness, oversees all, even the innermost thoughts of the wicked. There will be an inquiry into the dealings of the wicked and not even a whisper will remain hidden. With such images as God himself being the witness of the innermost thoughts of the wicked (v 6c), the assurance of a careful judge (v 6d), a resume of the speech of the wicked being sure to reach God (v 9), God having acute ears that hear everything (v 10), the outcome of the trial is equally made clear. No

---

For examples of the combination of ἐπίσκοπος with μάρτυς in extra-biblical sources, see D. WINSTON, *The Wisdom of Solomon*, p. 104.

[5] Justice (δίκη), personified as an avenger, is a common image in both Greek philosophy and drama:

> With him (God) followeth Justice always, as avenger of them that fall short of the divine Law (PLATO, *Laws*, 716A, cf. 872E).
> Count me a prophet false, a witless wight
> If Justice, who inspires my prophecy,
> Comes not, my child, to vindicate the right (SOPHOCLES, *Electra*, 472-475, cf. 528).
> See D. WINSTON, *The Wisdom of Solomon*, p. 105.

[6] "Another method consists in attacking slander, showing how great an evil it is, and this because it alters the nature of judgments, and that it does not rely on the real facts of the case" (ARISTOTLE, *The Art of Rhetoric*, III.xv.7-9).

wickedness perpetrated through falsehood and false accusation will stand undetected and go unpunished.

In the light of this trial background, the reader is exhorted to refrain from wickedness especially in the particular form of false speech which destroys the soul (v 11). This final verse of the second sub-unit begins to shift the discourse within the trial background to the author's ultimate reason for loving justice and refraining from wickedness - namely, the result of self-destruction which injustice and false accusation necessarily bring about.

The end result of wickedness is death. The negative exhortation in the final sub-unit (1:12-15) functions as a counterpoint to the opening positive exhortation of the unit. The author's call to love justice and to search for the Lord is juxtaposed to the author's dissuasion from inviting death. The dissuasion is expressed in perfect synonymous parallelism (1:12):

Do not invite	death	through the error of your life;
Nor bring on	destruction	through the works of your hand.

In this way, the stark reality of death is intimately connected with wickedness. The responsibility for death and wickedness resides in the very choices of the wicked themselves.

Just as wickedness is juxtaposed to justice (1:1-5) at the outset of the discourse, so too a radical demarcation is established between death and God (1:12-15). The precise nuance of meaning in these difficult and controversial verses is not easy to establish. But the general tenor communicated in the line of argument is the radical difference between God's desire for human beings and the death that is the result of error and wickedness. Just as God and the Spirit of wisdom were declared as ones who would not enter into a person associated with wickedness, so too the author declares that God does not have a part in the end result of wickedness, namely death.

The author takes pains to set a clear demarcation between God/creation and death. a) God is not responsible for death (οὐκ ἐποίησεν), b) the forces of the world are wholesome (σωτήριοι), c) the reign of Hades is not on earth. In dissuading the reader from wickedness by the introduction of the stark reality of death, the author has introduced into the exhortation the capital issues of the ultimate realities of life and death.

With a succinct sentence, the opening exhortation recalls the virtue of justice. The end result of wickedness, death, becomes counterpoised to the end result of justice, immortality:

Indeed, justice is immortal (1:15).

This sentence brings the sub-unit on death to a conclusion through the antithetical inclusion achieved in contrasting θάνατος (1:12) with ἀθάνατος (1:15), and it also brings the opening exhortation to a conclusion through the declaration regarding the end result of justice in the inclusion achieved in δικαιοσύνην/δικαιοσύνη (1:1,15).

Summary: In this brief, opening exhortation, the author has created a dramatic situation filled with tension. The exhortation to justice and to searching for the Lord is set against their opposites, wickedness and injustice. The juxtaposition between the Spirit of God and the very nature of wickedness is highlighted through the use of forensic terminology. The contours of wickedness are presented through the characteristic imagery of false speech and perjury. The background image of a trial, where the perpetration of false accusation is the crime under investigation, raises the reader's expectation for a decisive resolution between justice and wickedness. What is being examined through trial imagery in the author's opening exhortation to justice is wickedness that accuses falsely. The content of the false accusation at this point remains undefined. Moreover, the tension reaches dramatic proportions through the introduction of the images of death and Hades. Death is decisively disassociated from the realm of God. It is the ultimate result of wickedness and its particular expression in false accusation. The specific connotation of death remains elusive though it is decidedly and unambiguously pejorative. Death is the result of wickedness. It is the author's most dramatic image for catching the reader's attention to take the exhortation to justice seriously. It is the ultimate negative reason for avoiding wickedness. The positive reason for embracing justice is simply and briefly declared in the closing remark of the exhortation, which reiterates the theme of justice and counters the reality of death with immortality. The contrast is complete. Wickedness brings death; justice brings immortality.

Though justice is the theme which envelopes the opening discourse, it is not the central theme. Justice is presented as the final value to be embraced. The central and climactic issue of the exhortation is the damaging effect of wickedness and its ultimate result - death. It is the issue of death and its relationship to wickedness which clamors for clarification and judgment in the context of a trial which the author subtly constructs in the background. If the final value of justice is to be embraced, the challenge of wickedness and death must be unmasked and resolved for the exhortation to justice and to immortality to be fully credible. The opening exhortation presents death, the negative motive for embracing justice, as the problematic challenge to the love of justice.

C - 3.   The First Speech of the Wicked (Wis 1:16–2:24): an analysis of the dynamic of wickedness

C - 3.1   The introduction to the speech of the wicked

In 1:16 the attention of the author turns to the wicked themselves. Death is ultimately linked to the deeds and the words of the wicked. Personalistic language is employed to denote an intimate relationship between the two. Death is distant from God and justice, but it is on intimate terms with wickedness. Since the wicked pine away for death, considering it a friend, and since they have made a covenant with it, they are worthy to belong under its sphere. In this brief introduction to the speech of the wicked, the author lays responsibility for death unequivocally on the shoulders of the wicked.

The terminology employed in the author's short declaration of the wicked's responsibility evokes several biblical images. The idea of considering death or Hades as a friend echoes Prov 8:36, where personified wisdom declares: "All who hate me love death". The notion of the wicked having made a covenant with death evokes Isa 28:15: "We have made an agreement (διαθήκην) with Sheol, and covenants (συνθήκας) with death". Finally, the idea of the wicked being the portion (μερίς) of death recalls the Hebrew juridical terms denoting possession, חלק, (one's rightful share of booty or goods, Gen 14:24), מנה , (a rightful portion of food or of a sacrificial offering, Exod 29:26), and נחלה , (one's rightful claim of inheritance, Deut 9:26).

This latter image which describes the wicked as a possession of death is rather innovative on the part of the author. Ordinarily, the term, חלק , which is usually translated by μερίς in the LXX, designates mutual possession between the Lord and Israel or the rightful merit, positive or negative, which is due to people. For example, it is the Lord who is the possession of Aaron (Num 18:20). Israel is the Lord's possession (LXX Deut 9:26; 32:9). The idea that each person has a particular lot in life is amply employed in Qoh (cf. 3:22, 5:17, 9:6,9). But the author of Wis never employs the image of the just or the people of Israel as the portion of God. The just are said to be worthy of God or of wisdom (3:5, 6:16).

Y. Amir rightly draws a distinction between the typical biblical phrase 'man's portion in life' and the phrase 'the portion of death' (Wis 1:16) [7]. Israel never used the common term, חלק , for possession of persons among one another. However, in the LXX the term, μερίς, is

---

[7] Y. Amir, "The Figure of Death in the 'Book of Wisdom' ", *JJS* 30 (1979) p. 157.

employed exactly with the nuance it has in our phrase in Wis 1:16. In Ps 62(63):10-11, the psalmist announces the fate of enemies:

> They shall go down to the depths of the earth, they shall be given over to the power of the sword and they shall become the portions of foxes (μερίδες ἀλωπέκων ἔσονται).

The Greek, μερίς, translates the Hebrew, מנה, in Ps 63(62):11. It is this nuance that the phrase bears in our context. Just as the enemies will be the prey and the victims of foxes, so too are the wicked the prey and victims of death [8].

The announcement that the wicked are death's portion is an ominous declaration. The wicked belong to the power of death. The introduction to the speech of the wicked combines the responsibility they bear in their fate with the utter hopelessness that their choices imply.

The source of the fate for the wicked resides in their false reasoning and in their deeds. The combination of χερσίν and λόγοις (1:16) reiterates the source of their fate in both their deeds and their reasoning. To present the process of wickedness the author chooses to have the wicked speak out their reasoning for themselves, and this they do in a particularly eloquent manner. But at the outset of the speech, the reader knows that the source of death lies in the false reasoning of the wicked and in their choices for a life project which are derived from this false reasoning.

C-3.2   The direct speech of the wicked: an analysis of wickedness

1) *The underlying despair in the reflection on death*

The opening section of the direct speech is filled with images that describe the wicked's judgment regarding the fragility and the evanescence of human life. The negative judgment is clear at the outset, "short and bitter is our life, and there is no healing for the human end" (2:1). All the images concentrate on the fate of human beings which, in the eyes of the wicked, renders life meaningless. Humans have come to exist through mere chance, and when they have gone it will be as if they had never been (2:2). The images capture the poignant reality of physical death without ever calling it by its most usual name, the name the wicked use to impose death on the just (2:20). Instead of the usual term for death, θάνατος, other terms or phrases are used to soften the stark reality of death

---

[8] D. WINSTON translates 1:16d, "for they are worthy to be members of his party," thereby employing the nuance of party or faction for the term, μερίς, as in PLATO, *Laws*, 692B. D. WINSTON, *The Wisdom of Solomon*, p. 113.

(τελευτή, 2:1,5; μετὰ τοῦτο, 2:2). All the images point to the inescapable termination of human life with a seeming despair in that there is no healing, no escape (2:1,5).

2) *The eloquence of the wicked's speech*

Concomitant with the quality of despair underlying the speech, manifold images display what can only be described as an eloquent expression of the transience of human life. The breath, the heartbeat and the soul of human beings are compared to smoke, mist, a spark, air, all of which are described as dissolving or vanishing in a moment (2:1-4). There is an interplay between human existence in its bodily constitution (breath, nostrils, body, soul) and the transient aspects of natural phenomena. The explanation of the life forces is presented in a mechanistic manner in which human reality is reduced exclusively to a materialistic conception. The mechanistic and materialistic images insist on the permanence of human departure and on the irreversible destiny of a person being forgotten in time (2:1,4,5). To emphasize the insistence on time and the inescapable reality of human destiny, the wicked compare human life to a cloud which is pursued by the rays of the sun and is oppressed by its heat (2:4).

By presenting the wicked's pessimistic and materialistic judgment on human life in eloquent and expressive language, the author is subtly holding up for careful scrutiny what could be construed as an intelligent and convincing philosophy. The forensic terms, which described the damaging speech of the wicked in the opening section, have prepared the reader to view critically what the wicked actually present as the source of their belief and philosophy. The reader has been led into the argumentation of the author in which the background image of a trial is meant to focus the critical faculties on a subject filled with ambiguities and apparent truths, namely the issue of mortality and a human response to its reality.

3) *The wicked's despairing exhortation to enjoy life*

The grim evaluation of life and death issues in a concrete life project. With a series of subjunctives encouraging a line of action (17 occurrences in Wis 2:6-20), the wicked set forth their life project, which is the direct result of their negative evaluation of life and death. These subjunctives function as counterpoints to the imperatives to love justice and to seek God in the opening section. The dynamic of evil within the reasoning process of the wicked is expressed in a crescendo which starts with an exhortation to enjoy apparently innocent pleasures of life, but ends with the call to inflict physical death on the just, heartlessly and brutally.

The exhortation to innocent pleasures of life (Wis 2:6-9) continues the expressive, eloquent language of the preceding speech, which explains the wicked's assessment of life and death (Wis 2:1-5). What is advocated as the goal of this brief life is the enjoyment of good things. The good things are only vaguely presented through images which represent certain festivities of life. They are to enjoy creation intensely as in youth, with the best of wines, with myrrh, with spring flowers, and with crowns of rosebuds (Wis 2:6-8)[9]. This exhortation reaches frenetic proportions with the admonition not to be negligent in one's revelry, and to leave signs everywhere of one's enjoyment of life.

Though on the surface this exhortation to enjoy creation may appear innocent enough, a few terms within the speech, over and above the general context, function as signals that the revelry advocated by the wicked is heading towards a sinister end. For the most part, the verb, ἀπολαύειν, which is rarely used in the LXX, carries the nuance of an excessive enjoyment of illicit pleasure, but on one occasion it conveys the wholesome pleasure of enjoying God's creation[10]. At the end of the exhortation to pleasure (2:9), the tone of the festivity becomes clearly strained and exaggerated. The word, ἀγερωξία, conveys a sense of haughtiness or arrogance (cf. 2 Macc 9:7; 3 Macc 2:3).

The boastful claim, that such enjoyment and revelry is their proper share and lot, masks the underlying despair which is carried over from the negative judgment of physical death. This hint of despair is present in the reminder to the wicked that they are to crown themselves with rosebuds before they fade (2:8)[11]. The exhortation to take one's share in

---

[9] The brief images in 2:6-9 perhaps recall certain customs of the symposium, the festivity or banquet prevalent in Alexandria in the first century B.C. and adapted by Antony and Cleopatra. It was customary to spice the best of wines with perfumes and to be adorned with flowers. C. LARCHER, *Le Livre de la Sagesse*, p. 231.

[10] Prov 7:18; 4 Macc 5:9; 8:5; 16:18. In Prov 7:18, the sage warns the son against the lures of a woman who advocates the enjoyment of sexual love with the assurance that her husband is gone (ἀπολαύσωμεν φιλίας). In 4 Macc 5:9 and 8:5, the same verb is employed in the description of Antiochus' attempts to convince the old man Eleazar and the seven brothers to abandon their faith and to adopt the Greek way of life. Antiochus urges them to enjoy his friendship and not to ignore innocent pleasures.

"Surely it is sheer folly not to enjoy harmless pleasures, and it is wrong to spurn nature's good gifts" (4 Macc 5:9).

"Share in the Greek style, change your mode of living, and enjoy your youth" (4 Macc 8:5).

But the term also connotes the positive value of enjoying God's creation. In 4 Macc 16:18 the mother of the seven brothers reminds her children that it is for God that they have participated in the world and have enjoyed life (τοῦ βίου ἀπελαύσατε).

[11] L. ALONSO SCHÖKEL captures well the discrepancy between the tone of despair and the images of life in the exhortation of the wicked to pleasure. "En realida, ¿no es un grito desesperado este discurso de tonos victoriosos?, ¿no es un unisono estruendoso con que aturdir una tristeza abismal?" L. ALONSO SCHÖKEL, *Ecclesiastes y Sabiduría*, Madrid: 1974, p. 92.

the pleasures of life carries with it an aura of foreboding, based as it is on the negative motive of despair. And this foreboding is immediately realized in the appeal to power that is made in verse 2:10.

The exhortation to innocent pleasures takes a sudden, menacing turn (2:10-11). As part of their life project, the wicked advocate the oppression of the poor and the widow, traditional images for the weak and vulnerable in society [12]. They are to disregard the old [13]. A reliance on power and a despising of what is weak are the corollaries to the negative judgment of death and the masking of the void through transient pleasures. Power is their only law of right (2:11).

4) *The wicked's project to test the claims of the just*

In its turn, the exhortation to power over the widow, the poor, the elderly, leads to the advocacy of a specific oppression and aggression against the just one who does not accept their judgment of death nor their mode of life. The clear line of demarcation between the wicked and God in the opening part of the book surfaces here in a radical tension between the wicked and the just. The wicked contest the claim of the just to have a special knowledge of God (2:13), to hope in a blessed finality for the just, and to consider God as father (2:16). As a result, they condemn the just one to torture and to a shameful death as a verification of their own negative judgment of weakness and of physical death (2:19-20). The wicked intend to inflict physical death on the just as a rhetorical test of the claims of the just. This rhetorical test is meant to be a mockery of the life style of the just which differs from their own choice of sensuality, power and violence. The wicked intend to inflict on the just the very reality of physical death which they have judged to render life hopeless and arbitrary. This entire project is a direct consequence of their original judgment on physical death.

The dynamic of evil present in the speech of the wicked is a progressive movement. The negative judgment of physical death declares

---

[12] The word pair, poor/widow, is not frequent (cf. Isa 10:2, ἁρπάζοντες κρίμα πενήτων τοῦ λαοῦ μου ὥστε εἶναι αὐτοῖς χήραν). A common word pair to designate the weak in society is orphan/widow (ὀρφανός/χήρα, cf. Exod 22:22, Deut 10:18; 14:29; 24:17; Isa 1:17,23). Finally, the term for poor, πένης, frequently refers to the oppressed whom the Lord heeds and who require special protection (Exod 23:6; Deut 15:12; 24:14-15; Ps 81(82):3).

[13] According to the law, the old are to be respected: "You shall rise up before the hoary head, and honour the face of an old man" (Lev 19:32). In the context of the first speech of the wicked, the old who are to be disregarded clearly represent a vulnerable group. This group is in contrast to the youthful pleasures that had been advocated early in the speech. In itself, old age, for the author of Wis, does not guarantee honor if it lacks virtue (Wis 4:8-10, cf. Qoh 12:1-7; Sir 3:13-16).

life to be arbitrary; there is no remembering of one's name or deeds after death. This judgment leads to choices of a life style which simply mask the underlying despair in the adherence to transient pleasures. The concomitant side of the adulation of youthful pleasures is the despising of weakness and the reliance on power. Finally, the stance towards life of the just one, who resists this negative judgment of mortality with its turn to pleasure and power, is condemned to the test of a shameful death. In other words, the negative judgment of death leads in turn to the infliction of death on others as a verification of the original judgment. What the wicked have judged to be an inescapable proof of life's ephemeral value, they inflict on the just one who declares a life of justice to have absolute value in God. The dynamic of evil is intensified through the gradual progression from poetic images based on inanimate nature to the violent image of inflicting torture and death on the just. This dynamic highlights the tension between the appearance of innocence and the underlying wickedness. The wicked's mechanistic and materialistic reflection on human life, which negatives absolutely physical death, is motivated by a form of despair which eventually inculcates injustice and brutality.

The background image of a trial begins to take on new details in the author's argumentation. The victim who had been unnamed in the first part of the exhortation is here identified first of all as the vulnerable person and, more specifically, the just one. By resuming the wicked's speech with their own eloquent language, the author provides the life style under attack with a semblance of credibility [14]. The speech creates the expectation in the reader of a refutation of the wicked's claim.

In the argumentation of the author, the wicked are on trial for their false speech which includes: a) their false reasoning on physical death (2:1-5), b) their life choice of sensuality (2:6-9) c) their reliance on power (2:10-11) and d) the call to violence against the just as a test of their claim to belong to God (2:12-20). The pivotal issue on which their defense stands is the claim that death renders life meaningless. The shameful death of the just will have to be disclaimed effectively for the entire reasoning process of the wicked to be proven false. The call for the just's shameful death is the climax of tension and expectation. With their demand for torture and death, the wicked have put the just one's claim of absolute value to the test of death. But, in fact, within the larger context, it is the wicked who are on trial. The accusing speech of the wicked takes

---

[14] For ARISTOTLE, the introductions to epideictic discourse often borrow elements from forensic discourse where the arguments of the opponents are foreseen and tentatively rebutted (ARISTOTLE, *The Art of Rhetoric*, III.xiv.11-xv.9). See P. BIZZETI, *Il Libro della Sapienza*, Brescia: 1984, pp. 163-165; M. GILBERT, "Il giusto sofferente di Sap 2:12-20", [*L'antico testamento interpretato dal nuovo: il messia*, ed. G. DE GENNARO, Napoli: 1985] pp. 198-200.

on the quality of their own defense. The accusing speech ends with the defiant challenge of the correctness of their thought and decisions, which demands the death of the just.

C - 3.3   The conclusion to the speech of the wicked (2:21-24)

The speech of the wicked is enclosed by the author's comment on the error of the wicked's thinking. But a reason for their false thinking is added in the closure. Their evil has blinded them. In other words, the author is suggesting that there is a reality which the wicked are unable to perceive because of the reasoning they have employed. This other reality which they have not perceived is intimated through three images: the mysteries of God, the wages of holiness and the prize of guiltless souls. All these images point to a reality not readily visible. By introducing the concept of the wicked's blindness, together with intangible values, the author strengthens the dichotomy between appearance and reality disclosed in the speech of the wicked. There are realities which the wicked are unable to perceive. This dichotomy between appearance and reality will become a main feature in the author's rebuttal of the wicked's challenge.

The main thrust of the wicked's judgment is immediately challenged with the declaration that God had created human beings for immortality (ἀφθαρσία). The appeal to the Genesis narrative is unmistakable in the parallel stich where God is said to have made human beings in the image of his own identity or eternity[15]. This declaration counters the wicked's claim that humans have come to exist through mere chance and that after death it will be as if they had never been. In other words the negative judgment of physical death is being challenged by the declaration that human beings were created by God for immortality.

The separation between God and death, which the author took pains to establish in the introduction to the speech of the wicked, is reiterated in the conclusion with the added clarification of death's origin. Death is associated with the adversary, satan. It has entered the cosmos through the envy of the adversary[16]. Those who belong to the adversary actually experience death[17].

---

[15] ποιήσωμεν ἄνθρωπον κατ' εἰκόνα ἡμετέραν καὶ καθ' ὁμοίωσιν (Gen 1:27).
καὶ εἰκόνα τῆς ἰδίας ἰδιότητος ἐποίησεν αὐτόν (Wis 2:23).
The variant reading of ἀϊδιότητος (everlasting) instead of ἰδιότητος (identity) does not influence the similarity of the verse to Genesis. The idea of everlastingness, however, draws out more explicitly the author's point that life does not end in physical death.
[16] Y. AMIR studied the image of death in the Book of Wisdom from the point of view of the mythological background which underlies the author's perspective. Specifically in Wis 2:24, AMIR attempts to project a dualistic mythological vision in which

C-4. The Various Senses of Death

It is at this point perhaps more clearly than at any other in the author's argumentation that the ambiguity of the term death reaches its full force. For it becomes evident that death is being viewed from various perspectives with different contents. On the one hand, there is the view of physical death presented by the wicked which is under a severe critique by our author. This physical death is the test that the wicked intend to inflict on the just as verification of the correctness of their position. On the other hand, there is the view of an ultimate death which is the object of the author's concern in the introduction and conclusion of the speech of

there are two kingdoms with their respective fields of influence, God and the just, satan/death and the wicked. Amir recognizes that the author of Wis, however, downplays the mythological aspect (p.169). Y. Amir, "The Figure of Death in the 'Book of Wisdom'", *JJS* 30 (1979) 154-178. J.J. Collins likewise stresses that the framework of the author of Wis is more philosophical in the presentation of the arguments than it is mythological (J.J. Collins, "The Root of Immortality: Death in the Context of Jewish Wisdom", *HTR* 71 (1978) pp. 186-192.

The author's attempt to elucidate the origin of death, necessarily runs into the ambiguity and complexity associated with ultimate origins. Even the Genesis accounts of creation are silent on the origin of the temptation of the serpent. But Amir's claim that the author was careless about a possible relation between his dualistic myth and the narrative of Gen (p. 171) is valid only if by death in 2:24 one understands physical death. But in the context of the argument, it is not physical death which is distinguished radically from the realm of God. It is the final death which is in enmity with God, which the adversary promotes, to which the wicked succumb. The author does not personify death to the point of creating a mythological figure of the same grandeur of God. Use is made of personification only to express the relationship between the wicked and the final death as "the wicked's pining for death, making a covenant with Hades" (Wis 1:16).

[17] A.-M. Dubarle proposed to translate πειράζουσιν with a transitive meaning, with the objective pronoun, αὐτόν, referring to κόσμος. The meaning would be the following: the wicked, who belong to satan, tempt the world (A.-M. Dubarle, "La tentation diabolique dans le Livre de la Sagesse (2,24)", [Mélanges E. Tisserant, I, Rome: 1964] 187-195). See also A.-M. Dubarle, *Le péché originel dans l'écriture*, LD 20 (1958) pp. 86-89.

The idea that devils or spirits lead humans astray into folly was present in apocalyptic literature (cf. Jub 10:1-6). However, S. Lyonnet contended that the verb, πειράζω, acquired this active meaning of tempting in order to cause fault only in NT writings (Mark 8:11, 1 Cor 7:5). S. Lyonnet, "Le sens de πειράζειν en Sap 2,24 et la doctrine du péché originel", *Bib* 39 (1958) pp. 28-29.

In Wis, πειράζω is used in the transitive and intransitive voice, both of which focus on the act of experiencing or knowing. The intransitive meaning denotes 'to experience' (12:26, they will experience the deserved judgment of God; 19:5, that my people may experience a strange journey). The transitive meaning denotes the idea of 'testing in order to know' (1:2 - he is found by those who do not test him; 2:17 - let us test him to the end; 3:5 - God tested them; 11:9 - for when they were being tested). Within the perspective of its use in Wis, the verb, πειράζω, in our context is best understood in its intransitive mode meaning 'to experience, to know'.

the wicked. It is this ultimate death which provides the author's negative reason for embracing justice (1:12). It is this ultimate death which is not willed by God (1:13). It is this ultimate death which is the result of the free choice of the wicked, and which exerts a subtly attractive power over its adherents (1:16). Finally, it is this ultimate death which has entered the world due to the envy of the adversary (2:24).

In each case where ultimate death is implicitly intended by the author before and after the speech of the wicked, a qualifying phrase hinders the reduction of the word, death, to mean physical death itself. In 1:12, death is conceived as being the consequence of a personal, moral choice. In 1:13, the death that is not willed by God belongs to those who are worthy of it (1:16d). The death which entered the cosmos through the devil is experienced by those who belong to him (2:24).

The precise relationship between two aspects of death, the ultimate and the physical, remains to be studied. For PHILO such a distinction between spiritual and physical death had been commonplace. Though PHILO expressed a clear distinction between two kinds of death, namely death of the body and death of the soul, he had not coined a phrase that would have denoted explicitly in his writings the particular death under discussion [18]. Why is it that the author did not employ an explicit distinction in the argumentation, when in fact such a distinction would have been current at the time of the author? [19] This issue will become the

---

[18] PHILO's clear distinction between two kinds of death deserves to be quoted:
"That death is of two kinds, one that of the man in general, the other that of the soul in particular. The death of the man is the separation of the soul from the body, but the death of the soul is the decay of virtue and the bringing in of wickedness. It is for this reason that God says not only 'die' but 'die the death,' indicating not the death common to us all, but that special death (καὶ κατ' εξοχὴν θάνατον) properly so called, which is that of the soul becoming entombed in passions and wickedness of all kinds. And this death is practically the antithesis of the death which awaits us all. ... observe that whenever Moses speaks of 'dying the death,' he means the penalty death (θάνατον τὸν ἐπὶ τιμωρίᾳ), not that which takes place in the course of nature" (PHILO, Legum Allegoriae I, 105-108).

[19] Various terms have been employed to denote a distinction between the two kinds of death. I have chosen the term, ultimate death, as a contrasting term to physical death because of the author's concern with ultimate realities both in the speech of the wicked and in the author's rebuttal, as opposed to physical appearances (ἔσχατα δικαίων, 2:16, see also 3:17,19; 4:19e;).

An explicit reference to a death other than physical death occurs in Rev, a second death (Rev 2:11, 20:6,14, 21:8). Perhaps this phrase had already been in use by the Tannaim for the author of Rev to have employed it. See P.-M. BOGAERT, "La «seconde mort» à l'époque des Tannaïm", [Vie et survie dans les civilisations orientales, ed. A. THÉODORIDÈS, P. NASTER, J. RIES, Leuven: 1983] 199-207. G. SCARPAT notes the similarity and difference between the second death of Revelations and the 'double' death of PHILO and SENECA. They are similar in that the second death in both cases is a moral death. They are distinct in that the second death in Revelations is associated with a final judgment,

main focus in a following chapter where the results of the study of the
author's argument can be collated.

The conclusion to the rather developed speech of the wicked
reaffirms the error of their thinking with the claim that they wrongly
assessed physical death. Physical death is not the end of life. On the
contrary, as a result of their folly and their ensuing wickedness, it is the
wicked who will experience ultimate death. Because of their wickedness,
the wicked are already within the sphere of ultimate death. According to
the author's reasoning, they will eventually experience its ultimate effect
— conviction.

Just as the author concluded the opening exhortation with the
introduction of the dramatic figure of ultimate death, so too does the
conclusion to the wicked's speech restate the wicked's receiving a sentence
of ultimate death. Within the speech itself, physical death is discussed
twice, a) in the wicked's assessment of the transience of life (2:1-5), and b)
in the wicked's exhortation to inflict physical death on the just (2:19-20).

Ultimate death (1:12-16) ——————————————(2:24) Ultimate death
Physical death (2:1-5) ————————— (2:19-20) Physical death

While physical death is considered and presented as the enemy by
the wicked, it is ultimate death which is considered by the author to be in
enmity with God and, by their relationship to God, with the just. The
author's discussion of death both in the concluding commentaries
(1:12-15; 2:21:24) and in the speech of the wicked (2:1-5; 2:20) constitutes
the main objection and barrier to the opening exhortation to love justice
and to seek God. The wicked's condemnation of the just to a shameful
death creates a crisis which demands a resolution in the argumentation of
the author. This crisis parallels and completes the heightened tension
created in the opening exhortation where the author dissuades the reader
from inviting ultimate death.

The speech of the wicked with its introduction and conclusion
together constitute the author's formal treatment of the issue of death.

---

whereas for the Stoics and PHILO, moral death begins during life (G. SCARPAT, "La morte
seconda e la duplice morte", *Paideia*, 42 (1987) 55-62). For a plethora of terms to denote
the polarity between two deaths based on the metaphor of physical death see X.
LÉON-DUFOUR, *Face à la mort, Jésus et Paul*, Paris: 1979 [trans. T. PRENDERGAST, *Life and
Death in the New Testament*, San Francisco: 1986]: temporal death - final death, pp. 5-6;
physical death - spiritual death pp. xxi-xxii, 210-211; death - biological phenomenon,
eschatological death; being separated from God, definitive death, p. 213; wrenching death,
passage death, destruction death, p. 213.

In addition to the polarity of the two deaths, LÉON-DUFOUR charts a third level
meaning of death within the New Testament, primarily in Johannine texts, namely the
death that gives life — transfiguration death (p. 213).

For this reason, it will be helpful to summarize the presentation of the argument from three points of view: a) the role of the image of death in the author's argument, b) the progression of evil in the wicked's own argumentation, c) the contribution of the background trial image for the argumentation.

C-4.1 Ultimate death / physical death

The speech of the wicked had been prefaced, through the introduction of death in the conclusion of the opening exhortation, as the prime negative motive for embracing justice. This ultimate death, which is presumed to be a supreme deterrent in the author's exhortation, is associated with the wicked. Its introduction into the discourse focuses the argument onto the capital issues of life and death.

By creating fictitious characters who present the inner motivations for their life choice of injustice, the author holds up for careful scrutiny the subtle errors in the wicked's reasoning process. The subtlety is accentuated by the fact that the reasoning process of the wicked is intelligent, consistent and, at times, poetic. But the reasoning process of the wicked, which begins with a negative assessment of life in the face of the reality of their eventual physical death, ultimately leads to their demand for the violent deed of inflicting physical death on the just. Physical death encloses the speech of the wicked; the speech opens with their negative assessment of physical death and it closes with their infliction of physical death on the just. Both the deeds and the reasoning process of the wicked had been explained as their invitation of ultimate death (1:16). The entire speech of the wicked, therefore, is under the author's critical examination.

C-4.2 The progression of evil in the speech of the wicked

˙The speech itself contains a progressive dynamic. One judgment and assessment of death leads to a life choice of pleasure which, in turn, leads to the other life choices of exploiting strength and power against the weak, which, finally, is consumed by the radical opposition between the wicked and the just in the projected violent act of inflicting physical death.

The reasoning of the wicked is progressive both in the sense of causality and also in the sense of the quality of the judgments. In other words, their despairing ruminations and judgments on life are the immediate cause of their particular stance towards life. Even the wicked's projects that issue from their reasoning are progressively more sinister. The judgment regarding the ephemeral reality of human life contains

many truths that echo the language of the psalms, the prophets and
other sapiential writings which describe the fragility of human life. But
the absolute negative assessment in the speech of the wicked does not
lead to their appreciation of the mystery of life. Instead, it manifests
their despair which leads to the exhortation to pleasure that is based on
the choice to fill or mask the underlying void derived from the negative
judgment of physical death. The exhortation to pleasure is then
sustained by their deliberate choice to maintain pleasure through their
own power which justifies oppression of the weak. Finally, this choice
runs into direct conflict with the just, who separate themselves from this
dynamic of evil. The end result of the dynamic of evil is the unambiguous act of injustice which casts its shadow over the entire
reasoning process of the wicked. The exhortation to inflict death on the
just should call into question for the reader the wicked's initial negative
assessment on physical death, just as the wicked's option for power and
oppression of the weak calls into question the exhortation to seemingly
innocent pleasures.

C-4.3   The trial background

The image of a background trial is carried over into the speech of the
wicked from the opening exhortation. Within the wider context of the
author's argumentation, the wicked's reasoning and life project, take on
the characteristics and quality of a defense. For the first time, the victim
of their wickedness is clearly identified as the just one. God, who had
been introduced as the ultimate judge, is denied any such status by the
wicked's negative assessment of physical death. The very absence of an
absolute value that would transcend physical death subjects life to the
arbitrary power of the strong. Moreover, in their defense, it is the wicked
who accuse the just one of pretensions to absolute value in their
relationship to God. It is precisely in their accusation against the just that
they subject the just one to a trial of testing through physical death. In
this way, in the narrower context of the wicked's speech, the background
image of a trial goes through an inversion. The accused become the
accusers. It is this accusation which the wicked cast against the just that
was foreshadowed with the destructive false speech of the wicked in the
opening exhortation.
      The very defense of the wicked then consists of an accusation against
the pretensions of the just that an absolute value exists in the face of
physical death. Their accusation issues in their project to condemn the
just to the reality of physical death.
      The physical death of the just constitutes the pivotal issue in the
wicked's accusatory defense. The author must refute the claim of the

wicked that the physical death of the just is a confirmation of their negative assessment of life and death. The entire middle section of the first part of Wis (cc. 3-4) is the author's attempt to refute this claim of the wicked. And with this refutation, the entire reasoning process of the wicked falls backwards. On one hand, physical death is not the destroyer of meaning which renders life arbitrary and hopeless, reduced to the brief exploitation of pleasure with power. On the other hand, injustice is the concrete sign of participation in an ultimate death that is a separation from God and the just.

C - 4.4 Summary on the critical role of the image of death

From all three perspectives, death constitutes the problematic issue in the argumentation of the author. In the context of the overall argument to love justice and to seek God, death is presented as the supreme deterrent that raises the argument for the reader to a vital issue. In the context of the wicked's speech, the projected physical death of the just is their proof for the validity of their life style. And in the context of the trial background it is specifically the physical death of the just that becomes the evidence that the author must explain in order to bring about the conviction of the wicked. With the conviction of the wicked, the entire reasoning process of the wicked regarding death will be proven false. The author views the correct assessment of death as vitally important in the pursuit of justice and in the search for God. It is the issue of death then that constitutes the central and the critical theme of the first part of the Book of Wisdom.

C - 5. The Author's Rebuttal of the Wicked's Arguments in Four Diptychs (Wis 3–4)

The tension produced in the conclusion of the wicked's speech, regarding the projected death of the just, is resolved abruptly in the author's declarative statement on the fate of the just. "The just are in the hand of God" (3:1). The wicked intended the shameful death of the just to be conclusive proof of the legitimacy of their reasoning and their positions towards life. This proof is directly challenged by the author's assertion that in fact the just survive under the protection of God. But this rather daring, declarative statement by the author will need elaboration for its force to have full effect on the reader. How is it that the just who, to all appearances, have suffered an ignoble death are in the hand of God?

C-5.1   The author's procedure of defense and attack

With the image of the hand of God, representing power and
protection, the author challenges the wicked's boast regarding the
possibility of someone freeing the just from their power. From the point
of view of the wicked, the just had been in their hands (2:18), but in
reality they are in the hand of God (2:18,3:1). The image that the wicked
had employed in their boast of power is picked up in the rebuttal to
reveal the reversal of the situation. It is this assertion of the just's blessed
survival that will throw havoc into the entire reasoning process of the
wicked and will lead to a complete reversal of the paradigm
accuser/accused that had been launched by the wicked.

This declarative statement inaugurates the double procedure which
the author adopts to disprove the claims of the wicked: a) the
employment of declarative statements through images that reveal the
nature of the destiny of the just, b) the reversal of the meaning of images
or statements employed by the wicked. The images that the author
employs function as metaphors to aid the reader to understand the
possibility of the blessed destiny of the just.

With these metaphors the author's discourse does not follow the
model of philosophical discourse which would attempt to prove through
formal logical reasoning the possibility of survival after death, but rather
metaphorical discourse, where common images are employed and
condensed in order to point to a reality on another level. The procedure is
executed within the literary device of a diptych where the blessedness and
the reward of the just are contrasted with the fate and punishment of the
wicked.

All four diptychs function as the author's rebuttal of the wicked's
accusation within the background court scene. In their turn, the diptychs
constitute an explanatory accusation of the wicked's lawlessness that will
bring sure punishment at the time of accounting.

C-5.2   The first diptych (3:1-12) - the just / the wicked

1) *Appearance and reality* (3:1-5)

The declarative statements of the author regarding the blessed state
of the just are presented in sharp contrast to the shameful death projected
by the wicked. The just are said to be in the hand of God (3:1); they are
in peace (3:3); their hope is the fullness of immortality (3:4)[20]. The

---

[20] In the hand of God, Ps 94(95):4; in peace, Ps 4:9; 28(29):11, 54(55):19
(λυτρώσεται ἐν εἰρήνῃ τὴν ψυχήν μου ἀπὸ τῶν ἐγγιζόντων μοι); immortality, ἀθανασία,

contrast between these positive declarations and the negative perspectives of the wicked is mitigated by the author's distinction between appearance and reality. In other words, for the benefit of the reader, the author concedes the seemingly tragic and desperate fate of the just[21]. But at the same time, the play on appearances and reality invites the reader to change perspectives in the estimation of the values of the just and the wicked[22].

The appearance of the fate of the just is tragic and hopeless only according to the false perspective and reasoning enunciated by the wicked in c. 2. "They seemed in the eyes of the foolish to have died (3:2)"; "And indeed in the eyes of men it was as if they were punished (3:4)". Throughout their speech, the wicked consider themselves the central protagonists. But the author reveals that the real protagonist has been God (3:1,5,8).

Wis 4:1, 8:13,17, 15:3; this abstract concept of immortality is denoted by a rare word in the LXX, used only in 4 Macc 14:5, 16:13 outside of Wis.

[21] The contrast that the author develops between appearances and reality in the experience of the just has occasioned the interpretation that the author is denying that the just experience suffering or physical death. See J.J. COLLINS, "The Root of Immortality: Death in the Context of Jewish Wisdom (Sir WisSol)", *HTR* 71 (1978) 190-192; also B.R. GAVENTA, "The Rhetoric of Death in the Wisdom of Solomon and the Letters of Paul", [*The Listening Heart*, Essays in Wisdom and the Psalms in Honor of Roland E. MURPHY, K.G. HOGLUND, E.F. HUWILER, J.T. GLASS, R.W. LEE, eds., JSOTSupS 58, Sheffield: 1987], p. 134, "Wisdom counters the logic of the ungodly with the claim that the godly are in fact in God's hands. While they appear to have died, they did not actually suffer and are at peace (3.1-4)."

However, once the framework of the trial scene is understood, it is evident that the author is not so much denying the reality of suffering, weaknesses, and physical death in the case of the just, as much as he is denying the interpretation that the position of the wicked attributes to the human conditions of limitations and mortality. This is a very important difference of perspective for the argumentation of the author.

[22] Since the just in Wis 3 are denoted in the plural form, and since the onlookers of their death are described as fools (3:2) or simply men (3:4) rather than the wicked, a doubt could arise with regards to the identity of the just described in Wis 3:1-9 (see A. BARUCQ, "La gloire des justes (Sg 3,1-9)", [*AS* 96, Paris: 1967] 7-17). Do they refer to the just one in the wicked's speech? The projected death of the just one in c. 2 was a real project of the wicked within the hypothetical construction of the author. In the author's defense of the just one, the violent death of the just is presumed. A number of verbal references imply that in this diptych the author is refuting the wicked's interpretation of their projected violent death of the just one: βάσανος, κάκωσις, σύντριμμα, κολασθῶσιν, ἐπείρασεν. Moreover, in the second half of the diptych, the subject 'wicked' reappears with reference to the reasoning of the wicked (3:10). Note also that in the confession of the wicked in c. 5, the wicked refer to themselves precisely as 'fools' when they face the just one whom they had ridiculed (5:4b).

This would strongly suggest that the author is refuting the wicked's interpretation of the projected violent death of the just. The switch from the singular to the plural noun for the just simply refers to the author's defense of the violent death of all the just. For this second interpretation see also C. LARCHER, *Le Livre de la Sagesse*, p. 275.

This clear distinction between appearance and reality makes explicit the contours of a distinction the author had been drawing in the wicked's argumentation. There the dynamic of the wicked's argumentation began with a description of the evanescence of human life and led to an exhortation to enjoy life, a view which finally concluded in a tragic stance towards life. The final intention of the wicked to subject the just to tortures and to a shameful death as a challenge to his integrity had stripped away any appearance of a tenable position towards life.

By making a clear distinction between appearance and reality, the author is setting the conditions for a radical rebuttal of the perspectives of the wicked's reasoning. Just as the wicked's reasoning and life choices at first seemed innocuous and even 'poetic', but finally ended in tragedy, so too at first the projected tragic death of the just does appear like punishment and total destruction but finally ends in blessedness. The reader is drawn into the consideration of viewing the same reality of the just's plight from a totally different perspective and with a different line of argument. The author is constructing a new perspective through the double procedure mentioned above: through declarative statements and through images manifesting the reversal of fortune.

2) *Images expressing the transformed reality of the just* (3:5-9)

Having highlighted the difference between appearance and reality, and having introduced God as the main protagonist in the life of the just, the author turns the reader's attention to images that present the experience of the just in a new perspective. God is the one who had tested the just and found them to be worthy (3:5). With this presentation, the author is echoing a fundamental explanation for the experience of suffering and discipline from Israel's foundational desert experience. The desert experience of the exodus narratives had been interpreted as an experience of God's time of testing and inculcating discipline, particularly in the Deuteronomistic tradition [23]. This image of testing became incorporated into sapiential teaching as a value for the search and transmission of wisdom and knowledge [24]. In this way, the experience of the just is placed into the perspective of Israel's salvation history.

Two metaphors are employed to sustain the announcement of God's testing the just. "Like gold in a furnace he examined them, like a whole burnt offering he accepted them" (Wis 3:6). In both cases, fire is the crucible through which gold is purified and by which the offering rises to

---

[23] The desert experience is presented as a time of testing; Exod 15:25, 16:4; 20:20, Deut 8:16, and as a time for learning discipline; Deut 4:36, 8:2-5, LXX 32:10.

[24] Ps 26:2; Prov 3:12; Sir 2:1-5; 4:17.

the Lord[25]. With both images, the author raises the apparently tragic ordeal of the just to a perspective of transformation.

The outcome of God's testing the just is outlined with several images that connote their active blessedness. "In the time of examination they will shine forth, like sparks in the stubble they will flash to and fro" (3:7). The background image of fire is carried over from the images of testing to denote the active brilliance of the just. Finally, the just who had been passive and silent within the projections of the wicked will become the protagonists who judge nations and rule over peoples under the kingship of the Lord (3:8).

The concluding verse of the first part of the diptych focuses the blessing of the just into the wider context of the general faithful. "Those who trust in the Lord will understand truth, the faithful will remain in his love, for grace and mercy belong to his elect"(3:9). With this formulation, the author is appealing to the covenant promises of the Lord for his elect in sustaining the declarations and the explanations of the apparent tragedy of the just and the truth of their blessedness. The idea of trusting and being faithful was particularly applicable to the exigencies of the covenant. In reward for obedience the Lord would give his covenant love and his mercy to his elect[26].

3) *The reversal of images in the contrast between the just and the wicked*

The author takes pains to underscore the reversal of fortune between the just and the wicked by picking up terms that had been applied either to the just or to the wicked and reversing their significance. The resulting juxtaposition of the just and the wicked confirms the total separation and tension between God and injustice that introduced the discussion of death in the opening exhortation. The terms picked up and reversed from the wicked's project to oppress the just one are: ἐν χειρί (2:18 - 3:1), βάσανος (2:19 - 3:1), ἐπείρασεν (2:17 - 3:5), ἐδοκίμασεν (2:17 - 3:6), ἐπισκοπῆς (2:20 - 3:7), ἀλήθειαν (2:17 - 3:9)[27].

---

[25] For the image of gold or silver tested in fire see Zech 13:9, Mal 3:3, Ps 66:10 (silver); Prov 17:3, Sir 2:5. Since the procedure of testing gold separates the metal from impurities, the author could very well be implying a process of purification in the case of the just who die (C. LARCHER, *Le Livre de la Sagesse*, pp. 282-283).

The second image, 'like a whole burnt offering', literally reads as a 'whole-fruit offering'. The more common term for burnt offering is ὁλοκαύτωμα. However, ὁλοκάρπωμα always translates the Hebrew term,עלה, (Lev 5:10, 16:24; Num 15:3; Judg 16:16) where the offering is a burnt offering of animals. The term evidently became synonymous with ὁλοκαύτωμα, signifying a whole burnt offering.

[26] The terms employed in Wis 3:9 (χάρις, ἔλεος, ἐκλεκτοῖς) echo the terms of the covenant promises. See R.J. TAYLOR, "The Eschatological Meaning of Life and Death in the Book of Wisdom I–V", *ETL* 42 (1966) pp. 125-127.

[27] For a detailed list of repeated words in the first six chapters of Wis see

A number of these reversals are meant to highlight what the image of God testing the just had indicated: that the real function of protagonist in the experience of the just was not executed by the wicked, but in fact by God. The souls of the just are 'in the hand' of God who saves them 'from the hands' of the wicked. The wicked projected 'to test' the words of the just, but in fact it was God who 'had tested' the just. The wicked planned 'to examine' the endurance of the just, but in fact it was God who 'examined' them like gold in a furnace.

Other reversals highlight the complete transposition of the situation as understood by the wicked. These reversals highlight the difference between appearances and reality and promote the idea of a change or transformation in perspective. The wicked planned to inflict 'torture' on the just, but now no 'torture' will touch the just. The wicked mocked the belief of the just that there would be an 'accounting', and the just in fact will shine forth at the time of 'their accounting'[28]. The wicked mockingly planned to see whether the claims of the just were 'true', and in fact it is only the faithful who understand 'truth'.

From the wider context of the wicked's speech, the author likewise picks up terms the wicked employ for themselves and transforms their application in the rebuttal to underscore a radical difference in perspective. The wicked had employed the image of a spark (σπινθήρ,

---

F. Perrenchio, "Struttura e analisi letteraria di Sapienza 1,16–2,24 e 5,1-23", *Sales* 43 (1981) 33-34. Perrenchio's list is meant to confirm the unity of the structure. He does not purport to explore the quality or purpose of these repetitions apart from the issue of unity. Alonso Schökel, on the other hand, notes a number of the repetitions from the point of view of irony that highlights the reversal of fortune between the wicked and the just. L. Alonso Schökel, *Ecclesiastes y Sabiduria*, Madrid: 1974, 97-102.

[28] The precise nuance that the word, ἐπισκοπή, denotes must be determined by its context. As Larcher noted, this term is hardly known in profane Greek usage and therefore derives its meaning primarily from the Hebrew term, פקדה , which it translates C. Larcher, *Le Livre de la Sagesse*, p. 257). However, it also does convey its own etymological meaning of seeing in connection with Hebrew words describing 'seeing' (cf. E. Hatch, H.A. Redpath, *A Concordance to the Septuagint*, II Vol, Graz: 1975).

In cases where God is the subject, the term, ἐπισκοπή, denotes divine intention to intervene positively (Gen 50:24, Exod 3:16) or in judgment (Job 7:18). In both cases, the root meaning of פקד, to miss, to make a search, to take care of, is focused on divine attention to particular persons or events. In cases where the term is attributed to persons, it often denotes responsibility connected with overseeing as the Greek root meaning suggests (Num 4:16, 7:2). Finally, in connection with a future time, it refers to a day of accounting where God intervenes in the course of events to judge (ἡμέρα τῆς ἐπισκοπῆς, Isa 10:3; ἐν καιρῷ ἐπισκοπῆς, Jer 6:15). In Wis, the ultimate accounting is portrayed as a divine judgment which rewards the just and punishes the wicked. To this aim, the author employed the typical term, ἐπισκοπή (2:20, 3:7,13; 4:15; 14:11; 19:15), but also synonymous terms that highlight the function of God's scrutiny and judgment, συλλογισμός - reckoning, 4:20; ἐξετασμός - examination - 4:6, διάγνωσις - analysis, 3:18).

2:2) to describe the fragility and transient quality of the beating of the heart. But the just are described as flashing to and fro in the stubble like sparks (ὡς σπινθῆρες, 3:7). What had been an image of weakness and hopelessness for the wicked, the author transforms into an image of vivacity and activity for the just. The author had described the impious as being worthy (ἄξιοί, 1:16) of the one to whom they belong, namely death/Hades. But in God's testing, the just are found to be worthy (ἀξίους, 3:5) of him. The wicked had judged weakness to be useless (ἄχρηστον, 2:11), but the author declares that it is their deeds that are useless (ἄχρηστα, 3:11).

4) *The punishment of the wicked* (3:10-12)

In turning to the reversed situation of the wicked in the second part of the first diptych, the author announces that the impious will receive punishment according to the way they had reasoned. In both the introduction and the conclusion to the speech of the wicked, the author had reiterated the falseness of the reasoning of the wicked (λογισάμενοι οὐκ ὀρθῶς, 2:1; ταῦτα ἐλογίσαντο, καὶ ἐπλανήθησαν 2:21). Similarly, the author had placed the entire responsibility for the attainment of death, the prime negative reason for embracing justice, on the reasoning and life choices of the wicked. Here in the first diptych, the author draws a close connection between the false reasoning of the wicked and their punishment. According to the way in which the impious reasoned (καθὰ ἐλογίσαντο, 3:10) they will have punishment. Their judgment on the hopelessness of life in the face of death, their exploitation of transient pleasure, their turn to power and their projected infliction of physical death on the just will all turn against them. The punishment that the wicked encounter is not an external dictum, but has an internal coherence with the manner in which they had reasoned [29].

The punishment is envisaged by the author as taking place in the future, but its contours are already present in the life of the wicked. In contrast to the hope of the just (3:4), the hope of the impious is empty (3:11). Their labors and deeds are profitless and useless. And even the supposed fruitfulness of the impious is accursed: wives, children and offspring (3:12). With this new theme of the children of the wicked, the author introduces the topic of the second and third diptychs, namely the

---

[29] This is a characteristic understanding of the author of Wis who perceives an inherent relationship between the manner in which one sins and the punishment that one encounters. It is as if the punishment is simply the logical consequence of the reasoning and choices of the wicked. The author applies this principle in a developed and detailed manner in the subsequent sections of Wis which deal with the origins of false worship (11:16; 12:23-27; 14:30-31) and the punishments of the Egyptians in the presentation of the plague episodes (15:18–16:1; 18:4-5).

contrast of the moral fruitfulness of the just and the immoral fruitlessness
of the wicked.

C - 5.3 The second diptych - the sterile woman/the eunuch in contrast to the generation of the wicked (3:13-19)

1) *Temporal fruitlessness with integrity brings moral fruitfulness (3:13-15)*

The introduction of the two images of the sterile woman and the
eunuch continues the author's argument regarding the appearance of
punishment and the reality of blessedness [30]. The fruitfulness of children
was considered a major divine blessing, derived as it was from the initial
divine blessing at creation (Gen 1:28; Ps 128). Moreover, fruitfulness was
considered a major blessing within the context of the covenant promises
(Deut 30:15). As a consequence, the suffering of the just, along with the
apparent fruitfulness and success of the wicked, became problematic
particularly in sapiential circles (Job 21:7-34, 24:1-25; Qoh 4:1-3,
8:10-14).

In this diptych, the author prescinds from the difficulty of the
tension between the appearance and reality in the specific case of the
projected death of the just and relates it to the general context of the
appearance of fruitlessness. In this respect, the author's choice of the two
images of the sterile woman and the eunuch is remarkable [31]. Sterility
was considered a curse, and eunuchs were barred from the 'assembly of
the Lord' (Deut 23:2, cf. Lev 21:20).

The sterile woman and the eunuch both are declared to be blessed
and to receive reward because of their moral integrity (3:13,14). The
author goes so far as to employ the expression of the beatitude, μακαρία
(3:13), for states of life that were held to be a curse [32]. The radical change

---

[30] The theme of the two central diptychs taken together is the contrast of the
virtuous fruitfulness of the righteous and the hopeless fruitfulness of the wicked. The
contrast is structured in two parallel halves, each with two parts. In the first half, the
second diptych, the virtuous sterile woman and eunuch are contrasted to the fruit of the
wicked (3:13-19). In the second half, the third diptych, the strength of virtue without
children is contrasted with the apparent fruitfulness of wickedness (4:1-6). All four
diptychs constitute thereby a chiastic structure a b b' a'.

[31] The author's concentration on the images of sterility in righteousness that will
bear fruit has parallels with Isaiah. In Isa 54:1-8, the sterile woman is said to rejoice
because the creator is her husband who will show compassion with everlasting love. In Isa
56:3b-6, the Lord promises the eunuch who is faithful to the covenant a home within the
temple, a monument, a name which will be better than sons and daughters. See M.J.
SUGGS, "Wisdom of Solomon II,10–V: A Homily Based on the Fourth Servant Song",
JBL 76 (1957) 26-33.

[32] A. MATTIOLI, "Felicità e virtù. La dottrina della Sapienza nel brano macarico per
le sterili e gli eunuchi (Sap 3,13-4,6)", [*Gesù Apostolo e Sommo Sacerdote*, in Memoria di

in perspective, which the author promoted in the first diptych in the reversal of fortune between the just who is killed and the wicked, is here accentuated. The author is challenging the reader to evaluate what true and final blessedness is even in the context of temporal fruitlessness and weakness.

The qualifications that the author presents for the blessedness of the sterile woman and the eunuch are stated negatively at this point. The sterile woman is blessed if she is guiltless (ἀμίαντος) and has not known an unlawful union (3:13ab). Similarly, the eunuch who has not done what is unlawful by his hand (ἐν χειρὶ ἀνόμημα) [33] and who does not harbor rancor against the Lord is under the same declaration of blessedness (3:14ab).

In both cases, what appears to be a curse is transformed into a blessing because of moral integrity. The sterile woman will have fruit in the accounting of souls. The eunuch will receive special grace and a lot in the temple of the Lord. The temporal fruitlessness of the virtuous is reduced to mere appearance in comparison to the fruitfulness they will have in their virtue. The inclusion of καρπόν/καρπός (3:13c,15a) highlights the contrast of the appearance of sterility and the reality of fruitfulness. The author asserts that because of their integrity, the sterile woman and the eunuch will bear fruit.

The parallelism between the sterile woman and the eunuch, on the one hand, and the death of the just, on the other, adds force to the author's argument. The death of the just appears to be a final tragic event only in the eyes of the foolish. In reality, because of their righteousness, the just are in the hand of God. Similarly, the sterility of the virtuous woman and eunuch is tragic only from the same false point of view. For

---

P.T. BALLARINI, Casale Monferrato: 1984] 23-49; reprinted in a recent collection of articles by the same author, "Possibilità sia per le sterili che gli eunuchi di essere pienamente felici", [Le realtà sessuali nella Bibbia, Casale Monferrato: 1987] 189-204.

[33] There are various possibilities for the interpretation of the phrase, μὴ ἐργασάμενος ἐν χειρὶ ἀνόμημα, depending on the value attributed to ἐν χειρί, which have a bearing on the kind of eunuch the author is implying. LARCHER suggests that ἐν χειρί is redundant, included under the influence of Isa 56:2 MT. Its meaning would then be 'who has refrained from doing evil'. C. LARCHER, Le Livre de la Sagesse, p. 303.

MATTIOLI proposes ἐν χειρί to be a qualifying phrase which explains the personal responsibility of being a eunuch. Since the office of eunuch had lucrative consequences, some had deliberately chosen this state. The author would then be excluding from the discussion official eunuchs who were responsible for their state. A. MATTIOLI, "Felicità e virtù. La dottrina della Sapienza nel brano macarico per le sterili e gli eunuchi (Sap 3,13–4,6)", p. 31.

In both cases, however, it is evident that the author does not intend an official eunuch who is content with his state. The parallelism between the sterile woman and the eunuch would suggest states of life that the subjects experience as suffering and weakness — counterpoised to fruitful states of life.

the suffering and weak who have the root of understanding, temporal
fruitlessness is sublated by the fruitfulness of integrity[34].

2) *The children of the wicked will have a grievous end (3:16-19)*

In contrast to the moral fruitfulness of the sterile virtuous, the
author declares that the children of the wicked, whether they grow old or
not, will have no hope. If we understand 'τέκνα δὲ μοιχῶν' (3:16) simply
on a literal level as 'the children of adultery', the argument of the author
would be rendered somewhat awkward. In that case, the author would
appear to be condemning individuals, namely the children, regardless of
their own responsibility. However, the author has already made it evident
that the responsibility for making death one's lot depends on the free
choice of the individual (1:16).

The image of the hopelessness of the 'children of adultery' is more
nuanced than the literal sense would suggest. In prophetic teaching, the
terms for adultery were used to denote Israel's infidelity and apostasy:
Hos 2:2; 3:1; 4:2,13,14; Isa 57:3; Ezek 16:32. Since the background of the
author's diptych is the contrast of the fruitful virtue of the just and the
'fruitfulness' of the wicked that brings no hope, the image of the 'children
of adultery' represents the apparent fruit that the wicked have gained
from their wickedness[35]. It is this fruit which will not gain its expected
strength for the wicked and, in fact, will have a grievous end (3:19). This
means that the fruit of the wicked will not bring the wicked their hoped
for consolation. Their 'children' will remain immature (ἀτέλεστα) in that
they will not be a source of hope for the wicked, at the time of accounting[36].

---

[34] MATTIOLI comments on the uniqueness of the author's understanding of the
concept of happiness that emerges from the treatment of the sterile woman and the
eunuch. "Nessuno però, sino al tempo del sapiente alessandrino, aveva spinto così
avanti la soluzione del problema, sino a escludere i beni materiali dal concetto di
felicità, e a non escludere la coesistenza di questa con la sofferenza." A. MATTIOLI,
"Felicità e virtù. La dottrina della Sapienza nel brano macarico per le sterili e gli
eunuchi (Sap 3,13–4,6)", p. 35.

[35] LARCHER tends toward a metaphorical interpretation of the image 'children of
adultery'. "Antérieurement, l'auteur a parlé des foyers impies en général. Puis, de l'idée
d'une fécondité spirituelle assurée par la vertu, il passe à une fécondité charnelle qui
n'aura aucun prolongement car elle est viciée dès l'origine" (p. 308). LARCHER continues
that the author's choice of the word, μοιχός, could be explained by a rabbinic
interpretation regarding the illegitimacy of children from mixed marriages. These
children were not to be considered the rightful inheritors of the covenant promises. In
this light, the author would be highlighting the separation between the covenant
promises of God and the fruit of wickedness. C. LARCHER, *Le Livre de la Sagesse*, pp.
308-309.

[36] It is important to keep in mind that the author's argument in the second diptych
is related to the third. In the second diptych, the argument regarding the grievous end of

C - 5.4 The third diptych - the praise of virtue in contrast with the useless fruit of the wicked (4:1-6)

The diptych focuses on the source of the moral fruitfulness of the just - virtue, ἀρετή. Within the first two verses (4:1-2), virtue is personified as a mediator between God and humans[37]. The images with which the author characterizes virtue are reminiscent of the praise of virtue in Greek writings[38]. It is better to be childless with virtue because virtue is immortal and victorious (4:1b,2d). What was stated negatively in the second diptych (the refraining from evil), is stated positively in the third. The source of the happiness and reward of the sterile is their firm rootedness in virtue.

In contrast, the prolific brood of the wicked are declared to be of no use, and their children are compared to vegetation that does not become mature. This metaphor of vegetation that is employed to elaborate blessedness or curse is not a new literary invention of our author (cf. Ps 1:3, Jer 17:6-8, Ezek 17:22-24). However, the author uses the metaphor with greater precision, employing the progressive stages of vegetal growth: seedling, roots, boughs, branches, fruit. The illegitimate seedling represents the children of the wicked.

The particular aspect that the author stresses in the development of the image of vegetation from the seedling is the eventual uselessness for the wicked of the fruit of evil . Even though appearances may be to the contrary, their root is not deep; even if they sprout branches they will be shaken, they will be uprooted and their branches will be broken; their fruit will remain immature and not fit to eat. Even more than useless, the children of the wicked, namely all the fruit and apparent success of the wicked, become witnesses against the wicked at the time of examination (4:6).

---

the generation of the wicked is in contrast with the specific images of the sterile woman and the eunuch. In the third diptych, the author emphasizes that the children of the wicked will be of no use to the wicked and in fact at the time of accounting, the children become their accusers. The two diptychs should be interpreted in light of one another as their deliberate parallelism would suggest. In the second, the children of adultery represent the 'fruit' of the wicked in its extended sense. All of this 'fruit', contained in the image of 'the generation of the wicked', will have a grievous end. But the import of this image is completed in the third diptych where the author accentuates clearly that the 'prolific brood' of the wicked will be of no use specifically to the wicked themselves. The separation of the two diptychs does create a difficulty for the reader if each is interpreted separately.

[37] Cf. the personifications of σοφία in Prov 8, Sir 24, Wis 7, and of δίκη in Wis 1:8. In 4:1-2, ἀρετή similarily undergoes personification. "Virtue is known by God and humans, and she marches with the crown of victory through the ages, winning the contest for spotless prizes."

[38] D. WINSTON, *The Wisdom of Solomon*, pp. 133-134.

This metaphor of vegetation which represents the lives of the wicked, is set in juxtaposition to the brief reference to the sterile woman and eunuch who have the root of wisdom (ἡ ῥίζα τῆς φρονήσεως, 3:15) [39]. Even though this root of wisdom did not bring forth actual boughs, branches and fruit, it will bear fruit at the final accounting. On the contrary, the apparent strength of the actual boughs, branches and fruit that stem from the illegitimate seedlings will be of no use to the wicked because their roots are shallow.

The idea that the children of the wicked become witnesses of the evil of their parents summarizes and clinches the main point of the author's analysis of the relationship between the wicked and their children. The author is unmasking the apparent success of the wicked which is in contrast to the apparent failure of the virtuous. According to their own reasoning, the wicked regard weakness as useless and strength as their law of right (2:11). Therefore, the fruit and success of the wicked, in their own perspective, appears as a vindication of their own stance towards life. However, the author declares that this fruit and success is only apparent and that at the time of accounting the very fruit of the wicked becomes a testimony against them. The wicked will fail not specifically because their fruit will be destroyed, but because their fruit will not bring their hoped for success and will be a source of their own condemnation at the time of accounting.

1) *The reversal of images*

For the most part, the reversal of images regarding the virtuous and the wicked takes place internally within the two diptychs. The very structure of a diptych, which contrasts two scenes, accommodates images that highlight the reversal of meaning. The fruit which the sterile woman will have at the accounting of souls (3:13c) contrasts with the fruit of the wicked which will be useless (ὁ καρπὸς αὐτῶν ἄχρηστος, 4:5b). The root of understanding is unfailing (3:15b), but the root of the wicked will not be deep (οὐ δώσει ῥίζαν εἰς βάθος, 4:3b). It is better to be virtuous without children (ἀτεκνία, 4:1) than to be like the wicked whose children (τέκνα, 4:6) witness against them.

---

[39] The meaning of φρόνησις is nuanced in Wis. The term often translates the Hebrew, חכמה, in the LXX but not exclusively so as to make it a synonym to wisdom (see REDPATH). LARCHER notes the unique nuance of φρόνησις in 3:15b and 4:9a as referring to 'virtuous wisdom'. In other words, this wisdom is a knowledge of good and evil that stems from virtue and not simply from science in the socratic sense (C. LARCHER, *Études*, p. 358). This nuance fits well with the contrast between the wicked and the virtuous. The root of wisdom for the virtuous enables them to go beyond the appearances of sterility to choose a way of life that will be fruitful.

In addition to the internal transformations, there are a number of reversals of images that refer back to the speech of the wicked and to the first diptych. These, in turn, accentuate the change in perspective with regard to the just and the wicked. In their ruminations on the evanescence of life, the wicked lamented that no one will remember their deeds (οὐθεὶς μνεμονεύσει, 2:4); but in the memory of virtue there is immortality (ἐν μνήμῃ αὐτῆς, 4:1). The wicked in their frenetic boasting called for wearing crowns of roses before they fade (στεψώμεθα ῥόδων κάλυξιν, 2:8); but it is virtue that marches everlastingly carrying the crown (στεφανηφοροῦσα, 4:2). The wicked considered the enjoyment of their fleeting pleasures as their specific lot in life (ὁ κλῆρος οὗτος, 2:9); but it is the eunuch with integrity who will have an inheritance in the Lord's temple (κλῆρος ἐν ναῷ, 3:14). There will be no hope for the children of the wicked (οὐχ ἕξουσιν ἐλπίδα, 3:18); this assertion continues the alternation between the hopefulness of the just and the hopeless situation of the wicked (3:4,11). Finally, in their adherence to power and might, the wicked had declared weakness to be useless (τὸ γὰρ ἀσθενὲς ἄχρηστον, 2:11). But, in fact, the weakness of the just is victorious in virtue (νικήσασα, 4:2), whereas the brood of the wicked will be of no use (οὐ χρησιμεύσει, 4:3), and the fruit of the wicked will be useless (3:16).

The author's continuous play on the reversal of fortune between the just and the wicked, under the distinction between appearance and reality, challenges the reader to view critically the perspective of the wicked.

2) *The context of the trial in the central diptychs*

In the second and third diptychs, the day of accounting for the just and the wicked is particularly highlighted. This is the time when the apparent success of the wicked will be laid bare, whereas the true values of the just will be vindicated. The day of accounting is the critical moment of judgment when the true nature of the lives of the wicked and just will be clarified. As such, the concept of a final accounting is a pivotal issue in the argumentation of the author. By virtue of this concept of a final accounting, the author is forcing the issue of a critical view of the values of the wicked at the present.

Three synonymous expressions are employed in the diptychs to convey the idea of the final accounting. 1) The sterile woman will be fruitful at the accounting of souls (ἐν ἐπισκοπῇ ψυχῶν, 3:13c). 2) For the wicked there will be no consolation on the day of scrutiny (ἐν ἡμέρᾳ διαγνώσεως, 3:18b). 3) During the examination of the wicked (ἐν ἐξετασμῷ αὐτῶν, 4:6), their children become witnesses of their wickedness.

The first expression in 3:13 recalls the wicked's mocking remark in 2:20 against the just one, who believed in an accounting. Similarly, it recalls the expression in the first diptych (3:7) where the just are said to shine brilliantly at the time of accounting (cf. 1:6d). The second expression is unique in the Bible. The term, διάγνωσις, implies a juridical concept that refers to the resolution of a case by a competent authority[40]. The third expression (4:6) echoes the author's assertion at the opening exhortation that there will be an examination of the impious (ἐξέτασις ἔσται, 1:9). Both terms, ἐξέτασις and ἐξετασμός, are juridical terms denoting the examination of information in case proceedings. The irony of the last expression is complete when the children of the wicked, who on the surface level are signs of strength and hope, are said to be witnesses against the wicked[41].

By conjoining to the biblical expression of the day of judgment (ἐπισκοπή), the technical terms derived from juridical contexts, the author is highlighting the juridical nature of the ultimate judgment. It is the perspective of the ultimate judgment, with its juridical overtones, that the author is constructing in the argumentation against the reasoning of the wicked. It is this perspective which enables the reader to examine with the author the tension between appearance and reality in the case of the wicked and the just.

C-5.5 The fourth diptych - the contrast of the premature death of the just youth with the wicked (4:7-20)

1) *Early death as a paradox of divine blessing*

The final diptych, which elaborates the paradox of an early death as a sign of divine blessing, is in continuity with the central diptychs on fruitfulness. The old age of the wicked's children had been declared to be

---

[40] C. LARCHER, *Le Livre de la Sagesse*, pp. 310-311.

[41] MATTIOLI attempts to argue that the contextual meaning of the expression, ἐν ἐξετασμῷ, simply refers to common court proceedings where children actually do become witnesses against their own parents. "Forse... abbia voluto riferirsi a un qualche processo publico nel quale i figli si constituirono veri testimoni di accusa contro i genitori." A. MATTIOLI, "Felicità e virtù. La dottrina della Sapienza nel brano macarico per le sterili e gli eunuchi (Sap 3,13-4,6)", p. 47.

The image may very well have been drawn from such circumstances, but to deny a reference to the ultimate judgment goes against the main argument of the author. The use of the present tense, 'they are witnesses of evil against their parents in their examination', does not exclude a reference to an ultimate judgment. It is the perspective of a judgment that the author is bringing into the present argument for the benefit of the reader. This is corroborated in the actual vision of the future confession of the wicked (5:1-14), and the sentence that the wicked receive (5:15-23).

honorless (3:17), and their fruit said to be unripe (4:5). The paradox is transposed from the issue of fruitfulness to the issue of time. The just have acquired maturity in a short time (4:13).

The tension between appearance and reality is evoked and highlighted. Honorable age is not to be assessed by the number of years or by grey hairs (4:8-9), but by understanding and innocence (4:9). Even though the just have died prematurely at a young age, they will be in peace (4:7). People witness such events, but they do not understand (4:14). They will see the death of the wise but not understand what has been established for them by the Lord (4:17). With the insistent use of the verb ὁράω (4:14c,17a,17a), the author recalls the original challenge the wicked had set forth, "let us see if his words are true" (2:17). Through this play on appearance and reality the author continues to invite the reader to change the basis of one's perspective on physical death.

As in the cases of the sterile woman and the eunuch, the author has chosen an image which ordinarily evokes tragedy and divine wrath in his exploration of the tension between appearance and reality for the just. A ripe old age was considered the Lord's special blessing for faithfulness (Gen 15:15; 25:8; 35:29; Exod 20:12; Deut 4:40; Judg 8:32). Even in sapiential circles, old age was considered a sign of wisdom and a reward for right conduct (Prov 3:1-2; 10:27; 16:31; Job 42:7; Sir 1:12). An early death was a curse one wished on enemies (Ps 109:8).

The same transformation in perspective, which the author proposed for understanding the death of the just and the apparent fruitless lives of the innocent, is operative in the case of the early death of a just youth. Honorable old age (4:8) cannot be measured by grey hair or by the number of years, but by innocence (βίος ἀκηλίδωτος, 4:9) and inner maturity. The author advocates the idea of a progressive internal growth which becomes pleasing to God (4:10) and brings maturity even in a short time (4:13)[42].

The physical death of the youth is not a destruction but a dislocation — a removal from danger evoked by the verbs, μετατίθημι and ἁρπάζομαι in 4:10-11. Far from being a destruction of tragic proportions, the early death of a perfected youth is presented as a special divine blessing. Since the just youth became pleasing to God, the Lord quickly

---

[42] The idea of a progressive moral growth is suggested by the verb, γίγνομαι, in 4:10 (having become pleasing to God), and by the participle of τελείομαι in 4:13 (having been perfected in a short while). On the author's idea of moral life as a progressive growth presented in the treatment of the premature death of the just youth, see C. LARCHER, Le Livre de la Sagesse, p. 330; A. SISTI, "La figura del giusto perseguitato in Sap 2,12-20", BbbOr 19 (1977) pp. 135-137; F. LUCIANI, "Il significato de teleo in Sap 4,16", BbbOr 20 (1978) 183-188.

took the youth from the midst of evil, lest he be contaminated[43]. The Lord is the protagonist in the early death of the youth just as God was the protagonist in the death of the just one in the first diptych.

The image of the just youth who has come to maturity in a short time integrates both the first and central diptychs. From the first diptych, it integrates the idea of God's special intervention at the time of physical death for the sake of the just. From the central diptychs, it integrates the idea of maturity and completion.

The contrast of the youth who shows exceptional wisdom with elders who act foolishly or wickedly has biblical precedents. Elihu defends his right to speak precisely with an explanation that the source of wisdom resides in the breath of God and not in the aged (Job 32:6-9). Qoheleth praises the poor, wise youth over an old, foolish king (Qoh 4:13). Daniel is described as a youth with a holy spirit (τὸ πνεῦμα τὸ ἅγιον παιδαρίου νεωτέρου, Theodotion, Susanna, 45) whom God aroused to confound the wicked elders who were judges.

But only with our author is the possibility of youthful moral maturity highlighted in the context of a youth's early death. The images and language associated with the departure of Enoch facilitated the author's elaboration of the divine blessedness of a just youth who dies. Two clear verbal points of contact exist between the two accounts: a) Enoch was found pleasing to God, εὐηρέστησεν Ενωχ τῷ θεῷ (Gen 5:24a, cf. Wis 4:10a); b) God transferred him, ὅτι μετέθηκεν αὐτὸν ὁ θεός, Gen 5:24b, cf. Wis 4:10b). The author applies specifically the two ideas of special divine favor and translocation from the Enoch account to the early death of the just youth[44].

2) *The theme of judgment*

The background image of a trial is sustained with terms and images reminiscent of the first three diptychs. The author's favored term, ἐπισκοπή (4:15), alludes to the future day of accounting, "there will be

---

[43] While early death had not been interpreted as a special divine blessing in Israel, the idea was common in Greek mythology and poetry. "He whom the gods love dies young" (*Menander*, 425). For references of the idea of God snatching away from evil those whom he loves in Greek and Rabbinic literature, see D. WINSTON, *The Wisdom of Solomon*, pp. 140-141.

[44] Israelite tradition uses the character in the Enoch story from Genesis as a mouthpiece for intricate apocalyptic accounts of the creation of the universe (1-3 Enoch). In Heb 11:5 the phrase of Gen 5:24 was interpreted to mean that Enoch did not see death. In Jub 4:23, the idea of Enoch not dying is not directly stated, but could be easily inferred, "And he was taken from among the children of men, and we led him to the garden of Eden for greatness and honor."

an accounting for his holy ones"[45]. Moreover, the author highlights the active role that the just youth will play at the time of judgment. As the just will judge (κρινοῦσιν, 3:8) the wicked, so too will the youth who is quickly perfected judge (κατακρινεῖ) the prolonged old age of the unrighteous (4:16).

The contrast of the wicked in the second half of the diptych (4:16-20) anticipates the ultimate judgment by means of apocalyptic language. The Lord will react vehemently (ἐκγελάσεται)[46] to the wicked's despising of the death of the wise youth (4:18). The wicked will be thrown down headlong, and at the end they will be laid in waste and destroyed (4:19).

The diptych is brought to a conclusion in parallel fashion to the third diptych. The evil deeds of the wicked will accuse (ἐλέγχει) them on the day of reckoning (4:20), just as the children of the wicked become witnesses against their parents at their examination (4:6). The expression, ἐν συλλογισμῷ ἁμαρτημάτων αὐτῶν, continues the author's use of synonymous expressions to indicate the day of judgment[47].

---

[45] The fourth diptych bears several resemblances with the first. The introductory word in both refers to the just, δικαίων/δίκαιος (3:1; 4:7). The physical death of the just and the youth are interpreted as an intervention of the Lord, to test and to save (3:5; 4:10-11,14). In both cases those who observed the death did not understand its true significance (3:2; 4:14). Finally, those who have died in God's favor, the just and the perfected youth, will judge the wicked (3:8; 4:16).

It appears the author is deliberately balancing the two diptychs, by paralleling significant ideas and words within both. This explains the fluctuation in the manuscripts of the couplet, "For grace and mercy belong to the elect, there will be an accounting for his saints" (3:9cd; 4:15) (J. ZIEGLER, Sapientia, p. 107). In both cases, the couplet concludes the first half of the diptych, just as both had been introduced with the subject of the just. See LARCHER for a restructuring of the verses to the order 16,17,15,14c,14d,18 (C. LARCHER, Le Livre de la Sagesse, pp. 339-340).

[46] Cf. the similar context of the Lord's despising and laughing at the wicked in Pss 2:4; 36(37):13; 58(59):9.

[47] The expression has been interpreted by commentators in two manners: a) as a synonymous expression referring to the day of judgment, b) as an expression denoting the subjective analysis of their sins by the wicked themselves before God (C. LARCHER, Le Livre de la Sagesse, pp. 352-353). The idea which immediately follows the expression, namely that the sins of the wicked will accuse them, would lend force to the second interpretation. During their own reflection on their lives, their sins accuse them in their conscience. However, the continuation of the synonymous expressions for the day of judgment (1:9; 2:20; 3:7,13,18; 4:6,15,20) clearly establishes an ultimate judgment as the reason and basis for the accusation against the wicked. This interpretation of a final reckoning does not exclude the subjective anguish which the wicked are said to experience on the day of judgment. This subjective anguish will be highlighted by the author in the wicked's 'confession' at the day of judgment (5:1-14).

C - 5.6   **The impact of the author's choice of images to refute the wicked's accusation**

The contrasting diptychs, where the author systematically uncovers the true meaning of the death of the just, the final fruitfulness of the sterile woman and the eunuch, and the special divine blessedness of the wise youth, constitute the author's refutation of the entire reasoning of the wicked. The contrast of the wicked in each diptych goes beyond the refutation of the wicked's argument and constitutes an accusation with the assurance of a definite verdict against the wicked. Just as the speech of the wicked followed a dynamic progression, the refutation in the diptychs follows the same progression in reverse order.

The first diptych refutes the climactic challenge of the wicked who envisage a confirmation of their life style in the projected brutal death of the just. The second and third diptychs oppose the wicked's decision to oppress the righteous poor, the widow and the elderly. The paradoxical images of the blessed sterile woman and the eunuch counter the false judgment of the wicked who consider human frailty or limitation as meaningless. The apparent temporal fruit of the wicked will be as useless as their advocation of the temporal flight into pleasure. Their old age will be dishonorable. Finally, the fourth diptych on the wise youth who dies a premature death constitutes the author's refutation of the wicked's negative view of physical death itself, which leads to their desperate extolling of youthful pleasures.

The fourth diptych has much in common with the first in that, in both situations, the author takes the case of the just who die and receive blessedness. But the difference is that, in the first, the death of the just is specifically the result of the deliberate torture and execution of the wicked. In the fourth, the death of the just youth focuses simply on a premature death, without attributing it to any intentional cause of others, except the pleasure of God. In order to refute the wicked's negative view of the transience of life, which is derived from the ultimate reality of physical death, the author chose the poignant example of the premature death of a youth, whose death does not constitute ultimate meaninglessness.

The parallelism of the diptychs, in reverse order to the progression of the wicked's argument, highlights the intentionality of the author. Through the argumentation of the diptychs, the author is refuting not only the dramatic and accusatory attack of the wicked in their projected death of the just, but the entire reasoning process which issued in that attack. The author's refutation in turn becomes accusatory.

It is evident that the author did not simply choose at random the four images for the formulation of the refutation: the persecuted just, the sterile woman, the eunuch and the just youth. The author has organized the refutation following a pattern of images found in Second Isaiah. M.J. SUGGS has listed the various points of contact between Wis 2:10–5:23 and Isaiah [48]. For our purpose, it will be enough to note the order of the four images and the major differences the author has created.

The image of the just, who is persecuted in death and rewarded by the Lord (Wis 2:12–3:10), follows lines depicted of the suffering servant in Isa 52–53. Isa 54 introduces the song of hope for the sterile woman who surely will have more children than those married. Isa 56:4-5 is a prophetic oracle which assures the eunuchs who keep the sabbaths and the covenant that they will have a monument and a name in the house of the Lord. Finally, Isa 57:1-2 consists of a brief theological reflection wherein the death of the righteous is interpreted as a release from calamity and an entrance into peace [49].

However, there are major structural and thematic differences, primarily in the first and fourth diptychs, which highlight the fundamental change of focus in Wis. The author has organized the material into tightly organized diptychs which contrast the virtuous and the wicked. This structure is evidently more conducive to a formal refutation of the accusation against the just, which the wicked had launched in their speech. These contrasting diptychs invite the reader to be actively reflective in following the author's rebuttal. The reader is challenged both to formulate a judgment against the wicked's reasoning process and to assess the values of virtue which the author promotes.

The central issue of the redemptive suffering of the servant of the Lord for others is adapted by the author in the first diptych. Though the suffering of the just may be redeeming in his own case (e.g. the purification envisaged in the images of gold purified in fire and the burnt offering), the suffering of the just is not presented as being redemptive for the persecutors. The reason for this is clear when we realize that the diptychs are organized as a rebuttal of the wicked's reasoning process and constitute a counter-accusation against the wicked. The point of departure and arrival of the speech of the wicked is physical death: at the point of departure, physical death exemplifies for the wicked the hopeless transience of life; at the point of arrival, the projected physical death of the just is meant to ratify the wicked's life style. The author suppressed the idea of redemptive suffering for others in order to concentrate the rebuttal of the diptych against the reasoning process of the wicked.

---

[48] M.J. SUGGS, "Wisdom of Solomon II,10–V: A Homily Based on the Fourth Servant Song", *JBL* 76 (1957) 26-33. See also J. SCHABERG, "Major Midrashic Traditions in Wisdom 1,1–6,25", *JSJ* 13 (1982) 75-101.

[49] The two sections which constitute Wis 5, the confession of the wicked and the apocalyptic judgment against the wicked, continue a similar sequence to that found in Isa 59:9-19.

The author has formulated the fourth diptych around the early death
of a wise youth. The element of youth is not adverted to in the reflection
of the departure of the just in Isa 57. The explanation for this major
difference is self-explanatory when we recall the function of this diptych
in the author's rebuttal. The premature, natural death of the youth
refutes both the wicked's negative assessment of the transience of life, and
their superficial extolling of pleasures 'as in youth', which includes their
despising of all that is weak.

All four diptychs are meant to refute the entire reasoning process of
the wicked. To this end, the author did not advert to the element of
redemptive suffering for others, which would have been inappropriate in
the case of the challenge mounted by the wicked. In turn, the author
added the element of youth to the fourth diptych in order to counter the
wicked's absolute judgment against what is weak and against what in fact
from many points of view may be transitory.

C - 6. The Wicked's Confession of Guilt and God's Judgment (Wis 5)

After having refuted the argumentation of the wicked, by showing
the true nature of the experience of the just in four diptychs, the author
introduces into the discourse the prospective scene of an ultimate
judgment. The mere presence of the just one, who had been tormented by
his oppressors, constitutes irrefutable evidence against the wicked. It
confirms the author's declarations in the diptychs on the reward of justice
and virtue, and proves the reasoning of the wicked to be false. The scene
of confrontation elicits the wicked's confession, which is followed by the
Lord's reward of the just and the sentence of destruction of wickedness in
apocalyptic imagery. Just as the four diptychs refuted the entire reasoning
process of the wicked, so too does the confession of the wicked
recapitulate their original speech in reverse order.

The author's double procedure in the diptychs to disprove the
reasoning of the wicked (whereby the blessedness of the just is guaranteed
and the reversal of fortune of the wicked is assured) reaches a
culmination in the vision of the ultimate judgment. The author brings the
reader to the lofty heights of a divine perspective where the realities of
blessedness and moral tragedy shine clearly over against the appearances
of the power of injustice and the impotence of virtue [50].

---

[50] This setting of the stage whereby the reader is led to a higher divine perspective in
order to pierce through the mystery of the thriving of injustice is readily perceivable in Ps
73 and in God's answer to Job from the whirlwind, Job 38–41. See L. ALONSO SCHÖKEL,

C‑6.1   The introduction of the scene of judgment

The author introduces the scene of a future judgment by means of the temporal adverb, τότε (5:1). The establishment of a temporal change refers to the coming judgment that was described in the preceding verses of the last diptych (4:20). By bringing into the discourse the coming judgment, the author sets onto the scene the future confrontation between the wicked and the just one whom they had planned to kill. The just one will stand with great courage against his tormentors (ἐν παρρεσίᾳ πολλῇ, 5:1). The wicked will be shaken and confounded at the turn of the just's salvation (5:2).

The very presence of the just one before his adversaries is presented as a conviction of the wicked. The just one is said to stand (στήσεται) before his oppressors. The gesture of rising up or the posture of standing are positions that describe a formal function in biblical trial proceedings. The judge rises to pronounce judgment[51]. An accuser or witness stands to pronounce an accusation or to make a defense[52]. One who is not able to stand in judgment has nothing further to add for defense (cf. Ps 1:5). The standing of the just with great confidence (ἐν παρρεσίᾳ, 5:1) before his oppressors carries with it the nuance of a definitive accusation. No word need be uttered on the part of the just, for the very presence of the just who is to be rewarded by God accuses the wicked.

The accusatory defense of the wicked in Wis 2 clarifies the accusatory nature of the just's presence. Since the wicked projected the shameful death of the just as a defense and confirmation of their own position towards life, it is only with the blessed survival of the just that this position can ultimately be proved wrong. In their accusation, the wicked planned to put the just to death as a rhetorical test 'to see' (ἴδωμεν) if his position were true (2:17). Therefore, when the wicked 'see'

J.L. Sicre Diaz, *Job*, Nueva Biblia Española, Madrid: 1983, pp. 535-536, 596: "La teofanía indica el paso de lo sapiencial a la revelación, paso ya trazado en el salmo 73. Al presentarse Dios, aunque su temática parezca sapiencial, el punto de vista y el enfoque pertenecen al orden de la revelación. Job, como el orante del salmo 73, será invitado a compartir el punto de vista de Dios" (p. 535). See also the article based on the commentary that concentrates on the theophany, L. Alonso Schökel, "La réponse de Dieu", *Concilium*, 189 (1983) 75-84.

[51] For a brief analysis of the various Hebrew verbs denoting the rising of the judge in the act of pronouncing judgment see P. Bovati, *Ristabilire la giustizia*, pp. 210-212. Cf. Ps 81(82):1, Job 31:14.

[52] Bovati notes various nuances that rising implies during a court case apart from the final rising of the judge. An intervention in a court case is often introduced with the speaker's rising to accuse or to defend. Often such a rising to speak conveys a resolving or victorious intervention. P. Bovati, *Ristabilire la giustizia*, pp. 217-219. Cf. Deut 19:15-16, Job 33:5.

(ἰδόντες) the blessedness of the just, they are overtaken with fear (5:2).
Precisely this presence of the just one before the tormentors at the ultimate
judgment thus constitutes an irrefutable accusation against the wicked [53].
In face of this incontrovertible proof of their error, they react with stupor
and anguish. The following monologue of the wicked betrays their
confession of guilt in response to the definitive accusation of the just.

C - 6.2   The wicked's confession of guilt

Just as the author had provided the reader with the privileged
position of following the false reasoning of the wicked, so too does the
author allow the reader to 'listen in' on the confession of guilt that the
wicked express among themselves. The speech of the wicked is not a
confession of guilt in the technical sense of such an act. A genuine
confession of guilt implies recognizing one's guilt before the wronged or
before the judge at trial [54]. But in our case the wicked confess their guilt
only among themselves [55].

---

[53] LARCHER disclaims any nuance of accusation on the part of the just one who
stands by insisting on three elements: a) the passivity of the just, they do not utter a word,
b) the fact that the accusation already takes place in 4:20, their sins accuse them
(according to LARCHER's delimitation of the text, the fourth diptych ends at 4:19) and c)
the phrase, ἐν παρρησίᾳ, emphasizes the attitude of the just's complete confidence in
God, rather than confidence with respect to the wicked. C. LARCHER, *Le Livre de la
Sagesse*, pp. 352-355.
    These objections dissolve at once in the face of the underlying metaphor of the trial
scene. a) The fact that the just one does not utter a verbal accusation is explained by the
fact that his very presence convicts the wicked. The presence of the just speaks against the
wicked and his silence emphasizes the power of his enduring presence. b) The delimitation
of the fourth diptych at 4:19 does not respect the parallelism between the conclusions of
the third and fourth diptychs. The children of the wicked accuse their parents (4:6); the
lawlessness of the wicked will accuse them at the time of reckoning (4:20). Moreover, in
the first diptych, the author attributes to the just the active role of judging at the time of
judgment (3:8). c) The author's particular preference to underscore the just's confidence,
which reflects his relationship to God, rather than the tension with the wicked, does not
detract from the accusatory nature of the just's presence before his oppressors. It is the
blessedness of the just that confutes the wicked's false accusation uttered by them in
Wis 2.
[54] BOVATI has noted two essential functions in the biblical world of the guilty's
confession that should not be confused: a juridical confession within the context of a trial
and a confession in the context of a confrontation between two parties. In the first case,
the confession simply clarifies the validity of the accusation and facilitates the correct
sentencing of the judge (see the story of Achan who confesses his guilt and is promptly
executed, Josh 7:10-25). In the second case, the purpose of the confession is to elicit
reconciliation through reparation of the rupture. (P. BOVATI, *Ristabilire la giustizia*, pp.
105-107, 152).
    Our case definitely belongs to the first type, where the confession of the wicked first of
all confirms the defense and accusation of the author in the four diptychs and, secondly,

Within the background trial image, the effect of this personal confession of guilt among the wicked is the confirmation of the reasoning of the author in defense of the just and against the wicked. By having the wicked confess their own error, the author is adding weight to his refutation of the wicked's original arguments. At the end, even they will recognize with anguish and regret, at least among themselves, the error of their life.

The significance of the wicked's recantation of their error, in reverse order to the presentation of their philosophy, is to underscore the entire dynamic of evil which finally issued in the projected death of the just. In this respect, the author duplicates the order of the defense and attack in the four diptychs. First, the wicked recognize their error with respect to the just one whom they had persecuted (5:4-5). Second, they admit the error of their position towards life, characterized by arrogance and an accumulation of wealth (5:6-8). Third, they recognize the transient qualities of their values and acknowledge virtue as a source of the hope which they lack (5:9-13). The confession of error, therefore, covers the entire reasoning process of the wicked as enunciated in Wis 2.

Only two verbal repetitions appear between 5:4-5 and 2:12-20, the sections in both speeches which deal with the wicked's reasoning about the just one (ὁ βίος αὐτοῦ, 2:15, τὸν βίον αὐτοῦ, 5:4c; υἱὸς θεοῦ, 2:18, ἐν υἱοῖς θεοῦ). However, the thematic similarities leave no doubt as to the reversal of the just one's end. The speech of the wicked closed with their boastful victory over the just in the projection of his death, and their confession begins with the awareness of the just one's blessedness. The wicked restate their previous judgments against the just one by recalling how they had concluded that the just one was 'an example of reproach' (2:14 - 5:4ab), that 'his life was madness' (2:15 - 5:4c), and that 'his death was disgraceful' (2:20a - 5:4d).

The blessedness of the just proves to the wicked that the former is a son of God and that his lot is among the saints (5:5). But this realization on the part of the wicked does not mean simply that their error is limited to a miscalculation of the fate of the just. Their choices for a life program

---

justifies the sentence of condemnation that follows. The uniqueness of the wicked's confession in Wis is that they admit their error only among themselves. It is the trial metaphor that allows their confession to function as a confirmation of the accusation against the wicked, and as justification of the sentence that they receive.

[55] Various parts of the wicked's confession can be identified in sections of Isa: Wis 5:3-4 = Isa 53:3,10; Wis 5:6 = Is 53:6 (see M.J. Suggs, "Wisdom", *JBL* 76 (1957) 26-33). Moreover, after the brief description of the just one who is taken away in calamity (Isa 57:1-2) and immediately before the description of the Lord being armed to enact judgment (Isa 59:15-20), there is a brief confession of Israel's sin. The confession also employs images of wandering in darkness (Isa 59:9-13) similar to the image found in Wis 5:6.

of sensuality and power, which culminated in the projected death of the just, are unmasked in their own consciousness as being erroneous. From the realization that the blessedness of the just belies their false interpretation of his projected death, they pass immediately to the realization that their life project was based on falsehood.

In vv 5:6-8, the wicked repudiate their life project as presented in 2:6-11. They finally admit that the ways of their life were wrong. The author employs the underlying image of 'journeying' to emphasize the recantation of their conduct. They had strayed from the way of truth (5:6), and they did not know the way of the Lord (5:7c). The light of justice and the sun did not illuminate them in their travels (5:7ab). As a result, they took their fill [56] of paths of lawlessness and destruction, wandering in trackless deserts [57]. Just as the confrontation with the reality of the just concluded with a question of amazement, so too does the explicit recognition of the error of their life style conclude with a questioning of the futility of their boasting and of their accumulated riches (5:8).

The wicked's question regarding their riches leads in turn to a reflection on the transience of their previously held values. This reflection picks up, in parallel fashion, the opening reflection of the transience of life in their first speech. But the subject throughout this final reflection (ἐκεῖνα πάντα, 5:9) refers specifically to their arrogance and wealth (5:8).

---

[56] The image of the wicked taking their fill (ἐνεπλήσθημεν) of paths of lawlessness and destruction (5:7a) in their confession contrasts ironically with the parallel exhortation of the speech where they plan to take their fill (πλησθῶμεν) of costly wine and myrrh (2:7a).

Although ZIEGLER's emendation of the text according to the Arabic translation offers an intelligible and consistent reading, it is not a necessary emendation. Instead of 'paths' the Arabic reads the equivalent of τριβόλοις (thorns). With this reading the verb must be emended as well. Instead of ἐνεπλήσθημεν, ZIEGLER reads with BRETSCHNEIDER ἐνεπλέχθημεν (we were hindered), similar to Prov 28:18. This idea of being hindered by thorns of lawlessness and destruction would follow naturally the references to the lack of light on the way (J. ZIEGLER, Sapientia, p. 32). Another emendation of the verb has been proposed, ἐμπλαγχθῆναι - to wander, while retaining the noun, paths (C. LARCHER, Le Livre de la Sagesse, pp. 367-368). These emendations are unnecessary considering the common image 'being filled with lawlessness or wickedness' (Gen 6:11, Lev 19:29, Prov 14:14, Sir 23:11).

[57] In the wicked's confession of error, the author is presenting a subtle contrast between the wandering life of the wicked and the wandering of the Israelites in the desert. The Israelites were guided by a starry flame in their travels (Wis 10:17). They too traveled through an uninhabited wilderness but with different results (Wis 11:2). Similarly, the confession draws parallels between the wicked and the Egyptians in the midrashic treatment of the plagues. The wicked had no light to guide them in their journeys, and the Egyptians were stricken with loss of sight, surrounded by darkness (Wis 19:17).

Several expressive images portray the transience of their arrogance and riches. Two brief images, the shadow and the rumor, initiate the series of comparisons between their previous values and the transitory image. These are followed by the metaphors of the boat with its oars, the bird with its wings, the arrow flying towards its target. The idea emphasized throughout the metaphors is the transitoriness of the movements. All movements are transitory, 'leaving no trace'. No trace remains of the passing of a boat, a bird, an arrow. The images, then, while immediately referring to the subjects, arrogance and riches, are metaphors representing the entire life of the wicked which they traversed in arrogance and riches. Nothing of substance remains of their lives.

As a result of this reflection, the wicked realize that they have no signs of virtue to show that would survive the transience of their materialistic values (5:14). At the end, they recognize what they had denied in their reflection on the transience of life - a value that transcends the reality of physical death - ἀρετή. The author concludes the reflection on the wicked by underscoring their hopelessness at the time of judgment. Expressive images of transience emphasize the rootless hope of the wicked: chaff in the wind, frost in a storm, smoke in the wind, and the passing memory of an occasional guest.

The images of transience applied to the wicked's values of wealth and strength parallel the images of transience in the wicked's prior evaluation of life and physical death. The difference between the parallel reflections lies in their subject matter. In the first reflection, the images of transience accentuated their judgment that no value survives physical death. In the second reflection, the images of transience accentuate their recognition of personal responsibility for not having acquired the value of virtue that endures.

The author's penchant to resume the wicked's speech with eloquent language and in erudite images, even in their confession of guilt, is consistent with the tension between appearance and reality that had been inaugurated in their opening statements. On the surface level, the wicked remain polished and sophisticated in their speech, capable of imaginative reflection. For the sake of the reader, the author does not wish to strip away from the wicked the facade of their erroneous positions. The effect of the wicked's confession in eloquent language emphasizes the importance the author attributes to judging values beneath the surface. Though they spoke with eloquence in the presentation of their stance towards life, and though they had the signs of strength from their own point of view, the reality of death conceived as hopelessness and enmity with God and the cosmos is already taking effect, ready to be revealed fully at a future time.

C - 6.3   The scene of judgment (5:15-23)

The prospective scene of judgment, which the author presents before the reader after the wicked's confession, confirms the argumentation of the four diptychs. The just receive a kingly reward of life in God (5:15-16) [58], and the enemies are consumed in an ultimate, cosmic conflagration directed against wickedness (5:17-23). The final conflagration against wickedness is developed in two stages as declared in 5:17: a) the Lord is mobilized for battle (5:17-20), and b) the forces of creation itself join in battle against wickedness (5:21-23).

The Lord is presented as a warrior, which is consistent with apocalyptic imagery. Divine attributes are mobilized for battle through the device of an analogy where each weapon of a hoplite is compared to a divine attribute: zeal - armor, justice - breastplate, impartial judgment - helmet, holiness - shield, wrath - sword [59].

The analogy is an adaptation of Isa 59:17-19. The author has tightened the similar analogy by comparing divine zeal with the entire armor of a hoplite (instead of God's mantle as in Isa) and then by identifying each weapon with a moral attribute. However the author's major adaptation of Isa 59:17-19 is the expansion of the idea that the cosmos itself is armed to do battle against wickedness. This idea is present only metaphorically in Isa 59:19 where the Lord is said to come with wrath as a powerful torrent (ὡς ποταμὸς βίαιος). The author raises the brief metaphor in Isaiah into a principle of cosmology; namely, that the forces of nature are clearly on the side of God and justice against wickedness and foolishness (5:17b,20b).

The ultimate conflagration is presented through the forces of lightning, hail, waters, rivers, a mighty wind, a storm (5:21-23). These will ravish the earth as a result of lawlessness, and the thrones of governors will be overturned because of evil doing.

---

[58] The kingly reward is conveyed through the two objects which the just receive, βασίλειον and διάδημα - royalty and the diadem (Wis 5:16). The author's expression was most likely inspired by the verse in Isa 62:3, where the downcast of Zion are assured that they will become a crown of beauty and a royal diadem in the hand of the Lord: στέφανος κάλλους - διάδημα βασιλείας. The characteristic of a kingly reward for the just corresponds to the author's address in the exhortation to kings and to the judgment of kings.

[59] LARCHER changes τὸν ζῆλον into the nominative case (following S* and Vetus Latina) in order to make zeal the personified subject of the analogy instead of the Lord (C. LARCHER, Le Livre de la Sagesse, pp. 386-387). But the change of subject is not significant for the background image. In both cases, the Lord's zeal (either as complementary object or as subject) is mobilized in the analogy of armor through which the distinctive divine attributes are then specified by a particular type of weapon.

The author presents a restrained description of this final accounting, which had been continuously appealed to in the diptychs. Precious little can be deduced regarding the specific eschatological beliefs of the author from the apocalyptic account [60]. It appears he wished to commit himself as little as possible to the qualifications of eschatology such as the resurrection of the body or the definite annihilation of the physical cosmos or the location of blessedness [61]. The final conflagration simply affirms the kingly reward of the just and the destruction of wickedness perpetrated by the enemies of God (5:17) and by fools (5:20).

This somber accounting concludes the prospective situation of the court scene inaugurated by the exhortation to avoid death (1:12). It is this undesirable destiny of wickedness that the author presents as the ultimate negative reason for loving justice and seeking God. It is this undesirable destiny of enmity with God and the cosmos that characterizes the death which the author dissuades the reader from inviting into life through a false reasoning on mortality and weakness.

C-7. The Concluding Exhortation for Understanding and for Wisdom (6:1-21)

After the final conflagration has been presented as a conclusion to the discourse of the hypothetical case of injustice, the argumentation of the author returns to the explicit form of exhortation which underlies the entire first section of Wis. With parallels to the opening exhortation through imperatives and subjunctives, this section concludes the concentric structure of the first six chapters. But the chapter also turns the subject of the exhortation more specifically towards wisdom [62]. The exhortation to wisdom is an introductory link to the second part of the

---

[60] J.J. COLLINS critiques the tendency to define apocalyptic eschatology in terms of a presentation of the end times. The apocalyptic vision which extends into future eschatological realities has the effect of promoting a hope that transcends death in the present (J.J. COLLINS, "Apocalyptic Eschatology as the Transcendence of Death", *CBQ* 36 (1974) 21-43).

"In short, despite the fact that the term *eschatology* is normally used to describe it, the future hope of late postexilic and intertestamental Judaism cannot be defined with reference to 'the end' of something" (p.27).

"... while the present experience of righteousness gives rise to the hope of final vindication, it is also true that the hope of final vindication confirms and even makes possible the present experience of righteousness and divine approval" (p. 41).

[61] For a discussion on the deliberate vagueness of the author on eschatology in the scene of the apocalyptic judgment see C. LARCHER, *Le Livre de la Sagesse*, pp. 397-398.

[62] The author had briefly alluded to wisdom and to its function in human affairs in the opening exhortation, 1:4-6.

book, which presents a reflection on the positive values of the wisdom that comes from God.

Two major new arguments are presented in the author's exhortation to wisdom. The first argument (6:1-8) is expressed as an exhortation for the reader to apply the criteria uncovered in the elaboration on death, injustice and virtue (cc. 1–5), to one's own life. The second argument (6:9-21) shifts the motive of the opening exhortation from the negative reason of avoiding death to the positive reason of obtaining wisdom for a happy and full life. Both arguments unfold within the contours of an exhortation.

C-7.1   Kings are exhorted to understand and to learn (6:1-8)

The readers of the exhortation are addressed as 'kings', 'judges' (δικασταί), and 'rulers' (κρατοῦντες). The three distinct terms are synonymous with the opening title of the exhortation, rulers/judges (κρίνοντες, 1:1). Judgment is one of the prime tasks of a king and intelligence one of the qualities necessary for good management[63]. The emphasis in the opening part of this exhortation is on the need for kings to understand (σύνετε, μάθετε, 6:1). The object of the understanding is not specified. Since this exhortation follows the trial scene which the author had elaborated, the object of the understanding is supplied concretely by this elaboration. As if a king or a judge, the reader is encouraged to understand from the example of the trial scene which the author presented. The background trial image is thereby indirectly sustained even in the concluding exhortation. The court case that had been constructed for the imagination of the reader has ended, but the author calls for the application of the criteria exposed in the argumentation of the court scene to the governance of life. The reader is exhorted to understand and to judge rightly the court case that had been presented in light of the prospective of the ultimate judgment.

---

[63] The qualities of understanding and wisdom necessary for the good judgment of the king are exemplified in Solomon's dream and in the case of the specific judgment which follows (1 Kgs 3). H.A. KENIK, *The Design for Kingship: The Deuteronomistic Narrative Technique in 1 Kings 3:4-15*, Chico, CA: 1983, pp.99-119. There is no reason to look specifically for an historical reference in Wis, as if the kings and rulers addressed to in the exhortation are historical rulers. The device of addressing kings in exhortations was typical in Hellenistic academic circles for appealing to the intelligence of students or addressees in general (J.M. REESE, *Hellenistic Influence on the Book of Wisdom*, AnBib 41, pp. 146-152). See also D. BARSOTTI, *Meditazione sul Libro della Sapienza*, Brescia: 1976, "Per l'autore del libro l'uomo è essenzialmente re, l'uomo non vive la sua vocazione che in quanto governa, perché Dio creò l'uomo perché fosse re del creato. Salomone così è tipo dell'uomo che ha realizzato la sua vocazione" (p. 28).

The reader has been led through the author's argumentation regarding the negative reason for loving justice and seeking God. This argumentation unfolded withiñ parameters parallel to a court case: accusation, counter-accusation, defense, confession and sentence. In the concluding exhortation, the author is addressing the reader as a king whose task is to judge rightly with wisdom.

The exhortation calls for the reader's personal application of the criteria established in the preceding discourse for ascertaining just conduct. God is the source of the government of rulers (6:3ab); there will be an examination of their deeds and plans (6:3c,8); if they do not judge rightly (6:4), God's intervention will be swift and powerful (6:5). In this succinct exhortation, the author is calling readers to apply the results of the court case between the just and the wicked to their own situation. The exhortation calls for the same criteria to be applied to the reader, addressed as a king whose task it is to judge. The author is appealing to the critical faculty of the reader to participate in the judgment which the author had presented in a prospective form and, moreover, to appropriate the judgment into one's life [64].

C-7.2 The positive motives for learning wisdom (6:9-21)

If the opening exhortation quickly subsumed the character of dissuading the reader from bringing on death, the concluding exhortation moves into the presentation of the positive values of wisdom. Those who learn to love wisdom will find holiness and will have a defense (6:9-11). Furthermore, wisdom herself will seek out those who love her, so that finding her will not be overly strenuous (6:14) and will bring freedom from anxiety (6:15b). The concentrating on wisdom constitutes perfect understanding (6:15a).

The sorites, which draws the exhortation of the first part of the book to a close, highlights in explicit fashion the positive motive for seeking wisdom (6:17-20). It is through wisdom that one is brought close to God [65]. Through wisdom the opening exhortation to love justice and to

---

[64] It is interesting to note the parallelism the author draws between the formal judgment in the instance of a court case, and the understanding that is necessary to be able to judge wisely. The 'kings' are called to understand and to learn from the case that had been presented to them. If they do not judge correctly (οὐκ ἐκρίνατε ὀρθῶς), it means they have not understood, and the same judgment that the wicked had received in the hypothetical scene will come upon them.

[65] Verse 6:19 is literally quoted in IRENAEUS, *Against Heresies*, IV,38,3 (C. LARCHER, *Études*, p. 39). But it is interesting to note that IRENAEUS is not simply quoting a phrase from Wis, but has integrated it as the conclusion in his own sorites. This employment of

seek God can concretely be fulfilled. The surprising conclusion, typical of
sorites, identifies the state of proximity to God as a kingdom. This
concluding assertion that wisdom brings a kingdom recalls the royal
reward that the just receive at the time of accounting (5:16). It concludes
the exhortation to kings (6:1) and fittingly introduces the subject of the
praise of wisdom by a king, whom the reader soon will identify as king
Solomon, preeminent in wisdom.

The relationship between wisdom and her seekers is juxtaposed to
the relationship between the wicked and death. The wicked were
presented as those who invite death, considering him a friend; who pine
away for him; who come to an agreement with him (1:16). The seekers of
wisdom are assured that she is revealed to those who love her and search
for her (6:12). The wicked who are worthy of death belong to it (1:16d).
Wisdom herself seeks out those who are worthy of her (6:16a). The final
result of wickedness is depicted with apocalyptic imagery wherein the
thrones of rulers are overturned (5:23d). But the final result of seeking
wisdom is to obtain a kingdom by being in proximity to God (6:19-20).

The author's change in the tone of argument, from the negative
dissuasion of inviting death to the positive persuasion of loving wisdom,
follows consistently. In his dissuasion from inviting death, the author has
presented death to the reader on several levels. Ultimate death, which
culminates in a radical truncation from God and eternal life, is the
supreme negative reason for loving justice and seeking God. It exercises a
seducing power which the reader is challenged to overcome. This power
manifests itself by inducing a false reasoning in the wicked on the
meaning of physical death. From this false reasoning a whole series of
wrong judgments arises that involves the wicked in a dynamic of evil
which concludes with injustice and their own ultimate death. The
author's metaphorical court case unmasks both the dynamic of evil and
the true nature of ultimate death with its insidious origin in false
judgment. The appropriation of the correct understanding of appearance
and reality in the areas of ultimate and physical death is a logical

---

the identical phrase in IRENAEUS' construction of another sorites makes the parallel to the
Wis text even stronger.

> "It was necessary first that humans come into being,
> and once they have come into being that they grow,
> and once they have grown that they become adults,
> and once they have become adults that they multiply,
> and once they have multiplied that they become strong,
> and once they have become strong that they be glorified,
> and once they have been glorified that they see their Lord.
> For it is God that finally should be seen,
> and the vision of God procures incorruptibility,
> and incorruptibility makes one close to God."

preparation for the reader to appropriate the positive reasons for embracing wisdom. The elaboration of these positive reasons is begun in Wis 6 as a preparation for the eulogy of wisdom in 6:22–10:21.

C - 8.   A Summary of the Author's Argumentation in Wis 1–6

A brief overview of the dynamic of the author's argumentation in the first six chapters will permit the crystallization of the argument found not only in the first chapters but also in the context of the entire work. For the author applies the principles that are established in the argumentation on death to the liberation of the Israelites in the midrash on the exodus event.

The exhortation opens with the imperatives to love justice and to seek God. But the exhortation quickly presents wickedness and injustice as an obstacle to justice and as constituting enmity with God. In the contrast between God/justice and wickedness/injustice, the author dissuades the reader from injustice. Wickedness is presented in a general manner as being antagonistic to God within the terminology of false speech, which is reminiscent of false accusation and perjury. In this way, the author subtly prepares the background image of a trial scene [66].

The dissuasion from wickedness culminates in the author's introduction of the prime negative motive for avoiding wickedness — death. The author raises the topic of the exhortation to an issue of capital importance. It is wickedness that brings death — a death which God has not made and which God does not wish upon anyone.

In order to explain the dynamic of wickedness and its relation to death, the author has the wicked present the inner logic of their own reasoning. The hypothetical discourse of the wicked and the author's rebuttal of the accusation implied in the discourse unfold within the general contours of a court scene. The wicked's first speech functions as their defense against the accusation of false speech subtly introduced in the opening exhortation. Their defense ends in a counter-accusation against the just. The author's rebuttal in contrasting diptychs counters

---

[66] Since the author of Wis has employed the Fourth Servant Song from Isaiah significantly in the development of the argumentation in Wis 2–5 (M.J. Suggs "Wisdom of Solomon II,10–V", *JBL* 76 (1957) 26-33), it is valid to question whether or not the image of the trial likewise is borrowed from Isaiah. Though there are a few indices of elements of a trial even in Isaiah (for instance the presence of a judgment, 59:15b-19; confessions of guilt, 53:4-6; 59:9-13; accusations, 57:1-13), these indices do not follow the strict order of a trial, but belong more to the development of the theme of judgment particular to the major prophets. The Wis author has creatively focused the element of an apocalyptic judgment within the contours of a trial scene in Wis 1–6.

the entire reasoning process of the wicked. In the presence of the just, the wicked confess their guilt to themselves, and the confession is followed by the reward of the just and the sentencing of the wicked in apocalyptic imagery.

The author uses the metaphor of a trial scene in order to elaborate the dynamic of evil and to analyze the reality of death. With its primary tasks to uncover truth and to reestablish justice, the trial motif was a felicitous choice. The trial metaphor allows the author to juxtapose conflicting positions from differing points of view for the purpose of scrutinizing their strengths and weaknesses and to assess appearance and reality.

The task of the debate in court proceedings is primarily to establish the facts in order for the judge to be able to pronounce a verdict which re-establishes justice in so far as this is possible[67]. In our example, the facts of the case are represented by judgments which constitute stances towards life that consequently lead to gross injustice. Per se, the intentions and judgments of the accused lay outside of the primary level of the court proceeding which is to establish the facts. However, as a wisdom writer, our author shares the particular bent of sapiential writing, to elevate judgments and motives to a primary level of concern as sources of good and evil[68]. Our author is not content simply to attack a position towards life contrary to his own. Instead, he seeks to uncover the source of wrong in the false reasoning of such positions that have in their favor the luminous yet fragile strength of appearances.

The central issue in the speech of the wicked and in the author's rebuttal is the interpretation of death and the consequent results of different interpretations of it. The ambiguity of death stems, in part, from the different interpretations of physical death. The wicked conclude their defense with a decision to subject the just to physical death as proof of the validity of their stance towards life. The author's rebuttal in four diptychs aims at uncovering the true meaning of physical death and the hopeless situation of the wicked, which is destined to bring on their own death — separation from God and the cosmos.

---

[67] For the general scope of court proceeding and the specific task of its various components I have consulted the recent work of P. BOVATI, *Ristabilire la giustizia*, Rome: 1986. Regarding the general scope to establish truth in order to re-establish justice see the introduction to the second part of the work on 'il giudizio', pp. 151-152 and pp. 194-196. Regarding the specific scope of the components of the debate to establish the facts and to accuse, see pp. 197-198, 238-242.

[68] This sapiential concern to connect the results of evil and good with motivations, judgments and habits is particularly evident in the scope of teaching values through proverbs in Proverbs and Sirach, in the exploration of justice and injustice in Job and Qoheleth, and in the teachings of father to son in Sirach.

Finally, with the termination of the court scene, the author addresses the readers in their capacity to judge as kings and judges. The concluding exhortation entreats the readers to understand the implications of the court scene and to apply its insights to their conduct. With the reader's appropriation of the correct verdict from the trial scene, the obstacle to loving justice and to seeking God is overcome. The author then proceeds to exhort and entreat by means of the positive values that wisdom brings. These culminate in the reality of proximity to God.

The concluding exhortation presents wisdom as the positive means for loving justice and seeking God. The second part of Wis is dedicated concretely to the praise of wisdom. King Solomon, the unnamed speaker, presents a didactic reflection of his own relationship to the wisdom that comes from God. In his prayer for wisdom, he recognizes his task to be a judge over Israel (9:7,12). Only wisdom, which knows God intimately, will be able to enlighten him for judging justly. The need for the wisdom of God to understand what is right and the need for wisdom to be able to judge correctly are seen to extend backwards over the entire discourse of the first part of the book.

Finally in Wis 10–19, the principles enunciated in the treatment of death and in the praise of wisdom are confirmed in the author's interpretation of Israel's history: c. 10 for the pre-history of Israel, where wisdom is described as accompanying the biblical figures in their moments of difficulty, cc. 11–19 for the specific midrashic interpretation of the exodus and the digressions on false worship.

The contrast between the Egyptians and the Israelites is drawn out with ramifications similar to those between the wicked and the just. The author attempts to analyze the inner reasoning of the enemies of the Israelites in order to explain the judgment that occurs against them. The author does not employ the image of a trial, but the conclusion of the book has striking parallels with the final accounting of the first part. The Israelites, who are described as the just, experience the salvation of God's intervention. The Egyptians, because of their wickedness, experience the full wrath of God's judgment in a strange death. The elements of the cosmos defend the righteous, but punish the wicked (16:17, 17:20). The destruction of the Egyptians is presented in apocalyptic imagery similar to that found in c. 5, precisely because of the role of the cosmos in battling with God against wickedness (19:18-22)[69].

---

[69] The relationship between the judgment scene in Wis 5 and the author's development of the plagues as judgment in Wis 16–19 has been noted briefly in J.M. Reese, *Hellenistic Influence on the Book of Wisdom and its Consequences*, p. 138, and in M. Priotto, *La prima pasqua in Sap 18,5-25*, Bologna: 1987, pp. 132-135.

Whereas the principles of justice and responsibility are deduced and elaborated in the first part of Wis from the point of view of the individual, these principles are applied to the collectivity of the Israelites and the Egyptians in the latter part of the work.

C-9. Excursus: Sources for the language the wicked employ in their first speech

Various sources have been proposed as possible inspirations for the images and language that the author places on the lips of the wicked, notably, Qoheleth, Epicurus, Stoicism, Sadducees, Essenes. In order to follow the argumentation of the author, it is important to assess the significance that such influence would bear on the tenor and quality of this speech. There is a great deal of literature proposing various sources for individual passages, phrases and images of the wicked's speech [70]. The issue that is important for determining the tenor of the wicked's speech in the author's argumentation is whether or not the author meant to identify a particular group of individuals or a particular philosophy in the speech of the wicked. Different sources have been proposed for the three main sections that comprise the speech: 1) the judgment on death (2:1-5), 2) the call to exploit life (2:6-9); 3) the call to oppress the just (2:10-20).

C-9.1 The judgment on death (2:1-5), the call to exploit life (2:6-9)

The expressive and extended presentation of the universal transience of human life in 2:1-5 has few parallels in Scripture. An intense figurative expression of death, or more specifically of death in old age, is attested in Qoh 12:1-7. In this passage from Qoh, an analogy and a series of images attempt to convey the inexorable onslaught of time on human beings. The deterioration of the body in old age is compared to the closing down of a house at the approach of a storm [71]. And finally, through a series of

---

[70] For a synthesis of the various contacts between the speech of the wicked and extra-biblical sources see J.P. WEISENGOFF, "The Impious in Wisdom 2", *CBQ* 11 (1949) 40-65 and C. LARCHER, *Études*, 179-236.

[71] The underlying image can be interpreted in a literal or analogical manner. The literal interpretation would understand the closing down of the house at the approach of a storm as the underlying image of death. The analogical interpretation would understand further that the closing down of the house is described in an analogous manner to the deterioration of various parts of the human body. L. DI FONZO, *Ecclesiaste*, Rome: 1967. See also M. GILBERT, "La vieillesse en Qohelet XII 1-7, est-elle allégorique?", VTSup 32 (1981) 96-109.

brief, terse images which depict the breakdown of a well, a universal life source image, the reality of death is highlighted. The cord is snapped, the bowl is broken, the pitcher is cracked by the fountain, the wheel is smashed at the cistern (Qoh 12:6). But our passage in Wis bears little resemblance to this reflection on old age where the place of God in the over-all perspective is recognized.

Taken as a whole, then, there is no parallel passage in Scripture to the wicked's reflection on the evanescence of life. However, individual phrases and images bear resemblances to several passages found throughout the Scriptures, particularly in the sapiential writings.

2:1b short and sorrowful is our life:

> Job 10:20 LXX - Are not the days of my life few?
> Job 14:1-2 - Man that is born of woman is of a few days and full of trouble.

2:1c there is no healing for our end:

> Qoh 8:8c - One has no authority over the day of death.

2:1d no one has been known to free us from Hades [72]:

> Ps 48(49):10 - a man cannot ransom another or pay God his price (cf. Job 33:23-25).

2:2b and after this we shall be as if we had never existed:

> Obad 16 - they will drink and fall and be as if they never existed.
> Job 10:19 - and become as though I had never been.
> Sir 44:9 - they will perish as though they had never been.

2:2c for the breath in our nostrils is but smoke:

> Ps 101(102):3 - for my days pass away like smoke (cf. Pss 36(37)20; 67(68):2).
> Job 27:3 - As long as my breath is in me and the spirit of God is in my nostrils.

---

[72] The transitive meaning of ἀναλύω is preferable to the intransitive meaning which would translate, "No one has been known to return from Hades." The intransitive meaning is clearly intended in 5:12b, ἀνελύθη, but it is achieved through the passive voice. The active voice in 16:14 obviously intends a transitive meaning, 'a man in his wickedness kills another but he cannot bring back (οὐδὲ ἀναλύει) the departed spirit'. The author in Wis 16:13-14 is confuting the wicked's denial of a superior power that can free humans from Hades (against C. LARCHER, Le Livre de la Sagesse, p. 214).

2:3a when spent the body turns to ashes:

> Gen LXX 3:19 - You are earth and to earth you shall return.
> Job LXX 16:15 - I have sown sackcloth on my skin, my strength is spent in earth.

2:4a our name will be forgotten in time:

> Qoh 2:16 - there is no enduring remembrance, seeing that in the days to come all will have been long forgotten (cf. Qoh 9:5).

2:5 indeed our time is the passing of a shadow:

> Job 14:3 - He flees like a shadow and continues not.
> Qoh 6:12 - For who knows what is good for man in his life, for the few days of his vain life, he lives them like a shadow.

2:6 Come let us enjoy the good things and make use of creation as youth:

> Isa 22:13 - Let us eat and drink for tomorrow we shall die.
> Qoh 9:7 - Come eat your bread with enjoyment and drink your wine with a merry heart (cf. 11:9-10).
> Sir 14:14 - Do not deprive yourself of a happy day, let not your share of desired good pass you by.

2:8 Let us crown ourselves with rosebuds before they fade:

> Job 15:30 - the wind will make his blossom fade (cf. 24:24).

2:9c For this is our lot and this is our share:

> Deut 10:9 - For this reason the Levites have no lot or share among their brothers, the Lord is their share.
> Isa 57:6 - This is his lot and this his share.
> Jer 13:25 - This is your lot and your share measured out to you by me, says the Lord.
> Qoh 5:17 - Behold what I have seen to be good and fitting: to eat and to drink and to find enjoyment in all the toil which one toils under the sun for the few days of his life which God has given him, for this is his lot.

Despite these numerous contacts between the reflection on the evanescence of life in Wis and other biblical writings, there remain a number of expressions, images and turns of phrases which resonate more explicitly with the world of Hellenism in Alexandria [73].

---

[73] A. DUPONT-SOMMER, "Les «impies» du Livre de la Sagesse ne sont-ils pas des Épicuriens?", *RHR* 111 (1935) 90-109. J.P. WEISENGOFF, "The Impious in Wisdom 2", *CBQ* 11 (1949) 53-60. C. LARCHER, *Études*, pp. 201-223. D. WINSTON, *The Wisdom of Solomon*, New York: 1979, pp. 114-123. C. LARCHER, *Le Livre de la Sagesse*, pp. 211-263.

2:2 we have come to be by chance (αὐτοσχεδίος):

This notion of human existence arising through chance without purpose or design provided a common explanation for the origin of the universe and life in late Epicurean thought [74]. But it was also an idea diffused in preceding Greek philosophies such as Atomism represented by LEUCIPPUS and DEMOCRITUS [75].

2:2d our thought is but a spark in the beating of our heart

It was common for the ancients to collocate the reasoning process with the heart, and this was true for the Hebrews as well. For the 'pneumatics' the soul was formed in the heart through the mixing of blood and air [76]. However, our author is unique in ascribing the image of a spark to the function of reason. A. DUPONT-SOMMER attempts to ascribe this example of identifying reason with a spark to the Epicurean party that the author is deliberately associating with the wicked [77].

---

[74] LUCRETIUS, a later exponent of Epicurean thought, insists on the arbitrariness of the cosmic forces. "For certainty it was no design of the first beginnings that led them to place themselves each in its own order with keen intelligence... nor assuredly did they make any bargain what motions each should produce; but because many first-beginnings of things in many ways, struck with blows and carried along by their own weight from infinite time to the present, have been accustomed to move and to meet in all manner of ways, and to try all combinations, whatsoever they could produce by coming together,... at length those come together which, being suddenly brought together, often become the beginnings of great things, of earth and sea and sky and the generation of living creatures" (LUCRETIUS, *De rerum natura* 5.419-431, cf. also the parallel passages: 1.1021-1063, 5.67-191).

[75] D. WINSTON, *The Wisdom of Solomon*, p. 116; C. LARCHER, *Le Livre de la Sagesse*, p. 216.

[76] C. LARCHER, *Le Livre de la Sagesse*, p. 219.

The theory of Pneumatism was advanced by an Alexandrian in the 3th century B.C., ERASISTRATUS. According to this theory, life is associated with a subtle vapor denoted as pneuma. ERASISTRATUS drew a distinction between two kinds of pneuma, the first being the vital spirit formed in the heart, a mixture of blood and air, transported by the arteries; the second being a mixture of the vital spirit formed in the brain transported by the nerves.

[77] A. DUPONT-SOMMER, "Les «impies» du Livre de la Sagesse ne sont-ils pas des Épicuriens?", *RHR* 111 (1935) 9-109. DUPONT-SOMMER identifies the presence of πνοή and λόγος in 2:2 as corresponding to the Epicurean distinction between the two parts of the soul, anima/animus, as represented by LUCRETIUS. The animus dominates the soul as thought fixed in the breast. The anima is spread throughout the body and obeys the animus (pp. 94-96). The image of the spark instead of fire to designate reason would be the author's clever substitution of 'fire' by 'spark' to indicate the Epicurean claim of the superiority of reason to soul (pp. 97-100).

However, in the two verses 2:2-3, the author uses several words to express the disintegration of human existence, πνοή, λόγος, σῶμα,, and πνεῦμα (the significant term, ψυχή, by which EPICURUS designated the soul diffused through the body is lacking (ἡ ψυχὴ σῶμα ἐστι λεπτομερές - *Letter to Herodotus* § 66). It is therefore not clear that the

EPICURUS describes the atoms of the soul as being even rounder and smoother than those of fire (*Letter to Herodotus*, § 66). For both the Epicureans and the Stoics the association of the soul with fire was meant to express the superiority of the reasoning process to matter, and to be sure, the soul itself is not considered incorporeal (*Letter to Herodotus*, § 67). Now, contrary to this meaning, in the speech of the wicked, the association of reason with a spark is meant to express the transitoriness of reason itself. The spark is used as an image expressing fragility, transience, momentariness.

2:3 the spirit will dissolve like thin air:

They fear that when the soul leaves the body it no longer exists anywhere and that on the day when the man dies it is destroyed and perishes, and when it leaves the body and departs from it, straight away it flies away and is no longer anywhere, scattering like a breath or smoke (PLATO, *Phaedo*, 70 A).

2:5bc there is no avoidance of our end, it is sealed up and no one returns:

There is none who comes back from (over) there, that he may tell their state (A Song of the Harper, *ANET*, p. 467).

The sections of the wicked's speech regarding the evanescence of life that show the closest contacts with Greek thought are precisely those where a denial of an after-life is paramount. But it is impossible to identify simply one philosophical group as the source. The author is making free use of current positions to mold together an intelligible denial of an after-life [78].

2:6-8 come therefore let us enjoy good things: creation as youth... the best wine... perfumes... the spring flower... rosebuds:

This theme is so diffused in the literature of the ancient world that it is impossible to identify a single source exclusively. It became a motto for funerary inscriptions [79]. The exhortation to enjoy life while one lives

---

specifically Epicurean distinction is implied in the speech. The terminology used by the Wisdom author is more consistent with general Pneumatic theories on the origin of thought as being a mixture of blood and air in the heart. For further critiques of DUPONT-SOMMER's thesis see C. LARCHER, *Études*, p. 214; *Le Livre de la Sagesse*, pp. 218-221; D. WINSTON, *The Wisdom of Solomon*, p. 114; J.P. WEISENGOFF, "The Impious in Wisdom 2", *CBQ* 11 (1949) 40-65.

[78] "En réalité, l'auteur a cueilli dans les systèmes opposés à l'immortalité de l'âme différents traits qu'il a ensuite durcis à l'aide d'explications «médicales» transposées sur un plan métaphysique." C. LARCHER, *Le Livre de la Sagesse*, pp. 221-222.

[79] WINSTON quotes the Greek inscription from the tomb of Jason in Jerusalem,

often follows the grim declaration of the passing of life. In an extremely popular play of EURIPIDES, the hero, Heracles, utters this exhortation to the somber servant who is lamenting the death of the host's wife.

> This hearing then, and learning it from me,
> Make merry, drink: the life from day to day
> Account thine own, all else in fortune's power (EURIPIDES, *Alcestis*, 787-789 [80].

The images designated for the exhortation to enjoy life, wine, perfume, roses are diffused likewise in Greek writings. The same combination of images occurs in a quotation from Horace: "Hither bid slaves bring wines and perfumes and the too brief blossoms of the lovely rose, while Fortune and youth allow, and the dark threads of the Sisters Three", (HORACE, *Odes* 2.3.13-16 cf. 1.36.15).

These same images also were associated with the feasting attached to the symposium, the famous discussion-dinner party which originated with PLATO and which the disciples of EPICURUS promoted. Though EPICURUS expounded a frugal style of living for the pursuit of understanding, opponents to his school often labeled the gatherings as excessively wasteful. LUCIAN criticizes the waste connected to such celebrations.

> "It is they," said he, "who buy expensive dainties and let wine flow freely at dinners in an atmosphere of saffron and perfumes, who glut themselves with roses in midwinter, loving their rarity and unseasonableness and despising what is seasonable and natural because of its cheapness, it is they who drink myrrh" (LUCIAN, *Nigrinus* 31) [81].

"Enjoy yourselves, those who remain living ... drink and eat alike." D. WINSTON, *The Wisdom of Solomon*, p. 118.

The exhortation to enjoy life is also typical in Egyptian texts related to funerals and tombs. "Fais un heureux jour, ô prêtre! Qu'il y ait toujours des parfums et des essences pour ton nez, des guirlandes et des lotus pour les épaules et pour la gorge de ta soeur chérie, qui est assise auprès de toi..." from the tomb of a priest of Ammon, Nofrihotpou (G. MASPERO, *Études égyptiennes*, I, fasc. II, "Étude sur quelques peintures", Paris: 1886, p. 174); "... suis ton coeur, tant que tu existes. Mets des parfums sur ta tête, pare-toi de fin lin, oins-toi de ce qu'il y a de plus merveilleux parmi les essences de Dieu!" from a tomb of the XIth dynasty (pp. 181-182).

[80] For other references to the exhortation to enjoying life see D. WINSTON, *The Wisdom of Solomon*, pp. 118-119.

[81] Compare however the frugality associated with the garden gatherings as recounted in *Diogenes Laërtius* § 10-11. "This is stated by Apollodorus, who also says that he purchased the garden for eighty minae; and to the same effect Diocles in the third book of his *Epitome* speaks of them as living a very simple and frugal life; at all events they were content with half a pint of thin wine and were, for the rest, thoroughgoing water-drinkers." Certainly EPICURUS himself, even when postulating pleasure as the end to be sought, did not intend by pleasure a dissipated life, but rather the pleasure of sober reasoning (*Letter to Menoeceus*, § 131-132).

In light of the variety of sources that the author has made free use of to formulate the wicked's negative judgment on death, it is unlikely that the author wished to identify the wicked in the speech with a specific philosophical school. The Hellenistic claim to superiority with respect to culture and religion in the organization of the 'polis' obviously caused strains on the faith of many Jews in the diaspora, particularly in Alexandria [82]. The thriving yet precarious situation of the Jewish community in Alexandria suggests this city to be the most likely site for the addressees of Wis. Here, in the Delta section of the city, the Jewish community thrived not only economically and culturally but also numerically. It is in Alexandria that large segments of the community actually embraced Hellenism and integrated its achievements into the Jewish faith. PHILO's literary and philosophical achievements testify to this exchange of cultures and ideas.

At the same time, however, there were outbursts of antagonism between the communities (Greeks, Egyptians, Jews) due to political intrigues and disloyalties. The Greeks of Alexandria would prove to be aggressive with respect to Jewish faith and ideas. This aggressiveness would translate itself into concrete political restrictions and ostracism towards the Jewish community both religiously and juridically within Alexandria. On several occasions the Jewish community would be threatened with the restriction of rights, particularly access to the gymnasium. It would have been a particular challenge for Jewish youth in Alexandria not to be swayed by the power, the aesthetic beauty, the clarity of reasoning offered by Hellenism. It seems likely that the arguments of Wis are addressed to such a vulnerable Jewish group in Alexandria — a group familiar with, and appreciative of the values of Hellenism and, at the same time, challenged by the aggressiveness and restrictions of the inimical Greeks. It is in the general threat and challenge to remain faithful to their traditions, while integrating the good aspects of Hellenism, that characterizes the context for the arguments of the Wis author.

---

[82] For a contrary position see D. GEORGI, *Weisheit Salomos*, (Jüdische Schriften aus hellenistisch-römischer Zeit, III, 4, pp. 391-478), Gütersloh: 1980. GEORGI thinks it is not necessary nor possible to posit Alexandria as the site for the composition of Wis and proposes Syria in the 2nd century B.C. Reasons: Wis does not agree with Ben Sira on the relation of the law to wisdom. This would mean that Wis was written before Ben Sira or that the author of Wis did not know Ben Sira because he was not in Alexandria. PHILO does not quote it, therefore it could not have been in Alexandria (pp. 395-397). However, GEORGI is working under a considerable restraint by dating the work as early as the 2nd century B.C., which is difficult to maintain in light of the late Greek terms employed in Wis (see D. WINSTON, *The Wisdom of Solomon*, New York: 1979, pp. 21-25.

For a concise presentation of the various persecutions against the Jewish community in Alexandria see LARCHER's treatment of dating the book (C. LARCHER, *Le Livre de la Sagesse*, pp. 141-161).

The Greek 'polis', with its educational project effected through the 'gymnasium' and the 'ephebate', was the embodiment of the spirit of Hellenism [83]. Through the organizations of the 'polis' in economics, education and cult there was tremendous strain on local groups to integrate for the sake of the privileges and advantages that the gymnasium provided [84]. On the one hand, the privileges which Jewish communities obtained to abstain from local cults often enough caused strains with the local inhabitants [85]. On the other hand, many Jews sought the same privileges and recognition as their counterparts in

---

[83] "Instruction in the 'Greek School' was presumably divided into three age groups: school age from about 7-14/15, followed by the period of the ephebate which lasted one or two years, which was the real time of training in the gymnasium, dominated above all by physical exercise and also a degree of military training. This was in turn followed by the stage of the 'young men', who continued their instruction in the gymnasium until about the age of twenty," (M. HENGEL, *Judaism and Hellenism*, trans. J. BOWDEN [*Judentum und Hellenismus*, WUNT 10, Tübingen: 1973] vol I-II, Fortress, Philadelphia: 1974, p. 66). There is some controversy as to how exactly the age divisions of the various groups was actually carried out in different cities. H.I. MARROU puts the ephebate, as in Athens, between the ages of 18 and 20, (H.I. MARROU, *Histoire de l'éducation dans l'antiquité*, Paris: 1948, p. 152-153).

[84] Hellenization is a complex phenomenon which denotes both the Greek tendency (championed by Alexander the Great) towards an acquired and shared education and the antithetic Greek tendency towards exclusivity based on the feeling of Greek superiority over the 'barbarians'. The Hellene idea of spreading education was an ideal eloquently expressed by ISOCRATES, "the designation 'Hellene' seems no longer to be a matter of descent but of disposition, and those who share in our education have more right to be called Hellenes than those who have a common descent with us" (ISOCRATES, *Panegyricus* 4,50). However, this ideal was only too often countered by the struggle for power by the various Greek communities in the Greek cities. When a Greek group felt threatened by the loss of advantages they would tend to restrict access to the educational system by the attempt to maintain the 'purity' of their own children over against the 'barbarians'. An example of this takes place precisely in Alexandria with the petition of the Alexandrians to Augustus about 20-19 B.C. for the preservation of the purity of the ephebate and citizenship.

The transitive use of *hellenizein* is used for the first time by PHILO (*Legatio ad Gaium*, 147) where Augustus is praised for the Hellenization of the barbarians. This would suggest that the idea of spreading Greek civilization among the barbarians became a theme only at the time of the Romans, (see M. HENGEL, *Jews, Greeks and Barbarians*, trans. J. BOWDEN [*Juden, Griechen und Barbaren*, Stuttgarter Bibelstudien, 76, Katholisches Bibelwerk, Stuttgart: 1976], Philadelphia: 1980, pp. 53-54).

[85] "Much as freedom of religious conviction was allowed in the Greek *polis*, people could be very intolerant with their own citizens in questions of the official cult. At least *the Jew exposed to Hellenism in the Diaspora* could come up against difficulties if he wanted to undergo education in the gymnasium or acquire citizenship of his native town" (M. HENGEL, *Judaism and Hellenism*, p. 67).

"When by his famous letter of AD 41 Claudius finally deprived the sons of the Jewish aristocracy of entry to the gymnasium in Alexandria, which they coveted, and hence of the right to Alexandrian (and Roman) citizenship, it was a bitter blow against the leaders of Alexandrian Judaism and led the way to the rebellion and the annihilation

business and in social life[86]. Therefore, the picture of an aggressive
Hellenism, that universally sought to incorporate other cultures and
religions and to inculcate into them the spirit of Hellenism, is somewhat
inaccurate[87]. Yet at the same time it would be difficult for Jews wanting
to be faithful to their traditions not to feel threatened by Hellenism, and
particularly by the tendency of the Jews themselves to participate more
fully in Hellenistic life.

The pressure to accept or at least integrate Hellenistic traits in
Palestine as proof of a sophisticated culture is dramatically presented in 4
Macc 5–8. The tension between Hellenism and Judaism was most acute in
Palestine. In the diaspora, especially in Alexandria, there was a greater
readiness on the part of the Jewish community to participate in the
cultural achievements of the city (the museum, the library, the gymnasia).

Though there is definitely a strain of critique in Wis 2 regarding
foreign philosophies and customs, the author's sympathy towards Greek
terminology and literary styles is well known[88]. The author's critique of
the familiar positions enunciated in the speech of the wicked is partially
meant to challenge the reader to look under the surface of an attractive

---

of the Jewish Diaspora in Egypt in AD 115-117" (M. HENGEL, *Judaism and Hellenism*,
pp. 68-69).

[86] V. TCHERIKOVER, *Hellenistic Civilization and the Jews*, New York: 1970, pp. 26-28,
303-314. "Thus in Egypt, and here especially in Alexandria, the Jewish Diaspora
developed an extraordinarily lively spiritual life. At least the upper classes acquired an
often astonishing rhetorical and philosophical education — going beyond a knowledge of
Greek, which was taken for granted. That means that they gained access to the
educational institutions of the Greek world, the Greek school, the gymnasium and
advanced study in rhetoric and philosophy. Jewish names appear later on lists of ephebes
both in Cyrenaica and in Asia Minor. PHILO of Alexandria, with his extensive education,
was certainly not the only Jew who had a universal *enkuklios paideia*" (M. HENGEL,
Judaism and Hellenism, pp. 100-101).

[87] G.G. PORTON, "Diversity in Postbiblical Judaism", [*Early Judaism and its Modern
Interpreters*, eds. R.A. KRAFT, G.W.E. NICKELSBURG, Atlanta: 1986] pp. 57-80.
"In the past it was common to draw a sharp distinction between Judaism and
Hellenism and to argue that much of the history of postbiblical Judaism was a record of
the struggle between Jews loyal to Judaism and those who favored the new Hellenistic
ideals. The implication was that one could not be truly Jewish and Hellenistic at the same
time. Although W.R. FARMER, A. GUTTMANN, and A. FINKEL still favor this view, many
others have now rejected it. Writing in general terms, M. HADAS states that 'individual
alien elements may be assimilated without consciousness of surrendering and indeed can
themselves come to be regarded as part of the tradition which must be protected against
encroachment by Hellenism' " (p. 57). See also M. HADAS, *Hellenistic Culture: Fusion
and Diffusion*, New York: 1972, p. 9).

[88] See A.A. DI LELLA, "Conservative and Progressive Theology: Sirach and
Wisdom", *CBQ* 28 (1966) 139-154, also in *Studies in Ancient Israelite Wisdom*, ed. J.L.
CRENSHAW, New York: 1976, pp. 401-416; É. DES PLACES, "Le Livre de la Sagesse et les
influences grecques", *Bib* 50 (1969) 536-542 and J.M. REESE, *Hellenistic Influence on the
Book of Wisdom*, pp. 146-152.

or easy accomodation to Hellenism in order to grasp the inner reality and dynamic of such positions [89].

If a group contemporaneous with the author needs to be identified in the wicked as a source for the argumentation, a parallel could very well be found in Jewish apostates, or at least in a Jewish group's slackening of faithfulness to the traditions [90]. Since the author in the first section of Wis is exhorting the reader to love justice and to seek the Lord, it is reasonable to assume that the exhortation is meant to bolster the faith of the Jewish community as well. M. GILBERT notes that even if one does identify the wicked with renegade or apostate Jews, it nevertheless remains impossible to locate them precisely in history [91]. We have no evidence of large scale apostasy in Alexandria, but we do have evidence of a form of Judaism in Alexandria that integrated to a great extent the values of Hellenism, (e.g. ARISTOBOLUS, PHILO of Alexandria).

What the author is depicting in the wicked's negative judgment on death is not so much a particular group of apostates as much as the reasoning process which leads to positions that, according to the author, threaten the community. It is this reasoning process which prior to the speech (2:1) and afterwards (2:21) the author declares to be mistaken and false.

---

[89] "The Jews seem to have felt the new Greek way of life to be an 'aggressive' civilization which threatened to alienate them from the distinctive tradition of their fathers. They opposed it with their own tradition of the Law, which could be equally 'aggressive' i.e. could have just as great a missionary effect... However, the special element of this conflict is that the Jews attempted to counter the new civilization threatening them with their own forms of language, literature and thought. In this controversy we cannot mistake the fact that the Greek feeling of superiority with its contrast between 'Hellenes' and 'barbarians' was matched on the Jewish side by a sense of election, unique in antiquity, which was expressed in the contrast between 'Israel' and the 'nations of the world' " (M. HENGEL, *Jews, Greeks and Barbarians*, p. 78).

[90] "Anspielungen auf die Hl. Schrift (2c = Gen 2,7; 12 = Jes 3,10; 18-20 = Ps 21,8.9; παῖς κυρίου = Jes 40ff.) lassen vermuten, daß der Autor uns hier in erster Linie abtrünnige Juden vorführen will. Daß diese von der griechischen Bildung ganz unberührt geblieben seien, ist unwahrscheinlich, denn die Hellenistische Kultur übte auf die Juden der Diaspora, zumal auf die wohlhabenden Kreise, einen gewaltigen Einfluß aus. Aber jene Anklänge an die Hl. Schrift sind nicht derart, daß die Rede nicht auch im Munde von genußsüchtigen Griechen denkbar wäre" (P. HEINISCH, *Das Buch der Weisheit*, Münster: 1912, p. 41).

[91] "È chiaro dunque che, se bisogna vedere negli empi di Sap 2 dei giudei rinnegati e apostati, è impossibile dar loro un nome preciso. Sembra piuttosto che l'autore di Sap 2 abbia intenzione di abbozzare un quadro le cui linee siano generalizzate e schematizzate." M. GILBERT, "Il giusto sofferente di Sap 2:12-20", [*L'antico testamento interpretato dal nuovo: il messia*, ed. G. DE GENNARO, Napoli: 1985] p. 204.

C - 9.2   The call to oppress the just (2:10-20)

One of the major contextual difficulties of attributing the reasoning of the wicked in Wis strictly to a philosophical school in Alexandria in the first century is the turn to violence which the discourse suddenly takes (Wis 2:10-20) [92]. In this section, the author is firmly rooted both in the prophetic tradition with its image of the suffering servant and in the psalms of lament with their descriptions of the persecution of the just.

The three subjects that the author employs to introduce the longer section of the persecution of the just are the just poor, the widow, the aged (2:10). All three subjects are protected by Israelite law: the widow, Exod 22:22, Deut 14:28-29; the poor, Exod 23:6, Deut 15:12; the aged, Lev 19:32. The widow and the poor are subjects which are extensively employed in the prophetic writings and in the psalms in contexts describing oppression against the weak by the wicked or the enemy.

— Hab 1:4 the wicked surround the righteous so justice goes forth perverted.
— Ezek 18:12 The one who ... oppresses the poor and needy... shall he still live?
— Jer 7:6 If you do not oppress the alien, the fatherless or the widow, ... I will let you dwell in this place.
— Ps 12:5 "Because the poor are despoiled, because the needy groan, I will now arise," says the Lord.
— Ps 36(37):14-15 The wicked draw the sword and bend their bows, to bring down the poor and needy, to slay those who walk uprightly.
— Ps 81(82):3-4 give justice to the orphan and the destitute, maintain the right of the humble and the poor, be merciful to the poor and the humble.
— Ps 108(109):16 For he did not remember to show kindness, but pursued the poor and needy and the brokenhearted to their death.

---

[92] D. WINSTON summarized well this difficulty of the turn to violence regarding the issue of the wicked representing a specific group. "It should be clear at once that the wicked described here do not represent any particular philosophical group or political faction. The wicked of all ages have cynically culled whatever has suited them from the philosophical and scientific literature of their respective periods to bolster their frankly aggressive and opportunistic designs. Although the Epicurean emphasis on the finality of death, the denial of Divine Providence, and the legitimacy of pleasure have to some extent been harnessed by the godless crew described in this chapter to further their own ends, only a grossly distorted understanding of Epicureanism could conceivably reconcile that philosophy with the latter's crude and unprincipled brand of hedonism" (*The Wisdom of Solomon*, p. 114).

The image of the elderly (πρεσβύτερος) is employed as a subject denoting vulnerability to a lesser extent than the widow and the poor[93]. As an image of vulnerability, it is primarily employed in prophetic and late historical writings and in the sapiential circles.

— Isa 47:6 I gave them into your hand, you gave them no mercy, on the aged you made your yoke exceedingly heavy.
— Lam 5:12 Princes are hung up by their hands, no respect is shown to the elders.
— 2 Macc 5:13 Then there was killing of young and old, destruction of youth, women and children, and slaughter of virgins and infants.
— 2 Macc 8:30 ... and they divided much plunder, giving to those who had been tortured, and to the orphans and widows, and also to the aged, shares equal to their own.
— Sir 4:7-8 (S²) Bow your head low to an old man, incline your ear to the poor.

The main section (2:12-20), which describes in greater detail the explicit exhortation of the wicked to persecute the just, also is at home in the world of the psalms and the prophetic writings.

2:12a let us ambush (ἐνεδρεύσωμεν) the just one (τὸν δίκαιον) for he is inconvenient to us:

Ps 9:30 (the wicked) is ready to ambush (ἐνεδρεύει) like a lion in its den, he waits in ambush (ἐνεδρεύει) in order to seize the poor. Ps 36(37):11 The sinner will plot against the just (τὸν δίκαιον). This verse is almost identical to LXX Isa 3:10: εἰπόντες δήσωμεν τὸν δίκαιον, ὅτι δύσχρηστος ἡμῖν ἐστιν. However, it is also possible that the text of Wis had exercised an influence on the Greek manuscripts of Isa rather than the opposite, due to the lack of concordance between the MT and the LXX in Isa 3:10a[94].

---

[93] On occasion, when πρεσβύτερος is parallel to νεανίσκος, the terms function more as an hendiadys which conveys the totality of the destruction perpetrated rather than the idea of oppression against the vulnerable (cf. 2 Chr 36:17).

[94] Various possibilities have been proposed to explain the Greek translation of Isa 3:10. F. FOCKE considered Isa 3:10a to be dependent on an already existing Wis text. F. FOCKE, *Die Entstehung der Weisheit Salomos. Ein Beitrag zur Geschichte des jüdischen Hellenismus*, Göttingen: 1913, pp. 66-67. J. ZIEGLER noted the progressive alterations of the text in which the alternate reading ἀρῶμεν replaced δήσωμεν under the influence of collected texts. J. ZIEGLER, *Isaias*, p. 20. B. VELLAS suggested the possibility of Wis 2:12a having influenced later corrections of the Greek verse of Isa 3:10 (see C. LARCHER's review note in *RB* 49 (1940), p. 291). LARCHER concludes, therefore, that dependence is uncertain in that the verse fits the context well in Wis whereas it constitutes difficulties in Isaiah. C. LARCHER, *Le Livre de la Sagesse*, pp. 240-241.

A motif in the wicked's exhortation to oppress the just one is their claim of the just one's opposition to them. They describe the just one as opposing their deeds, reproaching them for their sins, recalling their mistakes, considering them base and staying away from them as unclean. This motif of the separation of the just from the wicked is frequent in the psalms and it echoes the separation between God and injustice in the opening exhortation of Wis.

— Ps 1:1 Blessed is the man who does not walk in the counsel of the wicked.
— Ps 25(26):4-5 I do not sit with false men, nor do I consort with dissemblers, I hate the company of evildoers and I will not sit with the wicked.
— Ps 37(38):20 Those who render me evil for good are my adversaries because I follow after good.
— Ps 138(139):22 I hate them with perfect hatred; I count them my enemies.

The wicked's exhortation to oppress the just includes a mockery of the trust that the just one places in God (2:18,20b). It is a common feature in the individual and community laments that the psalmists utter a declaration of trust that issues in praise out of the assurance that God will intervene on their behalf[95].

— Ps 12(13):6 But I have trusted in your mercy, my heart will rejoice in your salvation.
— Ps 26(27):13 I believe I will see the goodness of the Lord in the land of the living (cf. 53(54):7-9).

The wicked in the psalms likewise mock the trust which the psalmist places in God in their exhortation to pursue the psalmist.

— Ps 3:3 Many are saying against me, "There is no help for him in his God".
— Ps 21(22):9 "He placed his trust in the Lord, let him save him, let him deliver him for he delights in him".
— Ps 70(71):10b-11 those who watch for my life consult together saying: "God has abandoned him, pursue him and seize him for there is none to save him".

In terms of the prophetic writings, the most striking parallels to the persecution of the just one in Wis are found in the messianic songs of the

---

95 C. WESTERMANN, *Praise and Lament in the Psalms*, trans. K.R. CRIM and R.N. SOULEN, Edinburgh: 1981, pp. 77-81.

Lord's servant[96]. There are numerous thematic contacts in particular with the fourth poem on the suffering servant: a) the servant has a special relationship and intimacy with God, b) the servant is persecuted and killed, c) the Lord will assist the servant for the sake of justice.

Within these thematic similarities there are, however, only a few lexicographical contacts. The just one is said to claim to be a child of the Lord (παῖδα κυρίου, 2:13a). In LXX Isa, the Hebrew term to denote the servant of the Lord, עבד, is translated alternatively between παῖς (cf. Isa 42:1; 43:10; 44:1; 49:6; 52:13; 53:2) and by δοῦλος (cf. Isa 49:3,5). The term is meant to express a special relationship between the Lord and his servant, and this special relationship is presumed in the wicked's exhortation to oppress the just (Wis 2:13). The servant of Isa suffers an ignoble death and is despised by his adversaries (Isa 53:3,7), but the Lord will assist him (Ιακοβ ὁ παῖς μου, ἀντιλήμψομαι αὐτοῦ; Isa 42:1).

Though it is virtually certain that the author refers to the poems of the servant of the Lord in the wider context of Wis 2–5[97], it is also obvious that these poems are only one source among the author's reference points which are intended to aid the reader in the dramatization of the argument. For the actual description of the wicked's exhortation to destroy the just one, Ps 21(22) comes closer to the text of Wis[98]. Moreover, an essential feature in the poem of the suffering servant is the vicarious nature of the servant's suffering for the sins of the people (Isa 53:4-6,10-12). Now this feature is totally absent in Wis' presentation of the just, not only in the speech of the wicked, but even in the author's subsequent treatment of the just's vindication. The suppression of the redemptive task of the Lord's servant in Wis constitutes a clear indication that the author of Wis is liberally making use of biblical sources to construct and mold his own particular argument.

Another unique feature in the wicked's explanation for oppressing the just one is the attribution to the just of a special relationship with the Lord through images of fatherhood and sonship (Wis 2:13,18). In addition to the term which implies the uniqueness of the Lord's servant (παῖς), terms referring to the unique relationship of the davidic messiah are attributed to the just[99]. The wicked insinuate that the just considers

[96] M.J. Suggs, "Wisdom of Solomon II,10–V: A Homily Based on the Fourth Servant Song", *JBL* 76 (1957) 28-33.

[97] Other major contacts between Wis 2–5 and Isa consist of the themes of the peace of the just and the armor of the Lord used for judgment (Wis 3:1-3 = Is 57:1-2; Wis 5:16-19 = Is 59:15-18); see M.J. Suggs, "Wisdom of Solomon II, 10-V: A Homily Based on the Fourth Servant Song", *JBL* 76 (1957) 28-33.

[98] C. Larcher, *Le Livre de la Sagesse*, p. 254.

[99] M. Adinolfi, "Il messianismo di Sap 2,12-30", [*AttiSettBibl* 18, 1964, Brescia: 1966] 205-217.

God to be his father (καὶ ἀλαζονεύεται πατέρα θεόν, 2:16d). They mock
the implication that this special relationship of sonship should save the
just from their condemnation to a shameful physical death, "If indeed the
just one is a son of God (ὁ δίκαιος υἱὸς θεοῦ), he will help him" (2:18).
These attributions may allude to the messianic texts that refer to the
messiah's special relationship to God, which is based on the davidic
kingship. 2 Sam 7:17 - I will be his father and he shall be my son (cf. 1
Chr 17:13; 22:10; 28:6; Pss 2:7; 88(89):27.

Even apart from the messianic texts which employ the images of
God's fatherhood and the king/messiah's sonship, the two terms express
the unique relationship between God and his faithful one. God is referred
to as father in order to convey the caring and guiding relationship
between the Lord and Israel. Ps 67(68):6 - God in his holy place is a
father of orphans and a judge for widows; Ps 102(103):13 - As a father
pities his sons, so does the Lord pity those who fear him (cf. Deut 8:5).

The expression, the son of God (2:18), is attested throughout the
Scriptures in various contexts with different nuances (vocation, Hos 11:1;
belonging, Deut 14:1; holiness, Hos 2:1). Particularly in the later writings,
a tendency has been noted to limit the expression to faithful Israelites
with the nuance of an eschatological reality[100].

These terms denoting a special relationship between God and the
persecuted just one in Wis also reflect parallels to the Qumran writings.
This has led to a thesis of the possible identification of the persecuted
just one of Wis with the Teacher of Righteousness in the Qumran
writings[101]. The three main expressions which could be construed as

---

[100] TLevi 18:8 - For he shall give the majesty of the Lord to those who are his sons
in truth forever. TJud 24:3 - And he will pour the spirit of grace on you. And you shall be
sons in truth...

LARCHER notes the explanation of M.-J. LAGRANGE for the tendency to limit the
expression to denote Israelite faithfulness to the law in the writings at the turn of the eras:
"Cependant lorsque le discernement se fit, non plus entre Israël et les autres peuples, mais
entre les Israélites fidèles à la Loi et les autres, lorsque la religion fut davantage l'objet
d'un choix personnel, ce fut ce choix et cette fidélité qui permirent à un Israélite de se dire
vraiment fils de Dieu" (M.-J. LAGRANGE, "La paternité de Dieu dans l'Ancient Testament", RB 17 (1908) p. 486). For other examples of the expression, the son of God, see
C. LARCHER, Le Livre de la Sagesse, p. 252.

[101] A.-M. DUBARLE, "Une source du livre de la Sagesse", RSPT 37 (1953) 425-443.
M. DELCOR, "L'immortalité de l'âme dans le Livre de la Sagesse et dans les documents de
Qumrân", VRT 77 (1955) 614-630. M. PHILONENKO, "Le Maître de justice et la Sagesse de
Salomon", TZ 14 (1958) 81-88. C. LARCHER, Études, pp. 112-129. Y. AMIR, "The Wisdom
of Solomon and the Literature of Qumran", [Proceedings of the Sixth World Congress of
Jewish Studies, vol. III Jerusalem, 1977] 329-335.

Among the scholars who compare the Qumran writings with passages from Wis, it is
M. PHILONENKO who argues for the closest parallels. PHILONENKO goes so far as to claim
that the author of Wis utilized and paraphrased sections from the Qumran writings. The

points of contact between the description of the persecution of the just one in 2:10-20 and the Teacher of Righteousness are: a) the special knowledge that the wicked chide the just one for claiming (2:13a), b) the terms of fatherhood and sonship which denote a special relationship between the just one and the Lord (2:16d, 18a) and c) the brutal death which the just one is to undergo (2:19-20).

The Teacher of Righteousness is described as one "to whom God made known all the mysteries of His servants the Prophets" (1QpHab 7:4) [102]. The Hymns speak of the Lord as a father for the just, "For you are a father to all the sons of your truth" (1QH 9:35). The Teacher of Righteousness is identified with the persecuted just of the Hymns (1QH 2:23-24; 3:21-22; 4:35-36; 5:22-23; 8:33).

However, the similarities between the description of the persecution of the just in Wis and the Teacher of Righteousness remain exclusively on the thematic level. There is no expression or turn of phrase in Wis that would compel us to regard the Qumran writings as the prime source for Wis 2:10-20 [103].

Nevertheless, it remains possible that the author of Wis, in the description of the persecution of the just, is including an allusion to the ideas of the just who suffer in the Qumran writings among other allusions (e.g. to the suffering just of the psalms and the prophets). However, an allusion to the Qumran writings does not imply an allusion to the historical Teacher of Righteousness [104]. Even in the case of such an allusion to the

---

parallels to the suffering servant of Isaiah in Wis, then, are explained by the identification in the Qumran writings of the Teacher of Righteousness with the suffering servant and the persecuted just of the psalms (pp. 83-88). See J. STARCKY, "Les Quatre Étapes du Messianisme à Qumrân", *RB* 70 (1963) 484-505, for an evaluation of the development of Messianism in the Qumran writings in relationship to biblical writings.

[102] LARCHER argues against the identification of the phrase in 2:13 with the knowledge of unique mysteries which the Teacher of Righteousness is described as possessing in the Qumran writings. The knowledge of God is a rather typical characteristic attributed to those who have a special relationship with God (cf. *TDNT* I, pp. 696-698). "Les «mystères de Dieu» devraient être reconnus par les impies, sans doute à partir de l'Écriture, et ils demeurent accessibles à tous... En définitive, si l'auteur a repris une expression en faveur dans des cercles ésotériques, c'est pour désigner une forme de connaissance religieuse qui se rattache étroitement aux conceptions bibliques et juives" (C. LARCHER, *Le Livre de la Sagesse*, p. 244).

[103] M. PHILONENKO claims there is sufficient evidence in the Qumran writings to imply that the Teacher of Righteousness actually was put to death (M. PHILONENKO, "Le Maître de justice et la Sagesse de Salomon", *TZ* 14 (1958) p. 85, n.13. However, the evidence for such an historical assertion is not convincing given the diverse representations of the fate of the Teacher of Righteousness in the different documents of Qumran themselves. An allusion to the suffering of the just in the Qumran writings need not imply that the author was a follower of the sect, or that such an allusion refers to an historical event.

[104] In his introduction to the translation of the Qumran writings, G. VERMES notes the discrepancies regarding the fate of the Teacher of Righteousness from one document

Qumran writings, it would have to be understood exclusively on a secondary level, namely that the author employs imagery from various literary sources that would be known to his readers in order to create an ideal or a model of the persecution of the just[105]. There is no evidence that the author of Wis intends the descriptions of the just one's persecution to be associated historically or exclusively with the Teacher of Righteousness[106]. Such an interpretation would need to explain the relationship of the wicked described in 2:5-9 and the Teacher of Righteousness of Qumran. The wicked who exhort one another to exploit the pleasures of life, as a result of the negative judgment on physical death, are not described in terms of the 'children of darkness' as in the Qumran writings, but rather in terms of the images attached to the symposium and to traditional images of oppression in the psalms and prophetic writings.

C-9.3 Conclusion: the priority of the argument over an identification of a single group

What surfaces rather clearly in the analysis of possible sources for the author's composition of the speech of the wicked is that the primary

---

to another. In *The Damascus Document* the teacher did not suffer an ignoble death, but rather during his exile 'was gathered in', a euphemism for death which suggests natural causes. On the other hand, the wicked priest is described in terms similar to those in Wis 2 as one who was captured and killed by a rival. The relationship between history and imaginative representation in the Qumran writings creates difficulties for assessing the historical basis of the references to the supposed 'tragic' death of the Teacher of Righteousness. "It would be unrealistic, taking into account the vagueness of all these statements, the cryptic nature of the symbolism and the entire lack of any systematic exposition of the sect's history, to expect every detail to be identified" (G. VERMES, *The Dead Sea Scrolls*, Sheffield: 1987³, p. 27).

[105] Another possible allusion has been noted for the persecution of the just in Wis. M. ADINOLFI, "Il messianismo di Sap 2,12-30", [*AttiSettBibl* 18, 1964], Brescia: 1966, 205-217. In the philosophical discussion on determining who is just and unjust in PLATO's *Republic*, we read: "Though doing no wrong he must have the repute of the greatest injustice, so that he may be put to the test as regards justice though not softening because of ill repute and the consequences thereof. But let him hold on his course unchangeable even unto death, seeming all his life to be unjust though being just, that so, both men attaining to the limit, the one of injustice, the other of justice, we may pass judgment which of the two is happier" (*Republic* 2:362).

[106] This does not mean that the author intends the wicked's description of the persecution of the just to have no historical basis whatsoever. The author most likely intends the reader to identify in the just one who is to suffer the faithful Jews who do not share the false reasoning of the wicked. But the important issue for the author is to refute the arguments of the opponents and not so much to ostracize a contemporary opponent. See M. ADINOLFI, "Il messianismo di Sap 2,12-30", [*AttiSettBibl* 18, 1964] p. 209, "Gli esegeti oggi concordano nel vedere in Sap. 2,12-20 una realtà storica che, nella stragrande maggioranze, identificano con i Giudei rimasti fedeli all'ortodossia e perciò vessati dai loro correligionari apostati e dai pagani in combutta con questi."

source is Scripture itself (the psalms, prophetic writings and sapiential texts). Possible allusions to philosophical systems such as Epicureanism, to cultural customs such as the symposium, to religious movements such as the Qumran community, are not meant to identify the wicked with a particular philosophical group contemporary to the author and addressees. Rather, the author utilizes various sources to identify the characteristics of wickedness itself that is opposed to God and to justice.

This means that the primary importance for the author in the construction of the speech of the wicked is the argument in their reasoning. The speech is not so much an exercise to identify a partisan group (such as a philosophical system or Jewish apostates) as it is the author's technique to lay bare a false reasoning that leads to despair, to injustice and to sheer violence. The result of such false reasoning is death. It is this death which is the author's negative reason for embracing justice and seeking God. As such, death is the obstacle that the antagonists (the wicked) employ within the author's argument; it is this that must be overcome and defeated for the exhortation to justice to be effective.

If the analysis of the possible literary sources has been rather detailed, it nonetheless underscores the importance that the author attributes to the movement of the false reasoning of the wicked. The author has constructed the speech of the wicked through references and allusions to various sources precisely so as not to identify one single group or source and in order to highlight the argument itself. The various allusions to images that describe human existence as ephemeral have their counterparts in Biblical and Hellenistic literature alike. The exhortation to exploit life likewise has its counterparts in Biblical wisdom, Greek literature, as well as in the Greek custom of the symposium. The images that describe the oppression of the vulnerable and the persecution of the just are readily identifiable in the psalms of lament, in the Servant of Isaiah and, possibly, in Qumran texts. To seek to identify exclusively one single group in a part of the speech of the wicked presumes a truncation of that single part from the overall context of the speech.

The result of the analysis of sources for the speech of the wicked confirms the specific argumentation of the author in the speech as the primary level of interpretation. Inferences to the author's contemporary philosophies or events are so manifold so as to indicate a second level of meaning. These manifold allusions to a variety of philosophical ideas and cultural customs should inhibit the reader's focus on a particular group and, in turn, highlight the dynamic of the argument itself.

CHAPTER FOUR

THE INTERPRETATIONS OF DEATH IN WIS (1–6)

D-1. The Critical Function of the Theme of Death in Wis (1–6)

Throughout the dynamic of the author's argument, we have followed the critical role that death plays in the opening exhortation to justice. The final end of the author's exhortation is to promote a love for justice in relation to God, to oneself and to others. However, the critical theme which dominates the opening exhortation of the first six chapters is not so much justice or wisdom as it is the obstacle to the practice of justice, namely death. It is the theme of death with all of its ambiguity that is the motor in the argumentation of the author. From this critical theme, the author spins several arguments to dissuade the reader from bringing on death, the counterpart to seeking God through justice.

The false perception of death on the part of the wicked is the prime obstacle to the practice of justice. Their mistaken judgment on mortality, as being the last word on the dignity of human beings, ironically makes them part of a death which takes them far beyond the mortality which every human being experiences. The central argumentation in the author's defense of the just is aimed at refuting the false reasoning of the unjust with regard to life and death. The author aims the argumentation to the task of unmasking the subtlety of this false reasoning in order to promote a clear, intelligible choice for the value of justice.

The critical function of the theme of death in the first six chapters of Wis has not been sufficiently appreciated by scholars. For the most part, scholars have attempted to organize the entire book of Wis around the theme of personified wisdom which dominates the second part of the book. The first part had been labeled as "the eschatological book" because of the image of the ultimate judgment [1]. The theme of the book

---

[1] W. WEBER was the first to denote the first chapters of Wisdom as 'the eschatological book' and this title was adopted by many scholars (eg. E. GÄRTNER, R.J. TAYLOR) as characterizing the content of the section. W. WEBER, "Die Composition der Weisheit Salomos", *ZWT* 47 (1904) pp. 168-169.

had been somewhat repristinated under the theme of justice precisely because of the first part of the book [2].

To a certain degree all of these classifications of theme uncover a specific perspective in the text. It is a matter of what one understands by centrality or finality that determines the classification of theme. The final end of the opening exhortation is the love of justice. The positive means for loving justice is the acquirement of God's wisdom, presented in the second part (6–10). And finally examples from Israel's history in the third part (11–19), buttress the author's argumentation in the first two parts of the work. But the critical theme which generates the central argumentation of the author in chapters 1–6 is the theme of death. And the appreciation of the critical function of death will have a bearing on the clarification of this complex idea in the author's exposition.

D-2. Approaches to the clarification of death in Wis (1–6)

Various systematic attempts to clarify the notion of death in the Book of Wis were undertaken with the intention of specifying its formulation within larger theological issues such as original sin (A.-M. DUBARLE, 1950) and the idea of immortality (H. BÜCKERS, 1938, A. HULBOSCH, 1952; P. GRELOT, 1961; R.J. TAYLOR, 1966). Another approach focused on the development of the notion of death within the entire Old Testament from a thematic point of view (L. WÄCHTER, 1967; O. KAISER, E. LOHSE, 1977; O. KNOCH, 1977; L.R. BAILEY, 1979 [3]. Almost every commentary would dedicate an amount of space to the problematic of the author's idea of death primarily in Wis 1-2 (I. LORINUS, 1607; C.L.W. GRIMM, 1860; P. HEINISCH, 1912; C. LARCHER, 1983). Even the approach of literary analysis elicited short commentaries on the author's notion of death [4]. Given the critical role of the function of death in the author's argumentation in the

---

[2] L. ALONSO SCHÖKEL, *Ecclesiastes y Sabiduría*, Madrid: 1974. S. BRETON, "Libro de la Sabiduría o Libro de la Justicia? El tema de la justicia en la interpretación del Libro de la Sabiduría", *CuadBibl* 1 (1978) 77-104. B. CELADA, "El libro de la Sabiduría, recuperado para la causa de la justicia", *CuBibl* 37 (1980) 43-55. J. VÍLCHEZ, "El binomio justicia-injusticia en el Libro de la Sabiduría", *CuadBibl* 7, (1981) 1-16.

[3] A number of general works on death in the OT exclude the Book of Wis either because the scope of the study is limited to the Hebrew text, M. KRIEG, *Toderbilder im Alten Testament oder: 'Wie die Alten den Tod gebildet'*, ATANT 73 (1987); H.W. WOLFF, *Anthropology of the Old Testament*, London: 1981, (1st ed. Munich: 1973), or is limited to the restricted canon, R. MARTIN-ACHARD, *De la mort à la résurrection d'après l'Ancien Testament*, Neuchâtel: 1956.

[4] F. PERRENCHIO, "Struttura e analisi letteraria di Sapienza 1,16–2,24 e 5,1-23", *Sales* 43 (1981) pp. 41-42; U. OFFERHAUS, *Komposition und Intention*, pp. 232-234; P. BIZZETI, *Il Libro della Sapienza*, p.106.

the first six chapters, it is understandable that various approaches to the Book of Wis or to the theme of death in general would grapple with the author's complex notion of death.

The manifold positions regarding the author's understanding of death derived from the various approaches can be classified into three main categories. Each of them hinges on the respective interpretations of two parallel verses, 1:13 — For God did not make death, nor takes delight in the destruction of the living; 2:24a — Through the envy of the adversary death entered the world. The reason these two verses are critical for understanding the interpretation of the concept death is that here the author specifically comments on the nature and cause of death in relation to God and the cosmos.

The first position regards the death under discussion primarily as physical death which is envisaged as a punishment for sin, and spiritual death would be considered a necessary accompaniment. The second position understands death in these verses as spiritual death, namely the second death that comprises the loss of union with God. The third position, which eventually had become the most dominant, envisages a combined notion of death in these verses, both physical and spiritual death. The author is primarily concerned with spiritual death but at the same time this notion includes physical death as punishment for sin.

In the following critical exposition of the interpretations of death in Wis, I will choose a number of the main representatives for each group of interpretations. The dynamic of the argument uncovered in the previous chapter will provide a context for assessing the strengths and weaknesses of these various positions within the larger framework of the author's opening exhortation to justice.

D-3.   Death in 1:13 and 2:24 interpreted as 'physical death'

The commentary on the Book of Wis by LORINUS in the 17th century is a prime example of the interpretation of the author's concept of death as physical death [5]. The arguments which LORINUS brings to bear on the subject are primarily theological. He is concerned to render the latin text of Wis, on which he is commenting, consistent with his understanding of AUGUSTINE's theological construct.

In his commentary on 1:13, LORINUS notes the parallel between death and annihilation in the two stichs.

Quoniam Deus mortem non fecit,
nec laetatur in perditione vivorum.

---

[5] I. LORINUS, Commentarius in Librum Sapientiae, Lyon: 1607.

Both death and perdition are said to be extraneous to God. "Mors, & perditio peregrinum, & alienum est opus ab eo..." (p. 33). In this way, for LORINUS the concept of physical death is intended by *mors*, and spiritual death (animae mors) by *perditio*.

To emphasize the inclusion of the concept of physical death in the death which God did not make, LORINUS draws on the Pelagian denial of physical death as punishment for sin, and cites 1:13 as a biblical refutation of the Pelagian position [6]. Though the emphasis in LORINUS' explication is on death considered as a punishment, it is physical death that is the prime referent of the death that God did not make. The physical death that God did not make is consequently a punishment for sin.

This particular twist in LORINUS' explanation of the author's concept of death is even more evident in his commentary on the parallel stich in 2:24; Invidia autem Diaboli mors introivit in orbem terrarum. Drawing on parallels to Rom 5:12 and Gen 2:17, LORINUS concretely specifies the death which the devil introduced into the world as physical death and not spiritual [7]. In this way, LORINUS clearly opts for the interpretation that the author of Wis sustains a human etiology whereby mortality per se and without qualification is extraneous to original human nature and is incurred by the sin of the first parents.

The major difficulty in LORINUS' approach is the reduction of the argumentation to the specific verses under discussion. Instead of grounding the interpretation of these difficult verses in the overall argumentation of the author of Wis, LORINUS immediately draws on theological arguments of a particular theological construct without verifying the author's intentionality in the context of the verses.

Not only does the limited interpretation of physical death in these verses run into serious restrictions within the author's overall argumentation, but also within the immediate context. After both statements on death, the death that God did not intend and the death that the devil introduced into the world, the author of Wis adds a qualifying statement that is meant to specify the quality of death associated with sin (1:16d;

---

[6] "Error item Pelagianorum fuit, mortem nobis esse penitus naturalem, non poenalem, nec minus moriendum fuisse, quamuis Adam non peccasset, cuius proinde negabat ad nos peccatum originaliter derivari. Inter alias rationes, affertur una ex hoc loco, quia Deus mortem non fecit, hoc est, hominem non condidit obnoxium morti, sed concessit ei..." (LORINUS, *Sap.*, p. 33). (Likewise, the error of the Pelagians was that they considered death to be our natural condition, not a penalty, he would have nonetheless died even had Adam not sinned, accordingly he denied that original sin arrives to us. Among other reasons, one found in this place, it is deduced that God did not make death, that is, he did not establish man subject to death...).

[7] "... fuit mortis causa, quam comminatus erat Deus non animae, atque damnationis aeternae perse, quoniam ipsomet peccato per se incurritur, sed corporis" (LORINUS, *Sap.*, p. 75).

2:24b)[8]. But before presenting the importance of these qualifying phrases, it will be useful to display another tendency of interpreting death in these verses primarily as physical death, namely in light of their dependence on the Genesis account.

In a succinct article, M. GILBERT has presented the author's use of Gen 1-3 in the Book of Wis[9]. The interpretation of death in Wis as physical death (always within the spectrum of 1:13 and 2:24) is supported precisely by an equivalent interpretation in the creation and fall accounts of Genesis. By showing how the author in Wis 1:13-14 and 2:23-24 employs or adapts the creation narrative in Genesis, GILBERT tries to elucidate the nuance of death as certainly including physical death in these two verses[10].

The author's phrase, "God did not make death' integrates both the creation account (Gen 1) and the fall narrative (Gen 2-3). It integrates negatively the phrase of creation, "God made the heavens and the earth'. The idea of death is taken from Gen 2-3, primarily from the prohibition of eating from the tree of knowledge under the threat of death (Gen 2:17; 3:3,4). In asking the specific question regarding which kind of death God did not create, GILBERT answers that under the influence of Gen 2-3, it must mean not only the death that separates from God, but physical death as well[11]. In contrast to the death that God did not make, the following verse 1:14 stresses the prime motive of God's creation to be 'life'. This interpretation of death in Wis 1:13 as including human mortality presumes that the death under discussion in the creation and fall accounts is human mortality[12].

---

[8] LORINUS was working with a serious handicap by limiting himself to the Latin text. The Latin translation of 2:25 misses the nuance of limiting the experience of death to the wicked: "Imitantur autem illum qui sunt ex parte illius." LORINUS was aware of the discrepancy between the Latin and the Greek and notes the presence of the verb πειράζω, in the Greek text. But in understanding the verb by its later nuance of 'to tempt in order to injure' rather than 'to know through experience,' LORINUS failed to grasp the qualifying nature of this stich on the understanding of death. See LORINUS, Sap., p. 76.

[9] M. GILBERT, "Gn 1-3 dans le livre de la Sagesse", [La Création dans l'Orient ancien, LD 127] 323-344. This tendency to interpret a physical perspective on death in Wis based on the Gen narratives can be especially noted in the articles by P. GRELOT, "L'eschatologie de la Sagesse et les apocalypses juives", À la rencontre de Dieu, Mém. A. GELIN, Le Puy: 1961, pp. 166-168; the article is republished in De la mort à la vie éternelle, LD 67, (1971) 187-199; and by W. GOOSENS, "Immortalité corporelle", DBS 4 (1949) pp. 314-316.

[10] The first section of the article which deals specifically with these verses from Wis is entitled, 'Création pour la vie'. The following arguments are a summary of this section (M. GILBERT, "Gn 1-3 dans le livre de la Sag", pp. 323-328).

[11] "La mort n'était donc pas dans les intentions du Créateur. Mais de quelle mort s'agit-il? Pas seulement la mort spirituelle qui sépare de Dieu, mais aussi, selon Gn 2-3, la mort physique" (M. GILBERT, "Gn 1-3 dans le livre de la Sag", p. 324).

[12] See also L.R. BAILEY, Biblical Perspectives on Death, Philadelphia: 1979: "At the end of the former quotation (referring to Wis 1:13) one may hear an echo of Ezek 18:32,

The same procedure is applied to the interpretation of death in Wis 2:23-24. With two stichs, the author of Wis restates positively what had been stated negatively in 1:13, "God created humans for incorruptibility (ἀφθαρσία), he made them in the image of his own identity (ἰδιότητος) (Wis 2:23)". To interpret the sense of ἀφθαρσία, GILBERT reads these verses in the light of an interpretation of the context of Gen 2–3. According to this interpretation, immortality was included in God's original design. The entire person, spiritual and physical, was destined to 'incorruptibility'. The tree of life before the fall was meant to destine human beings to immortality. Only with the fall, does every person pass through physical death [13].

By including the concept of physical incorruptibility in the term, ἀφθαρσία, GILBERT establishes a correspondence with the juxtaposed term, θάνατος, in Wis 2:24. However, it is by no means certain that the author intended such a nuance. LARCHER notes that in Greek usage the term referred to all which was considered imperishable, hence, the sphere of the divine, even the eternity of the world, and the immortality of the soul. Even though LARCHER finally opts for a similar interpretation of a physical nuance included in the term, ἀφθαρσία, he does not add any other convincing reason except the similar imposition of the given interpretation of Gen 2–3 [14].

However it should be observed that the author employs the term, ἀφθαρσία, only on one other occasion, in the sorites in Wis 6:18-19, where the term unambiguously denotes an ethical value which brings one into union with God:

> "Fidelity to the law is sure incorruptibility
> and incorruptibility brings one close to God".

'For I have no pleasure in the death of anyone, says the Lord God; so turn and live.' The prophet speaks of premature death, but the author of the Wisdom of Solomon has expanded it to include other categories including mortality" (p. 76).

[13] GILBERT explains the concept of 'man made in the image of God's identity' (Wis 2:23b) as the author's particular adaptation of the Gen account of creation. The author of Wis combines the idea of God creating humans according to the image of God (Gen 1:26-27) with the idea of God's immortality as conveyed in the expulsion narrative, Gen 3:22, "Lest he become like one of us and live forever". See M. GILBERT, "Gn 1–3 dans le livre de la Sag", p. 327.

[14] "En I,13a, la mort physique semble bien incluse dans cette mort «que Dieu n'a pas fait» et le récit de Gn. II–III nous montre le premier homme promis à une sorte d'incorruptibilité: une vertu préternaturelle, symbolisée par l'arbre de vie, entretenait son corps dans une perpétuelle jeunesse ..." (C. LARCHER, Le Livre de la Sagesse, p. 267). However, the author of Wis does not speak of ἀφθαρσία as a prenatural virtue which has been forever lost in the fall. On the contrary, this incorruptibility is part of the original plan (Wis 2:23) and remains the proper destiny of those who seek God through faithfulness (Wis 6:18-19). Therefore, what has been introduced by the envy of the devil is a death which is not equivalent to mortality.

The term is opposed to the death which the wicked bring on themselves through injustice. It does not convey a nuance of physical incorruptibility.

GILBERT's answer to the specific question as to what kind of death the devil introduced into the world is even more emphatic than in the case of 1:13. With the interpretation of Gen 2:17 and 3:3, מות תאמות, "you will surely die" as implying punishment through the acquiring of mortality, GILBERT concludes that the author of Wis is at least intending physical death in the death introduced by the devil[15].

D-3.1   The complexity of the primeval accounts in Gen 1–3

This tendency to interpret the author's understanding of death in the two critical verses through a reading of the primeval accounts of Gen is understandable because the author of Wis alludes to these accounts in the development of the argumentation[16]. Numerous scholars who have broached the subject of death in Wis would summarize the author's etiology in light of the Gen accounts in order to render an intelligible notion of the author's concept of death[17].

However, we have to be careful not to read into the verses of the Wis author an alien reading of the Gen accounts. The primeval accounts of

---

[15] "L'homme a désobéi et la mort physique fut désormais son châtiment (Gn 3,19). Sg 2,24 parle au moins de cette mort physique, mais puisque celle-ci est la conséquence du péché, la mort spirituelle, qui prive de l'amitié de Dieu et de sa société doit être également comprise en Sg 2,24..." (M. GILBERT, "Gn 1–3 dans le livre de la Sag", p. 327-328; see also the conclusion on p. 342). L.R. BAILEY also collocates mortality and spiritual death together in an undifferentiated manner under the author's notion of death in 2:23, "Death in all its manifestations (metaphorical and biological) initially resulted from the devil's spite" (Wisd of Sol. 2:23-24) (L.R. BAILEY, *Biblical Perspectives on Death*, Philadelphia: 1979, p. 82).

[16] In an imaginative and synthetic reading of Wis, D. BARSOTTI comments on the preponderance of the themes of creation throughout the entire Book of Wisdom. "Tutti i temi dei primi due capitoli della Genesi, sono al centro della meditazione religiosa dell'autore ispirato" (D. BARSOTTI, *Meditazione sul Libro della Sapienza*, Brescia: 1976, p. 28).

[17] Such approaches for clarifying the notion of death with short summaries of the etiologies behind the Gen accounts often can be noted in the commentaries: C.L.W. GRIMM, *Das Buch der Weisheit*, pp. 60-63; P. HEINISCH, *Das Buch der Weisheit*, 1912, p. 23; see also G. ZIENER, "Weisheitsbuch und Johannesevangelium", *Bib* 39 (1958) p. 46; The attempt to clarify the notion of death through a reconstruction of the author's etiology is reflected in J.J. COLLINS, "The Root of Immortality: Death in the Context of Jewish Wisdom (Sir WisSol)", *HTR* 71 (1978) p. 186 and in Y. AMIR, "The Figure of Death in the 'Book of Wisdom'", *JJS* 30 (1979) 154-178 (note that AMIR's reconstruction suggests that the Wis author was not employing primarily the Gen narratives but rather was constructing his own mythological system which the author carelessly conjoins with Gen), see also B.R. GAVENTA, "The Rhetoric of Death in the Wisdom of Solomon and the Letters of Paul", pp. 132-135.

Gen which describe creation and disorder are complex accounts that are not easily reducible to one-sided interpretations. The very presence of two distinct creation accounts that are integrated into a broader unity within Gen points to their synthetic function. The two creation accounts complement one another. They sustain the ambiguous and manifold elements that constitute the human condition. The temporal succession of the events even within a single account is not so important as their relationship to one another. The relationship between mortality and the sin of disobedience of Adam and Eve is certainly not necessarily reducible to a relationship of causality as conceived in a succession of events[18]. Several approaches to the Gen narratives highlight the temporal suspension of the narratives. They have a "primeval function" of sustaining symbolically the many facets of the human condition in the universe and the experience of mystery[19]. To illustrate this widespread understanding of the Gen accounts as synthetic presentations of the human condition as understood by Israel, I will briefly draw on C. WESTERMANN, P. BEAUCHAMP and P. GIBERT.

In his summary on the purpose and thrust of Gen 2–3, WESTERMANN suggests:

> "... the narrative explains human existence in its essential elements as something which came about in primeval time, and indeed the created state in contrast to the state of humanity limited by death, suffering and sin. It is a misunderstanding of the narrative as a whole to explain it as a succession of historical or quasi-historical incidents."[20]

---

[18] The amount of scholarly reflection on the relationship between mortality and sin in the Genesis accounts testifies to the importance of these concepts for the articulation and formulation of one's faith. It is not possible to enter into a comprehensive overview of the respective positions held on the nuanced interpretations of the creation and fall in Genesis, given the specific intent of this work to understand the notion of death in Wis. One can consult a variety of works which introduce different approaches and positions: 1) W. GOOSENS, "Immortalité corporelle", *DBS* 4 (1949) pp. 298-317; 2) X. LÉON-DUFOUR, *Face à la mort, Jésus et Paul*, Paris: 1979, [trans. T. PRENDERGAST, *Life and death in the New Testament*, San Francisco: 1986]. 3) P. GIBERT, *Bible, mythes et récits de commencement*, Paris: 1986. The purpose of introducing the possibility of a general synthetic approach to the interpretation of these accounts is to inhibit the reduction of the Gen accounts to an interpretation which is not the Wis author's etiological perspective of Gen.

[19] With the term 'approaches' to the Biblical narratives, I intend simply the various methods of redaction criticism (as exemplified in C. WESTERMANN's commentary, *Genesis 1-11*, trans. J.J. SCULLION, {Genesis 1-11, Neukirchen-Vluyn: 1974}, London: 1984); literary analysis (as exemplified in P. GIBERT's treatment of the Gen narratives in P. GIBERT, *Bible, mythes et récits de commencement*, Paris: 1986.

[20] C. WESTERMANN, *Genesis 1-11*, p. 276. In support of this perspective, WESTERMANN quotes H. HAAG who commented on current views in the late 60's regarding the approach to the Gen creation and fall accounts. "The current view in Catholic and Evangelical dogmatics that the primeval state was a chronological period at the beginning of human

As such, this primeval narrative of Gen is to be viewed and understood as Israel's understanding of the relationship between herself and God. The narrative is an articulation of the complex experiences of life as a gift, filled with dignity, with guilt, with fear, with limitation and hope that make up Israel's experience of God in history[21].

Similarly, in a short study on the ethical dimension of the creation account of the Priestly writer, P. BEAUCHAMP concludes by highlighting the opening creation account in Gen as God's positioning of 'efficacious signs'[22]. The formulation of the creation account by the Priestly tradition underscores the gift of life which takes on the ethical challenge of responsibility. For BEAUCHAMP this combination of gift and task echoes the covenant as conceived by the exilic and post-exilic prophets, the gifts and demands of the covenant. What this means is that the creation account is not simply a presentation of origins through a spectrum of cause and effect in historical time. It is an account which points to the hopes and possibilities of humans to be realized in the future. Gen 1 is not only an account of origins, it also signifies the goal, the hopes and destiny of human beings. It is addressed to human beings who must decide their future in terms of the possibilities given by God.

> Ils ne le sont, ces signes, que situés par rapport à un homme marchant, orienté par sa mémoire, désirant, choisissant: ils s'articulent nécessairement sur l'ordre éthique (p. 179).

The importance of reading the accounts of creation in their entire unity and even with respect to the Exodus account has been especially highlighted recently by P. GIBERT in his study on origins in the entire Bible[23]. In light of his analysis of the narrative, GIBERT notes the necessity to read the stories in Gen 2–3 not simply as a succession of episodes, but equally according to the circularity of their movement which establishes their full meaning. Only by reading chapter two in light

---

history... does not accord with the Bible. It knows no 'man before sin' and so no primeval state" (quoted from H. HAAG, "Der 'Urstand' nach dem Zeugnis der Bibel", *TQ* 148 (1968) 385-404).

[21] C. WESTERMANN, *Genesis 1-11*, p. 276-277.

[22] P. BEAUCHAMP, "Création et fondation de la loi en Gn 1,1–2,4a", [*La création dans l'Orient ancien*], LD 127 (1987) 139-182. "Il faut ajouter que la création est position par Dieu de signes efficaces. En cela, la création n'est pas exactment position d'une nature, d'un ensemble d'étants. Elle pose un devoir-être, puisque la parole créatrice est injonction. Elle pose aussi un pouvoir-être. Ce devoir-être, qui est pouvoir-être, dit tout le contenu de la notion d'image" (p. 179).

[23] P. GIBERT, *Bible, mythes et récits de commencement*, Paris: 1986. The sections dealing with the crossing of the reed sea (Exod 13:20–14:31) and the crossing of the Jordan (Josh 3:1–5:1) point to the formulation of the creation accounts in Gen with similar terminology and imagery (pp. 176-185, 195-198).

of chapter three and vice versa does one trace the indissoluble unity of the stories which speak of humanity of all times [24].

The integration of two distinct creation accounts (Gen 1, 2–3), which employ different styles and contain diverse emphases points to their complementarity. Both accounts are stamped by the context and milieu of their origin [25]. The understanding of the synthetic succession of the creation accounts points to their function of sustaining the various facets of the entire human condition: its desires, fears and hopes. The stories project back into origins the sketch of human destiny, in its essentials, as conceived and understood by their authors and their milieu [26].

If then the stories of creation are to be read in their synthetic unity and not as an historical succession of events, this has a bearing on the interpretation of the events narrated in the accounts [27]. The purpose of

---

[24] "Par conséquent les chapitres 2 et 3 doivent être lus non seulement selon les lois de la succession des épisodes, lois constitutives de la trame dramatique propre à tout récit, mais ils doivent l'être également selon une *circularité* de sens, le chapitre 3 ramenant sans doute au chapitre 2 autant que le chapitre 2 conduit au chapitre 3. Car c'est l'ensemble indissociable de ces deux chapitres qui rend compte, dans sa circularité même, de l'humanité de toujours et donc dans ses origines" (P. GIBERT, *Bible, mythes et récits de commencement*, p. 108).

[25] The accounts of Gen 2–3 employ a dramatic, narrative style in which the characters on the scene act and react. The latent mythical elements in the narrative testify to its ancient origin and setting in Canaan. The account of Gen 1, on the other hand, employs a poetic, descriptive style in which the sole hero of the narrative is God. It is through God's word, who remains the only witness to the absolute origin of the universe, that the order of the world comes into being. Israel's encounter with Babylonian culture and religion marks the context for a new comprehension of expressing the origin of the world. But the new expression of origins did not supplant the previous. Rather the ordered and descriptive account of origins in Gen 1 introduces and complements the dramatic narratives of Gen 2–3 (P. GIBERT, *Bible, mythes et récits de commencement*, pp. 146-151).

[26] "A travers un jeu d'images *et* de faits, qui ne doivent pas donner le change, le texte de Gn 2–3 rend compte de ce que tout être vit de plus fondamental dans sa destinée. L'ensemble du récit, tel qu'il est ici conçu, viserait donc *à projeter aux origines* l'épure de la destinée humaine, telle que l'auteur et son milieu la concevaient pour l'essentiel" (P. GIBERT, *Bible, mythes et récits de commencement*, p. 87).

"Le chapitre 1 de la Genèse pouvait devenir *préface* à l'histoire d'Adam et d'Eve, non seulement par son style et son ton, mais aussi par le «détail» de ses données. Il la compléterait aussi, le jardin d'Eden avec ses plantes et ses animaux n'indiquant en effet pas grand-chose sur l'univers céleste et terrestre dans son ensemble" (p. 150).

[27] For a recent study of the creation accounts in Jewish circles one may consult B. OCH, "The Garden of Eden: From Creation to Covenant", *Judaism* 37 (1988) 143-156. Here too OCH insists on the importance of situating the accounts within the larger perspective of the covenant. Unfortunately, he seems to be completely oblivious to Christian scholarship in this area that for three decades has been insisting on the wider context of the creation accounts. In lamenting the silence in Jewish scholarship on the creation narratives, OCH curiously explains:

"It is important to point out that this Christian interpretation of the history of mankind is not grounded in the Biblical text when viewed as a whole. The isolation of the first three chapters of Genesis, while basic to dogmatic Christian theology, has resulted in

the accounts is not so much to explain cause and effect within a succession of events as much as to present the essential aspects of the human condition in relation to God and the world.

Three moments in the Gen creation narrative that have a particular bearing on the subject of death are: 1) the first prohibition (Gen 2:16-17); 2) the punishment (Gen 3:14-19)[28]; 3) the expulsion from the garden (Gen 3:22-25). In all three cases, the synthetic reading of the text does not easily accommodate the interpretation of a causal relationship between mortality and sin within a succession of events. Rather it points to the general presentation of a disordered relationship rooted in disobedience between humans with respect to God and the world.

WESTERMANN discusses the difficulties exegetes have had in determining the meaning of מות תאמות in 2:17[29]. The term has a fixed juridical meaning. It is the oft used formula for the death penalty, the ultimate penalty. Two extreme positions are: 1) that the phrase is a threat whereby immediate death is threatened as a direct consequence of eating from the forbidden tree, 2) that the phrase is a threat whereby mortality in general is the result of eating from the forbidden tree. The difficulties with both extreme positions arise because of the absence of the announcement of the death penalty in the following narrative.

To mediate between these two extremes, WESTERMANN draws a distinction between threat and warning[30] in the case of the prohibition in Gen 2:17, "In the day that you eat of it you shall die".

> This is not in fact a threat of death, but rather the clear expression of the limit which is the necessary accompaniment of the freedom entrusted to humanity in the command. To say no to God — and this is what freedom allows — is ultimately to say no to life; for life comes from God (C. WESTERMANN, *Genesis 1–11*, p. 224).

In other words, with the prohibition, God warns Adam and Eve of a new situation that will arise from disobedience. A warning need not imply

---

a fundamental misunderstanding of the Biblical teaching concerning man and the world" (p. 143, n 1).

Cf. C. WESTERMANN "Sapiential and Covenant Themes in Genesis 2–3", [*Studies in Ancient Israelite Wisdom*, ed. J.L. CRENSHAW, New York: 1976] 468-480.

[28] This description of punishment/curses as a result of disobedience in Gen 3:14-19 is most likely an insertion in the original story which had the expulsion from the garden as the direct consequence of disobedience. Such an explanation of the present state of the text stems from the fact that the punishment/curses in 3:14-19 have no direct relationship to the offense. Moreover the parallel that lies behind Ezek 28:13-16 does not mention the curses between the offense and the expulsion from the garden (C. WESTERMANN, *Genesis 1–11*, p. 256-257).

[29] C. WESTERMANN, *Genesis 1–11*, pp. 223-225.

[30] For a similar interpretation of God's prohibition as a warning see L. WÄCHTER, *Der Tod im Alten Testament*, Stuttgart: 1967, "Tod als Warnung Gottes", pp. 203-204.

a precise delineation of the negative consequences. The warning of the death penalty in the mouth of God denotes, with juridical language, the supreme negative motive possible for eliciting obedience[31].

In the subsequent narrative, where God explains the punishment to the serpent, to Eve and to Adam (Gen 3:14-19), the death penalty is not mentioned. This absence should at least bring into serious question the reading of the prohibition in 2:17 as a threat of mortality.

The results of disobedience, described in God's announcement of punishment, consist of a transformed relationship between humans and their world that can best be described by hostility. Eve and Adam experience the limitations in their lives as pain and punishment. It is their relationships that have changed as a result of disobedience. P. GIBERT, in commenting on the description of punishment, states that, not only is physical death not the punishment for disobedience, but rather, death denotes the *limitation* of the punishment[32], "... until you return to the earth, from which you were taken, for you are dust and to dust you shall return".

Having been formed from the earth, Adam was mortal and remains mortal[33]. What has been transformed through disobedience is Adam's relationship to his mortality, to the entire sphere of his limitations. Separation from God introduces disharmony into the relationships of humans to their world[34].

---

[31] It is interesting to note that the immediate consequence of Adam and Eve's disobedience is the fear they acquire of their nudity. To be in harmony with one's nudity and in the nudity of another remains a deep-rooted human desire. The original harmony portrayed in the primeval account signifies precisely this longed for harmony. The result of disobedience is the fear of one's limitation and vulnerability. Adam and Eve immediately after disobeying are in disharmony with God, separated from God; it is they who run and hide from God. Cf. P. GIBERT, *Bible, mythes et récits de commencement*, p. 106.

[32] "Contrairement à ce qu'on entend dire parfois, la mort n'est pas ici *conséquence du péché*, mais plus simplement la *limite du châtiment* dû au péché, comme un retour à l'ordre des choses inauguré au début du chapitre 2, lorsque «YHWH Dieu modela l'homme avec la glaise du sol»" (P. GIBERT, *Bible, mythes et récits de commencement*, p. 107). Cf. L.R. BAILEY's brief treatment of the relationship between disobedience and mortality in Gen 2-3 (L.R. BAILEY, *Biblical Perspectives on Death*, Philadelphia: 1979, pp.36-39).

[33] "Der Mensch ist aus Erde geschaffen worden wie der Schöpfungsbericht deutlich sagt (2,7), und muß daher einst wieder zu Erde werden. Es wird ihm damit nicht etwas genommen, was er vorher besessen hätte: eine ursprünglich von Gott geplante Unsterblichkeit des Menschen wird ja nirgends behauptet. Der Mensch ist irdisch und damit sterblich, das wird nüchtern als Faktum hingestellt" (L. WÄCHTER, *Der Tod im Alten Testament*, p. 201).

[34] Cf. R. MARTIN-ACHARD, *De la mort à la résurrection d'après l'Ancien Testament*, Neuchâtel: 1956, p. 23: "...l'auteur fait ici une simple constatation, il n'annonce pas une punition - «il a été tiré de la terre... car il est poussière» (Gen. 3.19b,c); d'autre part s'il peut devenir immortel, c'est qu'il ne l'est pas auparavant (Gen. 3.22s)... Son châtiment ne

Finally, even the expulsion from the Garden, motivated specifically to bar access to the tree of life, cannot be interpreted simply as a punishment of mortality for disobedience[35]. On the contrary, echoing the theme of the search for immortality in the Gilgamesh Epic, the barring from the tree of life is an unequivocal reminder that humans are mortal, "you are dust and to dust you shall return". Mortality cannot be overcome or eliminated by a quasi magical potion. Humans must live out their lives according to the limits and possibilities set by God in creation[36]. The question of immortality becomes an issue in the narrative only from the point of view of disobedience[37]. From the point of view of sin, the human conditions of nudity, limitation, and mortality have taken on a frightening appearance[38]. Without God, humans are left with a hopeless mortality[39].

---

change pas sa nature, mais sa situation, il doit vivre désormais dans un monde hostile, sur un sol maudit (Gen. 3.19a)". See also P. HUMBERT, *Études sur le récit du paradis et de la chute dans la Genèse*, 1940, p. 149.

[35] For a discussion on the two trees in the Garden and the function of the expulsion narrative in its final redaction see C. WESTERMANN, *Genesis 1–11*, pp. 223-225; 271-273. See also L. WÄCHTER, *Der Tod im Alten Testament*, Stuttgart: 1967, pp. 201-203.

[36] It is interesting to draw a comparison between the expulsion from the garden because of Adam and Eve's disobedience and the barring of the Israelites from entering the promised land because of their disobedience (Deut 1:19–4:46). The result of the Israelites' disobedience at Kadesh Barnea was God's sentence that they must wander in the desert, until the generation of disobedience expires. Under Deuteronomistic perspectives, Moses is described as interpreting this experience of wandering in the desert as a precious time for learning obedience and faithfulness to the Lord (Deut 8). The Israelites are to remember that the gift of the Land is purely that of God. It is not through their might or power that they acquire the land. The expulsion from the garden has this similar concrete aspect of expressing the limitation of human beings that cannot be circumvented. As creatures, humans cannot acquire life through their own power or through some external magical power that bypasses their relationship to God, but only in obedience to God.

[37] C. WESTERMANN, *Genesis 1–11*, p. 271; O. KAISER, E. LOHSE, *Tod und Leben*, 1977, p. 18.

[38] "Es kann also keine Rede davon sein, daß der Mensch nach der Meinung des Erzählers unsterblich geschaffen wurde und seine entsprechende Qualität durch den Fall verloren hätte... Durch die Sünde hat der Tod seinen Schrecken bekommen" (O. KAISER, E. LOHSE, *Tod und Leben*, p. 16). Cf. the reflection of X. LÉON-DUFOUR on the understanding of death from the New Testament perspective in *Face à la mort, Jésus et Paul*, Paris: 1979, [trans. T. PRENDERGAST, *Life and death in the New Testament*, San Francisco: 1986]. "From Adam I inherit not only my humanity but also my mortal condition, which is a consequence of sin's entry into the world. In this sense, I am congenitally bound to Adam's sin, but, it must be carefully noted, Adam only opened the door to sin; it was sin that conferred on death its aspect of a violent tearing away" (p. 213-214).

[39] In late Judaism, mortality was attributed to sin, though even among the Amoraim there were exceptions. For references to the rabbinic understanding of the relationship between sin and death see E.E. URBACH, *The Sages: their concepts and beliefs*,

From the synthetic perspective, the purpose and thrust of the
primeval account is to show human destiny to be in harmony with God,
with oneself and with the world. As an intrusion in this destiny lurks the
reality of disharmony and alienation which is brought about from human
disobedience[40]. This setting provides an introduction for the relationship
between Israel and God which likewise is expressed through the
over-arching image of the covenant: the story of God's gift of blessings,
and Israel's disobedience.

How exactly the author of Wis understood the primeval accounts of
creation is not easy to establish, since the allusions to the Gen narratives
are not the central issue of the exhortation. But it should be clear that the
interpretation whereby human mortality is taken as the consequence of
Adam's disobedience is not self evident in Wis. Moreover, the interpretation of the allegorical tradition of Gen as exemplified in PHILO
would certainly have been known to our author. PHILO had interpreted
the death of God's warning precisely as a spiritual death, namely a death
which consists of the disharmony occasioned by separation from God[41].
The two qualifying phrases which restrict the experience of death to the
unjust (1:16d, 2:24b) certainly invite an alternate reflection on the notion
of death within the author's exhortation to love justice and to search for
God.

D-3.2   The restriction of 'death' to the wicked (1:16d, 2:24b)

1:16d - They are worthy to belong to it.

From the context of the exhortation, we have seen how the image of
death introduced in 1:12 ("do not seek out death') functions as the prime

---

Jerusalem: 1975, pp. 421-431. An interesting quote from R. Me'ir records the idea that
even mortality has its positive function and beauty in creation.

"The view of R. Me'ir is an exception. The very style of its transmission by one of the
great Haggadists among the Palestinian Amoraim testifies to its unusual character. 'R.
Samuel bar Nahman said: I was riding on my grandfather's shoulder and going up from
my town to Kefar Hanna by way of Bet Shean, when I heard R. Simeon b. R. Eleazar, as
he was sitting and expounding in the name of R. Me'ir, say: And, behold, it was very
[dam me'od] good — and, behold, death [tôm môt] is good'" (p. 429, see also n. 29,
p. 877).

[40] Cf. C. WESTERMANN, *Genesis 1-11*, pp. 276-277.

[41] For PHILO's explicit distinction on two kinds of death see *Legum Allegoriae* I,
105-108. For PHILO's allegorical elaboration on sin and virtue in the context of the Genesis
narratives see also *Questions on Genesis* Bk I: 6-53, Bk II: 1, 22-57. The points of contact
between PHILO and the Book of Wis are well known; see C. LARCHER, *Études*, c. 5, "Sag. et
Philon d'Alexandrie", pp. 151-178. Even though LARCHER concludes that the Wis author
did not draw on the works of PHILO, he insists that they must come from the same milieu,
drawing on the same traditions while employing different literary styles (*Études*, p. 161).

negative motive for loving justice and seeking God. Death is the antithesis to union with God. As such, it is a negative image which conveys
what is supremely undesirable. At this point in the text, the image is open
to conveying the negativity of physical and spiritual death[42]. In the
ensuing argumentation, the image is qualified with growing intensity as a
reality distant from God and unwilled by God. Finally, in 1:16 the image
is connected solely to the wicked. Since the wicked call upon death with
their deeds and thoughts[43], they are worthy to belong to it.

This final phrase qualifies the notion of death which had been
discussed in the last four verses. It is a death which is in complete
opposition to God and which the wicked bring on themselves through
their injustice. What had been intimated in the introductory phrase of
1:11d, "a lying mouth destroys the person", is clarified with greater
precision. The death that is in opposition to God and the consequence of
wickedness, is the sole property of the wicked, or more precisely, that the
wicked become the property of death. Since mortality is the common
experience of the wicked and just alike, the death the author is concerned
with in this passage is not mortality as such[44]. Rather, this death is the
supreme negative consequence of wickedness, ultimate separation from
God. What is excluded from this death in the qualifying phrase is the
mortality common to the just. But the physical death of the wicked,
which they experience with all the hopeless anguish of their negative
judgment of mortality, is not excluded from their death. The explanation
of the dynamic of the introduction of this ultimate death into life follows
in the subsequent speech of the wicked, which concludes specifically with
the projected infliction of physical death on the just.

2:24b - They experience it who belong to him.

The author employs the same procedure of introducing a qualifying
phrase in the parallel passage of 2:24 to 1:16. The author has presented
ultimate death to be in complete opposition to God. The parallel passage

---

[42] The preceding phrase 1:11d, however, prepares the reader for interpreting the
negative image of death as something much more than physical death, "a lying mouth
destroys the person (ψυχήν)".

[43] There are three possible referents to the four pronouns in 1:16: θάνατος (1:13a),
ᾅδης (1:14d), or the θάνατος of the presumed lost stich supplied by the Vulg (1:15b). The
different possible referents to the pronoun in 1:16d do not change in substance the
qualifying characteristic of the last stich in particular, since all three referents imply the
negative image of death or its synonym Hades.

[44] The fact that mortality does not play a negative role in Wis, contributes to this
distinction the author is implying between the death which is separation from God and
mortality. See particularly the diptychs regarding the mortality of the just (Wis 3-4), and
the mortality described of Solomon (Wis 7:1-14; 9:5-6).

confirms the opposition between God and death by explaining the presence of a death God did not create or intend, a death which has entered the world through the envy of the devil. God has destined humans to life. The qualifying phrase reiterates the experience of this death as belonging solely to the wicked, in this case, to those who belong to the side of the devil. Since this explanation of the origin of death follows the wicked's projected death of the just, it becomes obvious, that the author is constructing a distinction between the death not willed, nor created by God and the mortality common to all.

Just what the relationship between mortality and physical death as punishment consists of in the argumentation of the author remains to be studied. But at this point, what should be clear is that the two qualifying phrases restrict the negative image of death to the sole result of wickedness. It is a death which implies the ultimate antithesis to God brought about by one's thoughts and deeds of injustice.

D-4.   Death in 1:13 and 2:24 interpreted as 'spiritual death'

The specific observation of the qualifying nature of the phrases (1:16d, 2:24b), which limit the punishment and experience of death to the wicked, has elicited the counter interpretation of a 'spiritual' or 'ethical' notion of death. The death that God has not made and the death that the devil's envy has introduced into the cosmos refers to the second death, the inner moral death which leads to a final condemnation which the author describes in apocalyptic language. Such an interpretation accounts for the author's restriction of death to the wicked, and excludes from the scope of the term, death, the mortality of the just.

Numerous exegetes have preferred this solution for the complex notion of death in Wis [45]. For our purpose, it will be enough to review

---

[45] For a list of the main proponents of this interpretation of a spiritual death, one may consult, R.J. TAYLOR, "The Eschatological Meaning of Life and Death in the Book of Wisdom I–V", *ETL* 42 (1966) pp. 102-113. More recent proponents of the spiritual or ethical interpretation include, F. PERRENCHIO, "Struttura e analisi", *Sales* 43 (1981) p. 43; U. OFFERHAUS, *Komposition und Intention*, pp. 232-234. A. SCHMITT denies both the possibility of reducing the meaning of death to its physical aspect and the distinctions between physical and spiritual death by sustaining the meaning of death simply as punishment (Straf-Tod). "Eine Beschränkung auf den biologischen und physischen Aspekt des Todes wird weisheitlichem Denken nicht gerecht. Keine Distinktion zwischen einem leiblichen und seelischen oder einem zeitlichen und ewigen (eschatalogischen) Tod. Der physische Tod und damit ein Zustand ursprünglicher Unsterblichkeit, den der Mensch erst infolge der Sünde verloren haben soll, liegen außerhalb der Betrachtung" (A. SCHMITT, *Das Buch der Weisheit*, Würzburg: 1986, p. 40). In his commentary on Wis 2:23-24, ALONSO SCHÖKEL speaks of a 'definitive death' that the author intends in the

the key arguments proposed by its main proponents in order to note the limits of this solution.

C.L.W. GRIMM in confronting the difficulty of whether or not the wicked are viewed as being destroyed out of existence clarifies the option of understanding death in its ethical sense[46]. As a solution for this difficulty, he points to the juxtaposition of ἀφθαρσία (2:23;6:18) / ἀθανασία (3:4,8,13) to the term, θάνατος. Just as the terms for incorruptibility and immortality refer to the blessedness of the just in relation to God, so too does the term for death relate to the unblessedness of the wicked in their distance from God in Hades. In this way, GRIMM concludes that the notion of death underlying Wis 1-2 must refer to an ethical perspective of death[47]. Death must be viewed as what would later be called 'the second death' (Rev 2:11, 21:8)[48].

Furthermore, for GRIMM, the author's perspective of death combats a dualism which would render matter or the cosmos an inimical force to the spirit and to God. The use of the term, κόσμος (2:24), to denote the locus of the death introduced by the devil is not the world of matter, but the world of human beings. "Dass hier unter κόσμος nicht das Weltganze, sondern die Menschenwelt... zu verstehen sey, erhellt daraus, dass sowohl unmittelbar vorher (Vs.24), als auch im gleich folgenden Gliede von den Menschen die Rede ist[49]." Since the cosmos is wholesome from the beginning, and in the end the cosmos itself will combat against wickedness at the side of God, the death which the wicked call upon themselves and which the devil introduces into the world, refers to the inner death of the soul as GRIMM postulates for 1:13.

---

argumentation as opposed to the death that is a passage to life: "Por todo el contexto se ve que el autor piensa en la muerte definitiva, no en la muerte que da paso a la vida, como es la del justo. La imagen de Dios, no deformada por el pecado, permanece en el hombre como germen de inmortalidad y vence a la muerte física" (L. ALONSO SCHÖKEL, Ecclesiastes y Sabiduría, Madrid: 1974, p. 93).

[46] C.L.W. GRIMM, Das Buch der Weisheit, Leipzig: 1860, pp. 59-61.

[47] "Es ist also θάνατος in den hier in Betracht kommenden Stellen im Wesentlichen dasselbe, was Apok. 2,11. 21,8 δεύτερος θάνατος, in der Kirche mors aeterna... (versteht)" {C.L.W. GRIMM, Das Buch der Weisheit, pp. 60-61}.

[48] For R. SCHÜTZ the author's notion of death is emphatically spiritual. He summarizes the author's view in the following manner: "L'homme seul cause sa mort, car Dieu ne l'a pas fait. En effet, il a tout créé pour que l'homme puisse vivre cette vie opposée à la mort de l'âme. Toutes les créatures du monde sont salutaires, elles aident l'homme à conserver et à développer la vie et, d'autre part, elles ne contiennent rien qui puisse donner la mort spirituelle à l'homme" (R. SCHÜTZ, Les idées eschatologiques du Livre de la Sagesse, Paris-Strasbourg: 1935, p. 56).

[49] C.L.W. GRIMM, Das Buch der Weisheit, pp. 82-83. The author's positive view of creation and cosmos is reiterated in both the introduction to the speech of the wicked (1:14) and in the cosmic judgment (5:20). See R.J. TAYLOR, "The Eschatological Meaning of Life and Death", pp. 108-109, for a discussion on the author's view of the cosmos in light of the intentionality of God at creation.

F.R. TENNANT offers the identical solution of understanding an 'ethical' death for the obscure passage of the apocalyptic judgment against the wicked (4:19). The death that the author describes in Wis 1–2 is not a total annihilation after a final judgment. Rather, "... it is simply what later theology has called 'second death', death in an ethical rather than an ontological sense, supervening immediately on the separation of soul and body[50]." Therefore, TENNANT excludes from the term death employed in 1:13 and 2:24 an understanding of physical death. "Physical death can hardly be present at all to the writer's thoughts. θάνατος here is the deprivation of a blessed immortality."[51]

J.P. WEISENGOFF has offered the most compelling study in defense of the 'spiritual interpretation' of death in Wis. After his exposition of previous explanations of the notion of death in 1:13 and 2:24, WEISENGOFF notes the two possible interpretations: either death means both physical and spiritual death, or death means spiritual death alone[52]. In opting for the latter, WEISENGOFF advances essentially three main arguments.

The first argument refers to the qualifying phrases which restrict the phenomenon of death to the wicked. Since the author reserves death to the wicked as a consequence of their sin, and since physical death is the common lot of both just and unjust, the author must be implying spiritual death. The second argument is drawn from the opposition the author postulates between death and immortality. Since immortality has nothing to do with unending existence of the body, death must be the privation of everlasting blessedness. The third argument for limiting death in Wis 1–2 to spiritual death is the relative non importance that the author attributes to physical death in the ensuing argumentation. The mortality of the just far from being subsumed under the dark image of death is actually presented as God's purification of the just (3:5-6) and as a special divine favor (4:10-14)[53].

---

[50] F.R. TENNANT, "The Teaching of Ecclesiasticus and Wisdom on the Introduction of Sin and Death", *JTS* 2 (1901) p. 217.

[51] F.R. TENNANT, "The Teaching of Ecclesiasticus and Wisdom on the Introduction of Sin and Death", *JTS* 2 (1901) p. 218.

[52] J.P. WEISENGOFF, "Death and Immortality in the Book of Wisdom", *CBQ* 3 (1941) p. 113.

[53] J.J. COLLINS suggests that the author of Wis may be denying the reality of death in the case of the just. He concludes that the author's distinction between appearance and reality leads to an undermining of the significance of appearances. "If physical death is illusory, then there is imminent danger that physical life is illusory too!" This position he attributes to the platonizing tendency of Wis. However, the author does not deny the reality of mortality in the case of the just. This is emphatically the case in the wicked's projection of the death of the just. What the author of Wis adamantly refuses to do is to ascribe the appearance of mortality that the wicked maintain, namely a mortality which

In this way, WEISENGOFF excludes mortality from the notion of death in Wis 1–2. The author of Wis holds that personal wickedness deserves physical death as a punishment, as in the case of the punishment of the Canaanites (12:20) and in the cases of disobedience and sin (10:6-7, 18:12). But the author does not maintain a causal relationship between mortality and sin on the ontological level [54]. As in the case of P. GIBERT, WEISENGOFF claims that for the author physical death is rather the point or limit of maintaining or establishing friendship with God [55].

Though I am in fundamental agreement with the exclusion of mortality from the dark image of death which the author draws in the opening chapters of Wis, such a distinction between physical death and spiritual death does not cover the dynamic between mortality and death which the author subtly has drawn in his argumentation. It is not enough to list the cases in which the author intends physical death or mortality and in which he intends a wider death to understand the author's complex notion of death [56]. In the author's argumentation, the dark image of death, which is in opposition to God, to justice and to immortality, is specifically related to mortality through the wicked's ruminations on their lot and in their projected death of the just. The relation is not one of causality. But the question of their relation needs to be clarified.

D - 5. Death in 1:13 and 2:24 interpreted as both physical and spiritual death

The complexity of the notion of death in Wis does not lend itself to a fine line of demarcation between physical and spiritual death. Though the

---

destroys all meaning and value, to the case of the just. The just are immortal. J.J. COLLINS, "The Root of Immortality: Death in the Context of Jewish Wisdom (Sir WisSol)", *HTR* 71 (1978) pp. 190-192.

[54] In his summary of the author's etiology, WEISENGOFF partially contradicts what he had deduced in the specific case of the relationship between sin and physical death. Since he presumes that the Gen accounts draw a causal connection between mortality and the sin of Adam, he cannot imagine the author not holding such a position. Therefore he concludes that the author understood bodily immortality to have been lost by Adam's sin and blessed immortality to be lost by personal sin. J.P. WEISENGOFF, "Death and Immortality in the Book of Wisdom", *CBQ* 3 (1941) p. 128.

[55] J.P. WEISENGOFF, "Death and Immortality in the Book of Wisdom", *CBQ* 3 (1941) pp. 114-115.

[56] The scholars who subscribe to a distinction between physical death and spiritual death often limit their scope to naming the cases of spiritual death as Wis 1:12-13, 2:24, and physical death as 2:20, 12:20 (G. ZIENER, "Weisheitsbuch und Johannesevangelium", *Bib* 39 (1958) p. 48; C.L.W. GRIMM, *Das Buch der Weisheit*, pp. 60-61).

underlining distinction is necessarily present in the author's argumentation, because of the radical difference of the perspective on death
between the author and the wicked, the author does not draw a clear
distinction through an allocation of different terms. The differences must
be deduced in the mind of the reader through the confrontation of the
qualifying phrases introduced into the argument by the author.

Due to the complex notion of death that presents itself to the reader
in the opening chapters of Wis, several scholars have opted for an
understanding of death that necessarily implies both a physical and
spiritual perspective of death. Even GRIMM who had championed the
'second death' interpretation, asked himself whether or not, or in what
sense physical death is to be included in the author's understanding of
spiritual death [57].

The difference between this latter interpretation and the first which
viewed death primarily as physical death is one of emphasis and
perspective. These scholars view the author's fundamental concern in the
opening chapters as focusing primarily on the ethical or spiritual death
towards which the wicked hurl themselves. Physical death is necessarily a
part of spiritual death because it is a punishment of sin which heads
towards spiritual death. But the author in his argumentation is stressing
the ethical dimension of death [58]. This third position accepts the
fundamental orientation of the spiritual death interpretation, but insists
on a relationship with physical death. The problem is to see how the
author understands their relationship.

A.-M. DUBARLE studied this issue of death in Wis from the
perspective of the biblical development of the theory of original sin [59]. In

---

[57] "Ob und in wie weit in diesem Begriff des θάνατος der leibliche Tod (2,20. 16,13.
18,12.16.20. 19,5), den auch die Gerechten sterben, mit einzuschliessen sey, darüber s. zu
2,24. 3,2" (C.L.W. GRIMM, *Das Buch der Weisheit*, p. 61).

[58] There are various shades of meanings that scholars attach to the relationship they
conceive the author to be holding between physical and spiritual death in cc. 1–2. For an
excellent summary of the development of these positions see R.J. TAYLOR, "The
Eschatological Meaning of Life and Death", pp. 106-116. HEINISCH understood the author
to be primarily concerned with spiritual death and only secondarily with mortality (P.
HEINISCH, *Das Buch der Weisheit*, Münster: 1912, p. 59). BÜCKERS proposes that the author
has taken sin and death together. Physical death is punishment for sin in the present life
and spiritual death is punishment in the next life (H. BÜCKERS, *Die Unsterblichkeitslehre
des Weisheitsbuches*, Münster: 1938, pp. 19-21). HULSBOSCH insists on the semitic character
of the author which would not easily tolerate a dichotomy between a physical and
spiritual death. Personal sins involve the death of the body, but the death the author
intends must be much more, and this death which is more than bodily he calls
eschatological (A. HULSBOSCH, "De eschatologie van het Wijsheidboek", *StudCath* 27
(1952) pp. 118-119).

[59] A.-M. DUBARLE, "Le péché originel dans les livres sapientiaux", *RThom* (1956)
597-619. A.-M. DUBARLE, *Le péché originel dans l'Écriture*, LD 20 (1958).

determining the shades of meaning to be attributed to the author's notion of death, DUBARLE notes the relative non importance of mortality the author holds in relation to the importance of ethical choices for justice and wickedness. The author describes eternal beatitude in spiritual terms: grace, friendship with God, knowledge of truth, peace and kingship (Wis 3–5). DUBARLE concludes that if the author had held that corporal immortality had been lost through the first sin, it is strange that no reference is made to mortality in the latter part of the book where wisdom is said to have protected and saved the first man from his fall (10:1-2)[60]. Furthermore, for the just, mortality is no barrier to beatitude whatsoever. Therefore one cannot affirm that the author drew a causal connection between sin and mortality[61].

But while DUBARLE excludes mortality from the author's notion of death from the point of view of a direct dependence of causality, he does not attribute to the Wis author a rigid distinction between physical and spiritual death. Thus DUBARLE disclaims positions that would call for distinctions between earthly and eschatological punishment for sin, and between physical and spiritual death[62].

This integrating position recognizes a dynamic between mortality and eschatological death at work in Wis, but is at pains to draw the necessary distinctions and relations for intelligibility. DUBARLE appears caught in a dilemma whereby he excludes a causal dependence of mortality on sin from the author's notion of death and at the same time includes mortality in the author's vision of death as punishment.

> La mort n'est pas pour l'auteur de la *Sagesse* le simple fait du décès; ce n'est pas uniquement le malheur terrestre, comme pour un bon nombre de textes prophétiques ou sapientiaux, ce n'est pas uniquement la «seconde

---

[60] "Quoi qu'il en soit, la béatitude éternelle est décrite en termes exclusivement spirituels: grâce et familiarité de Dieu, connaissance de la vérité, paix, royaume. Si l'auteur avait pensé que le premier péché avait fait perdre l'immortalité corporelle, il aurait été normal qu'il montrât comment cet effet désastreux était réparé grâce à la Sagesse: le silence ici ne se comprend pas en dehors d'une certaine indifférence au sort du corps" (A.-M. DUBARLE, *Le péché originel dans l'Écriture*, p. 89).

[61] "... on ne peut affirmer que l'auteur ait mis un lien entre le décès corporel et le péché" (A.-M. DUBARLE, *Le péché originel dans l'Écriture*, p. 90); also: "La conviction manifestée que les hommes sont mortels en vertu de leur descendance du premier homme, formé de terre (7,1), prouverait aussi bien que le premier père était mortel en vertu de son origine terrestre. Rien n'indique que l'auteur pense ici à une mortalité provoquée par le péché" (p. 95).

[62] "Cette mort dont parle notre livre, ce n'est pas la simple dissolution corporelle, commune aux justes et aux pécheurs; ce n'est pas non plus le péché en tant qu'acte libre séparant de Dieu; c'est l'existence douloureuse, honteuse et sans valeur du pécheur... Il n'y a pas lieu de distinguer entre la phase terrestre et la phase eschatologique de ce châtiment: l'auteur les voit en continuité l'une avec l'autre" (A.-M. DUBARLE, *Le péché originel dans l'Écriture*, pp. 89-90).

mort», c'est-à-dire le châtiment eschatologique; c'est, à la fois et dans le prolongement l'un de l'autre, le malheur terrestre et la seconde mort destinés aux pécheurs [63].

In his attempt at reconciling the spiritual and 'nuanced' physical interpretations of death in Wis, LARCHER also proposes a complex notion of death whereby both forms of death interact in the author's single notion of death [64]. To shed light on this interaction between physical and spiritual death, LARCHER proposes the contrast between different positions towards physical death, namely that of the wicked and the author. The wicked recognize only the reality of physical death. The author recognizes in their physical death another death, the privation of divine beatitude [65]. The intermingling of the two notions of death takes place in the contrasting positions between the wicked and the author. For LARCHER the complex notion of death is the continuous relationship between physical death and spiritual death for the wicked:

> "La perspective d'une mort eschatologique prolonge donc la mort physique; ou, si l'on veut, une mort affreuse attend les impies car elle marquera l'entrée dans la Perdition". [66]

However, the same difficulty remains as with DUBARLE. What then is the relationship of the mortality of the just to this complex death? Is mortality to be included in the death that God did not make, which the devil introduced into the cosmos? DUBARLE would exclude it [67]; LARCHER includes it, because of his interpretation of Genesis [68]. The author's treatment of the mortality of the just and of the unnamed Solomon exclude mortality in itself from the realm of the sinister reality of death. But this does not mean there is no relationship between mortality, physical death as punishment and 'true' death, to use LARCHER's term. Nor does this mean that the author's notion of death is emptied of any reference to mortality. The problem is to grasp the relationship the author conceives of this dynamic within the overall argumentation that he constructs.

In a major work which focuses on the notion of the afterlife in Wis, R.J. TAYLOR also dedicates a chapter to the clarification of death within

---

[63] A.-M. DUBARLE, *Le péché originel dans l'Écriture*, p. 90.
[64] C. LARCHER, *Études*, pp. 289-292.
[65] C. LARCHER, *Études*, pp. 289-290.
[66] C. LARCHER, *Études*, p. 290.
[67] A.-M. DUBARLE, *Le péché originel dans l'Écriture*, p. 89.
[68] C. LARCHER, *Études*, p. 287. See also C. LARCHER, *Le Livre de la Sagesse*, pp. 197-198.

the first five chapters of Wis [69]. At the outset, it is clear that TAYLOR also interprets death in Wis as a notion which combines both physical and spiritual death. According to his argument, the complex notion of death certainly cannot be restricted to mortality, since the wicked plan to inflict physical death on the just. Nor should it be limited to an exclusive spiritual dimension, for God inflicts death as a punishment within the latter part of Wis (10:6-7; 12:20; 18:12) [70]. Furthermore, TAYLOR notes the stress of the ethical dimension within the author's notion of death:

> He was showing that life was to be conceived of in terms of moral quality rather than of traditional longevity, and this too must have a bearing surely on what he understands by death (p. 107).

But how exactly the two are related under the one notion of death within the author's argumentation is not so easily decipherable. On the one hand, TAYLOR excludes mortality, the natural condition of human beings, as a condition or state to which the author alludes in the treatment of the negativity of death [71]. On the other hand, physical death is included in the death God did not intend and which was introduced by the devil [72]. Death for the Wis author has two sides of a single coin comprising physical death and the loss of beatitude:

---

[69] The clarification of the notion of death in Wis is preceded by a valuable study of synonymous terms for death in Wis: ἀπωλεία, ἀποκτείνειν, ἐκβάσις, ἔσχατα, ἔξοδος, πορεία, ὄλεθρος, τελευτᾶν, τέλος, τελυτή, θνητός. The term, θάνατος, itself is rarely used in the first part of Wis (4 times), but the idea dominates the section in view of the challenge it poses for the just. R.J. TAYLOR, "The Eschatological Meaning of Life and Death in the Book of Wisdom I-V", *ETL* 42 (1966) pp. 102-106.

[70] "Given the use of *thanatos* in the physical sense which the impious inflict upon the just, it cannot be simply that which the author wishes to explain as coming from the devil" (R.J. TAYLOR, "The Eschatological Meaning of Life and Death", p. 107). "For if, as many commentators say, in 1,16; 2,23, for the interpretation of *thanatos* the author must mean 'spiritual death' as that which the devil brought into the world, for he was perfectly aware that all men alike were subject to physical death, it must be maintained as at least a possibility that he was aware of that too while writing the third part, but yet he still chose to give the traditional Old Testament interpretation of death in that context... However, it scarcely seems necessary to restrict the meaning of death in the first part to a purely spiritual affair, as we shall see below" (p. 103).

[71] "But despite Solomon's mortality he was still capable of being immortal, thanks to Wisdom, which begets justification, which in turn begets immortality; and this latter is the state of 'being close to God', 6:13-19. But in all this there is no affirmation that it is not normal for a man to be mortal. Indeed mortality would seem to define one essential aspect of man, since it was invoked to show that Solomon satisfied that definition" (R.J. TAYLOR, "The Eschatological Meaning of Life and Death", p. 106).

[72] "So we must therefore accept that the reference to death in our present context refers not just to the mere unexpected and retributive physical act of dying. Rather it is a way of speaking about man's final negative dispositions with regard to God: God did not predetermine man's final option against him. He did not force this death on him, a

It seems to us that it is best to think of death as having a twofold aspect
for the Wisdom author, namely that it is a punishment for sin here below
in its physical aspect, and that it is a continuation of that in the next life,
simultaneously involving suffering as well as distance from God (p. 113).

For TAYLOR, as with DUBARLE and LARCHER, it would appear that
the relationship between physical death and spiritual rests in the
retributive function of physical death which is conductive to spiritual
death. And this is certainly an element which stands in great relief in the
author's argumentation. The wicked will experience their own physical
death, as they themselves had described it, in negative terms, and the
ultimate outcome of their life choices will be divine wrath and judgment.
In other words the ultimate death which involves the loss of divine
beatitude does not exclude the experience of physical death as a
punishment and as an entrance into ultimate death.

But then what meaning does the author attribute to the mortality of
the just and of Solomon (Wis 7:1-14, 9:5), and what bearing does this
meaning have on the complex notion of death that the author
conveys [73]? These are questions that remain unanswered even within the
presentation of death as a complex notion with several levels of meaning
for the author of Wis.

D - 6. Conclusion: the distinctions between mortality, physical death as punishment and ultimate death

The various solutions to the author's complex employment of the
notion of death differ primarily in the emphasis placed on a particular
aspect of death: physical death as punishment or the ultimate death that

---

condition which is an alienation from everything which the fullness of life was intended to
be... . Death in the context is a way of talking about the final disposition of not being with
God, and if from the beginning this death was never intended to be, neither was physical
death which is the expression of this alienation, so that every time a man dies, even now,
it can still be regarded as the result of sin, and its punishment, though this is a very
secondary thought on the part of our author" (R.J. TAYLOR, "The Eschatological
Meaning of Life and Death", pp. 107-108).

[73] TAYLOR notes this discrepancy and attributes it to the fact that the author was not
trying to present a consistent thought system. "Thus he did not occupy himself with the
meaning of the actual physical death for the just, which he writes off as a mere semblance
of death" (R.J. TAYLOR, "The Eschatological Meaning of Life and Death", p. 114).
However, if the author held mortality to be a natural human condition which forms a
constitutive part of the human destiny to immortality, then it is possible the author is
drawing a distinction between mortality in general and physical death as a punishment
for sin.

is a privation of divine beatitude. Of course, it is obvious that the author employs the notion of death differently in various contexts, at times intimating mortality, or implying physical death as punishment and at other times denoting a death charged with moral consequences in its contrast to virtue and immortality. All would agree with this observation. The notion of death in Wis is ambiguous and complex. What has not been sufficiently noted, however, is the operative distinction in the author's argumentation between mortality and physical death as punishment. The dynamic of the author's argument presumes such a distinction and even presents their relationship in the reasoning of the wicked [74].

We have noticed that the issue becomes problematic specifically in the more spectacular declarations of the author, where death is said to be radically separated from God and intimately bound to the wicked. These declarations present a novelty; for traditionally the power over death and life is said to belong to God. The problem then revolves around the question as to what aspect of death the author is contrasting to God and attaching to the wicked. To establish the various possibilities, scholars had studied the manner in which the author presents these aspects of death in other contexts in Wis. There is the issue of mortality in general as a normal human condition. There is the issue of physical death as a punishment for wickedness. There is the issue of an ultimate death which signifies an ultimate separation from God and beatitude. All three aspects of death are operative in the author's construction of the argument against the injustice of the wicked. A coherent exposition of the author's understanding of death must take into account the relationship the author draws among all three aspects of death.

The author is working with an ambiguous notion, namely that of death, and prefers to leave it ambiguous within the unfolding of his argumentation. The reason for this ambiguity must be accounted for [75].

---

[74] A. SCHMITT presumes such a distinction in his interpretation of the death brought about by the envy of the devil. "24a meint ebenso wie 1:12,13,16 nicht den physischen Tod, der jeden trifft, nicht nur jene, die sich durch die Sünde auf die Seite des Teufels geschlagen haben, sondern den (Straf-)Tod, den der Mensch aus eigener Schuld über sich bringen kann" (A. SCHMITT, *Das Buch der Weisheit*, Würzburg: 1986, p. 54). Unfortunately, SCHMITT did not explicitly advert to this distinction operative in his interpretation of the verse. To place into relief the underlying distinctions the author draws between mortality, physical death as punishment and ultimate death will be a key to understanding with greater clarity the complex and profound notion of death which is operative in the author's argumentation.

[75] The ambiguity of the notion of death within Wis and specifically within the author's argumentation corresponds in part to the inherent ambiguity in the phenomenology of death. Human reaction to death is ambiguous, to say the least, for death is a notion that covers various strata in human experience. See P. RICŒUR for an interesting treatment of the inherent ambiguity of the human situation in the creation

Perhaps new light can be shed on the author's understanding of death by following the dynamic of the argumentation on death as a whole. We have noted the critical function of death in the author's opening exhortation. Death is the negative motive in the exhortation to justice, which immediately becomes the critical factor in the argument. The author sets out to disprove the serious claims on death of the wicked, and to give answer to the challenge of death imposed on the just. By following the lines of the author's argument I hope to explain with greater clarity the ambiguities of death the author deliberately constructs and the relations among the various components of the ambiguous notion of death: mortality, physical death as punishment, ultimate death.

---

accounts: humans created good and become evil. "This ambiguity, this twofold reference of human 'nature' to its original destination and to radical evil, stands out in high relief in the case of the divine interdiction" (P. Ricœur, *The Symbolism of Evil*, trans. E. Buchanan, Boston: 1970, p. 246). But the reason the author deliberately chose to maintain an ambiguity within the argumentation needs exploring.

Note also the interesting review that J. Ratzinger offers on the reference to Wis 1:13 and to 2:23-24 in *Gaudium et Spes*, art. 18, n. 14 (H. Vorgrimler, ed., *Commentary on the Documents of Vatican II*, vol. 5; "Pastoral Constitution on the Church in the Modern World", Part I, Chapter I, J. Ratzinger, trans. W.J. O'Hara, Freiburg: 1969). After elucidating the ambiguity of death as a natural phenomenon and as an experience of dread, using the categories of existential philosophy, Ratzinger critiques the formulation adopted in the constitution as being somewhat unintelligible to contemporary thought.

"On the basis of this phenomenon of absurdity, shown above all in dread, as well as on that of the difference between authentic and inauthentic life, it would have been possible to make clearer the meaning of the statement which appears rather disconnected in the latter half of the article, to the effect that man would have been immune from bodily death if he had not sinned. This thesis in its classical dogmatic form is scarcely intelligible to present-day thought, but could be made so by means of an existential analysis of the constitutive features of human life which established a distinction between death as a natural phenomenon and death as seen in the personal categories proper to human life" (p. 141).

CHAPTER FIVE

THE AMBIGUITY OF DEATH

E - 1 The Context of Death's Ambiguity

The complexity of the author's notion of death has been underscored throughout the presentation of the various interpretations and views of death proposed by scholars. The image of death in Wis is multi-leveled and viewed from different standpoints, from the wicked and the just. For this reason, the varied image of death lends itself to function as a catalyst for reflection in the author's argumentation. Death, as an object of human fear, is complex and ambiguous in itself according to the reasoning of the author. It is an apt negative image that raises the issue in the opening exhortation to one of universal and capital importance for the reader. Throughout this work a key proposition has been that the dynamic of the author's argument, charged and sustained through a concentrated literary structure, provides the widest context for understanding the intelligibility of death's ambiguity in the author's reasoning. What remains to be done then is to apply the results of the study of the dynamic of the author's argument to the levels and viewpoints of death constructed by the author of Wis.

The context of death's ambiguity in Wis is the dynamic of the extended argument of the author. The author has constructed an argument in the contextual form of a trial scene, which views, analyzes and critiques the reality of mortality and death. The argument as a whole is the locus for comprehending the author's complex and profound psychological understanding of death. The broad lines of the author's argumentation then will be highlighted as a basis for situating the specific meanings and views of death discussed in the argumentation. These broad lines of the argumentation will be presented under two major headings uncovered in the dynamic of the author's argument:

a) the author's refutation of the false reasoning of the wicked (E-2);
b) the unfolding of the argument through the image of the trial scene (E-3).

The nuances of the author's presentation of death throughout the argumentation will then be studied under three sections:

c) perspectives of mortality, physical death as punishment and ultimate
   death (E-4),
d) the relationship among the various aspects of death in the development of the argument (E-5),
e) the reasons for the author's sustaining of a surface ambiguity in the
   argumentation on death (E-6).

Where necessary, confirmation of the specific aspect of death under
discussion in the argumentation in Wis 1–6 will be established from the
author's arguments in other sections of Wis.

E-2   The Author's Refutation of a False Notion of Death

The argument which the author constructs in his analysis of death
begins with the presentation of the negative motive for loving justice and
seeking God — the avoidance of death (Wis 1:12). As a negative motive
in the exhortation, the dissuasion from death is meant ultimately to
engage the reader positively to love justice and to seek God through the
aid of wisdom. Both the opening and closing exhortations (Wis 1; 6)
contain positive counsels to choose the values of justice and wisdom.
However, the positive and enriching attributes of justice and wisdom are
elaborately explored only in the second section of the book, in Wis 6–10,
through the discourse of the unnamed master of wisdom, Solomon. In
the first section (Wis 1–6) the author's argumentation is aimed at
overcoming the prime obstacle to the practice of justice and the search for
God, a collusion with death exemplified in the reasoning of the wicked
that leads to injustice.

The first section of Wis is dominated by the author's analysis of the
source of death in human beings which constitutes a critique of the false
reasoning that ultimately leads to the embracing of this death. Through
the analysis of the false reasoning of the wicked, the argumentation
removes the barrier of a false notion of death which prepares the reader
for the appreciation of justice and wisdom.

The false reasoning of the wicked is conceived as the prime barrier
to justice, to wisdom and to God. The wicked bring onto themselves the
reality of a dark and somber death by their false reasoning on mortality.
Their false notion of death unleashes a dynamic of wickedness that is
the cause of their ultimate death. On the contrary, for our author,
faithfulness to the law leads to a life of virtue which brings one close to
God. Physical death is not the tragic end of a virtuous human existence,
nor are the experiences of suffering and limitations signs of a meaningless life.

E-3 The Analysis of Death through the Image of a Trial

The background image of the trial scene provides a critical context for the author's argumentation that induces the reader to exercise judgment. Throughout the argumentation, the reader is drawn into the discussion to follow the accusation and defense of both the wicked and the author with an eye to distinguishing truth from falsehood, reality from appearance.

What is of capital importance in the trial scene is the interpretation of death on the part of the wicked and that of the author. Death had been introduced by the author as the ultimate negative motive for loving justice and seeking God. This dark image of death is presented as exercising an attractive yet illusory force which conducts human intelligence to a concession ultimately towards injustice (Wis 1:16; 2:24). For this reason, the author dramatizes the function of death in a trial scene in order that it be analyzed from the points of view of truth and falsehood, appearance and reality. The appearance of power and attraction that underlies the reasoning of the wicked which leads to death must be recognized for what it is (a mistaken view of death based on despair) for the author's exhortation to wisdom and justice to take full effect.

To resume the salient points of the background image of the trial scene it will be enough to review the role of the image of death in the unfolding of the argument.

Early in the exhortation, the dark image of death raises the dramatic level of the argument to one of vital importance to the reader. A tension had been drawn between God, justice, wisdom, and the spirit on the one hand and injustice, wickedness, and folly on the other. Death, injustice and wickedness are the antitheses to God, justice and wisdom. The dissuasion from bringing on death both accentuates the tension the author has drawn between goodness and evil and opens the argument to the mystery as to how this death originates for the wicked. The source of the dark reality of death is not to be found in God, but in the false reasoning of the wicked.

The speech of the wicked functions as an eloquent defense of their stance towards life. It is preceded and concluded by the author's comment which asserts the false reasoning of the wicked to be the cause of death. Without trust in God, the wicked are left with a rather nihilistic reflection on life. In their reflections, the wicked view the conditions of their life under the spectrum of mortality. The wicked conclude that this human condition excludes absolute values. Their negative assessment and judgment of mortality in turn unleashes a dynamic of evil which progressively hardens until it culminates in the project to inflict physical death on the one who challenges their positions. The physical death of the just should be self-evident proof of the validity of their own positions. Mortality is the evidence of the wicked for their dismissal of any importance of a divine being or of spiritual values [1].

The author's rebuttal of the wicked's challenge and defense unfolds in four diptychs whereby the entire reasoning process of the wicked is proven false. Each diptych attacks the negative interpretation that the wicked give to human limitations, suffering and mortality. The author's favorable interpretation of the lot of the just who would have been killed attacks directly the wicked's assertion that their project to kill the just one validates their positions. The author's defense of the virtue of the sterile woman and the eunuch counters the wicked's negative assessment of human weakness exemplified in their comments on the just poor, the widow and the aged. Finally the author's praise of the perfected virtue of a youth who has died early counters the wicked's despairing exhortation to youthful pleasures and their negative judgment of mortality. The diptychs refute the entire reasoning of the wicked in the reverse order of their argumentation.

The arguments of the author are subsequently confirmed by a literary 'tour de force'. The author provides a view of the confrontation of the wicked and just in the future judgment, where the blessedness of the just whom the wicked had despised is established for a certainty in the presence of God. This elicits a confession of error among the wicked thereby confirming the author's argumentation. The eloquent description of their consequent state no longer is a mere comment on their human condition, but on their desolate moral condition acquired through an utter lack of virtue. It is an anticipation of the immanent sentence to be pronounced according to the sequence of the trial.

The future confession is followed by the sentencing of God whereby the just are to be rewarded and the wicked are to be destroyed. Though the term death is not employed by the author in the description of the final conflagration, the apocalyptic language of destruction which describes the fate of the wicked in ultimate terms suggests this state to be the death which the wicked have brought on themselves through their false reasoning and wickedness. This is the death the author dissuades the reader from bringing on oneself through false reasoning and injustice.

---

[1] The author introduces the reader to the reasoning of the wicked concretely with their negative reflection on human life. Underlying this negative reflection is the denial of the existence of God. The wicked's reflections could easily be representative of Jewish apostates or also atheists who reject the Jewish law. But the author's purpose of criticizing the wicked's hypothetical position on the human condition is to strengthen the faith of Jews who see their community facing disadvantages, suffering, persecution and even death.

The capital punishment of the wicked is depicted as an ultimate and final separation from God and the cosmos.

The author's argumentation on death through the image of a trial has presented perspectives on death from two points of view, namely from that of the wicked and the author. But these different perspectives on death are not simply different views of a single reality. They are perspectives of different conceptions of death. It is the interaction of distinct notions of death through the sifting of appearances and reality that constitutes the tense conflict within the background image of a trial. Three distinct yet related perceptions of death are operative in the author's argumentation: mortality, physical death as punishment and ultimate death.

E-4 Perspectives on Mortality, Physical Death as Punishment and Ultimate Death

E-4.1 Perceptions of mortality by the wicked and by the author

For the author, the false thinking of the wicked hinges specifically on their misrepresentation of mortality (Wis 2). They judge mortality to be the ultimate and tragic end of human destiny. This judgment is emphatically presented through the transient imagery that describes their negative assessment of the fragility of human life. In their judgment, there is no value capable of evoking belief or faith that provides hope for going beyond the reality of mortality. The human mortal condition is not open to a divine reality but collapses in on itself in death. This is the essential negative consequence of their judgment.

What is implied in this negative judgment is a rejection of hope to find meaning beyond mortality. Their reasoning does not exactly exemplify an objective assessment of the human condition with a view to making the most of life. It is a despairing view of human destiny that elicits a project in life which masks, in so far as possible, the inevitable reality of death[2]. Their judgment on mortality and their ensuing life

---

[2] The reflection of the wicked on their mortality constitutes a judgment that expresses a nihilistic view. It is not as if they tremble before the reality of death. But physical death for the wicked is proof of the meaninglessness of life. The negative assessment of mortality elicits the escape from the void of this meaninglessness into pleasure, power and violence. An interpretation that would suggest the wicked are simply expressing a light attitude towards physical death does not take into consideration the unity of the wicked's speech. What the wicked accept is that mortality is a sign of

project represent various attempts to escape from their meaningless mortality and from its presentient experiences of limitation and suffering.

The refusal of the wicked to accept mortality as a human condition open to divine life or spiritual values is expressed subtly in their unwillingness to name death by its common evocative term. Instead of the common term for death, the wicked employ images that reflect the stark reality of human transience in naturalistic, poetic language. Life is short and bitter, there is no escape from the human end, no one to bring humans back from Hades. Life began as an accidental whim and ends as if it had never been, passing like an extinguished spark, like dissolving air, like a shadow, with no remembrance. The end of humans is sealed and there is no escape (Wis 2:1-5).

The common denominator in all of these images leaves no doubt that human mortality is the subject matter of their reflection. And the negative judgment in this reflection issues in the definitive conclusion that there is no value that can go beyond the turning point of physical death. With the denial of a divine role both in creation and in an ultimate judgment, the wicked are left with a despairing view of their own transient horizon.

The author has conveyed the structure of the wicked's reflection and argument on mortality through an appeal to various philosophical systems. The very mixture of mechanistic creation theories with Epicurean and Stoic reflections reveals that the author is not attacking a particular philosophical school, but rather is tackling a common attitude towards one of the great mysteries of life, the issue of mortality. For the author, a negative judgment on human weakness, suffering and mortality, that does not allow for openness to spiritual values attained through virtue, finally leads to a dynamic of evil that results in ultimate death. Within such a position, mortality itself becomes proof of the validity of its negation of belief and hope in a divine being.

It is important to assess the wicked's reflection of their life situation in light of the project that follows the reflection. The author has formulated the entire speech of the wicked as an articulation of their defense within the sustained metaphor of the trial. It is the entire speech that represents for the author the false reasoning of the wicked. If there is any doubt on whether the wicked judge mortality negatively in their

---

meaninglessness. The tragedy of death for the wicked is proof enough of the correctness of nihilism and the falsity of hope. Against A. SISTI, "Vita e morte nel libro della Sapienza", *BbbOr* 25 (1983) 49-61, "Per gli empi la morte non è un problema e tanto meno un dramma, ma solo un punto di riferimento, da cui prendere orientamento per la propria esistenza" (p.55). See also M. CONTI, "L'umanismo ateo nel libro della Sapienza", *Anton* 49 (1974) 423-447.

ruminations on their lot, their concluding project towards the just renders the subject unambiguous.

The negative judgment of mortality on the part of the wicked is succinctly represented in their final project to inflict a shameful death on the just one. The wicked name death by its common term precisely in their project to eliminate the just one who opposes them (Wis 2:20). They plan to inflict a tragic experience of mortality on one who expresses hope in going beyond death in order to prove the validity of their negative view of mortality. This plan is their justification of the validity of their negative view of mortality and their life project of illusion, power and violence.

The wicked's negative judgment of human life under the spectrum of mortality is also emphasized in their despising of weakness (Wis 2:10-11). They judge weakness to be useless and plan to oppress those who are weak: the just poor, the widow and the aged. Human weaknesses are relative in comparison to the stronger. They are necessarily a reminder of the limitations of human existence which is stamped by mortality, being limited in space and time.

The reasoning of the wicked towards weakness is quite consistent in their negative judgment of mortality. Their appeal to power and might manifests their attempt to escape from the limitations of weakness and mortality. The judgment of a meaningless mortality on the part of the wicked reveals an underlying despair in the ultimate meaning of human life. Their life project is a plan merely to mask their despair of human mortality in the illusion of youthful pleasures, in the appeal to transitory power, and in the plan to inflict violence, as proof of the validity of their position.

The negative judgment of mortality and all its manifestation constitutes the beginning of the dynamic of evil for the wicked. The end of their wickedness concludes with the plan to inflict physical death on the just who opposes their reasoning and positions. Does the author offer any explanation for the origin of their false reasoning that unleashes this dynamic of evil? In the conclusion to the wicked's speech, the author intervenes with the assertion that their wickedness blinded them from perceiving the purposes of God in creation (2:21-23) and that the sinister reality of death entered the cosmos through the envy of the adversary (2:24). If there can be any explanation for their entanglement in false reasoning, it is their lack of faith in God and obedience to the law (2:12-13). They become enmeshed in a vicious circle. The wicked's lack of trust in a divine being confers to mortality its tragic and hopeless reality. In turn, mortality becomes their evidence and proof for denying any positive role to God in the overcoming of mortality and human limitations.

The author presents quite an opposite assessment of mortality with its expressions of suffering and weakness in the lives of the just. The author counters the negative view of mortality advocated by the wicked with the enduring values of virtue exemplified in the just. Mortality is not a tragic end of a virtuous human existence and neither are human weaknesses and deficiencies to be considered the last word for a human being who practices virtue.

The author dedicates the four central diptychs to proving that mortality, human weaknesses and limitations do not destroy the meaning of a virtuous life. The mortality of the just one and of the perfected youth is conceived in relation to God. It is God who purifies and accepts the lives of the just at the time of their departure and passage (Wis 3:6). In the case of the perfected youth, it is God who liberates the youth into union with the divine at the point of physical death. The just's experience of death, which in the eyes of the wicked is conceived as punishment (3:4), is a passage to beatitude. In the case of the just, the experience of mortality is a final self-surrender to God who is faithful in his covenant love (Wis 3:1,9).

Even the constant reminders of our state of mortality, experienced in weaknesses, incompleteness and suffering, are not presented as ultimate tragedies for those who live a virtuous life. The sterile woman, the eunuch and the fruitless will have life because of their virtue. The author has not shrunken aback from transforming traditional biblical images of curse into representations of beatitudes in order to drive home the point that mortality and suffering are not a barrier to eternal life. For the author, suffering, weakness and mortality are aspects of human life that remain within the power of God.

This counter view of mortality is confirmed in the second part of the book, where the author praises the virtues and values of wisdom through the figure of Solomon. Solomon's reflection on his fragile human condition is a counterpoint to the wicked's despairing ruminations on their mortality (Wis 7:1-6). Through the mouthpiece of Solomon, the author presents mortality simply as a human condition that expresses solidarity among humans.

> I also am mortal, like all humans,
> a descendant of the first-formed child of earth...
> there is for all humankind one entrance into life,
> and a common departure (Wis 7:1,6).

There is no breath of despair in the voice of Solomon which articulates this sober assessment of the human condition. On the contrary, this reflection on mortality in Solomon leads directly to an opening up to wisdom and to the divine.

Therefore I prayed, and understanding was given me,
I called upon God, and the spirit of wisdom came to me (Wis 7:7).

This same pattern, where the humble recognition of the fragility and mortality of the human condition leads to an openness to the divine, is repeated in Solomon's famous prayer for wisdom [3].

For I am your slave and the son of your maidservant,
a man who is weak and short-lived, with little understanding
of judgments and laws... (Wis 9:5).

Send her (wisdom) forth from the holy heavens
and from the throne of your glory send her
that she may be with me and toil
and that I may learn what is pleasing to you (Wis 9:10).

For the author, acceptance and recognition of the limitations of human existence in faith lead to an openness to the divine through which immortality is achieved [4]. Mortality is not conceived as a tragic, hopeless and fatalistic condition, as is the case in the reasoning of the wicked. Mortality is the human context from which humans seek the wisdom of God. It is a human condition which specifies concretely the limits from which humans become open to the divine. Accepting one's limitations and mortality implies accepting one's limited condition, shared by all humans — that one is a being created by God ultimately to be realized in union with God [5]. Negatively expressed, the experience of limitations,

---

[3] M. GILBERT, "La structure de la prière de Salomon (Sg 9)", *Bib* 51 (1970) 301-331.

[4] It is Solomon's realization and acceptance of his limitations that leads him to seek the wisdom of God and to pray for knowledge to be able to govern his life. Through unity with the wisdom of God comes immortality. "Because of her I shall have immortality, and leave an everlasting remembrance to those who come after me" (Wis 8:13).

[5] This positive view of the function of mortality in man's relation to God which the author establishes through discourse and imagery has a unique expression in contemporary philosophy and theology. Mortality, in its positive function, has been expressed as a condition for the possibility of human freedom. This is an aspect of mortality which surfaces in the theology of H.U. von BALTHASAR. In one of its aspects, physical death is seen as a constituent which positively opens the horizons of man towards ethical decisions. Being limited in space and time is a condition for the possibility of human freedom. See H.U. von BALTHASAR, *Theodramatik*, "Prolegomena", Vol. I, Einsiedeln: 1973, pp. 350-352; where under the aspect of 'death as a pointer to life' (Deuter des Lebens) BALTHASAR comments on mortality's relation to life. See also *Theodramatik*, "Die Handlung" Vol. III, Einsiedeln: 1980, pp. 455-456, where all seven aspects of death are discussed in a synthetic manner as treated in Vol. I: "Sieben Aspekte des Todes wurden unterschieden und mit Beispielen aus der Dramatik illustriert: Tod als Verhängnis, Tod als Deuter des gelebten Lebens, Tod als Immanenz

suffering and mortality is a constant reminder of the impossibility of completion and perfection without the enduring virtue of justice that leads one to the divine. Positively speaking, mortality is an expression of the human condition which is a constituent of becoming that thrusts humans to extend their horizon outside of themselves to the divine for ultimate completion. It is the rebellion against this meaning of limitation and creatureliness contained in mortality that characterizes the reasoning and decisions of the wicked.

The author of Wis presupposes this positive aspect of mortality, in the assessment of the mortality and suffering of the just [6]. In the specific

---

in allem menschlichen Dasein, Tod als entscheidende Lebenstat, Tod als Sühne, Tod als Ausdruck der Liebe, Tod als Stellvertretung."

The same idea is explicitly treated in *Christlicher Stand*, Einsiedeln: 1977: "Ist es nicht gerade die drängende Endlichkeit seines irdischen Raumes und Horizontes, die heilsame, verborgene Immanenz des Todes in jedem Augenblick seines Lebens, die ihn zur Höhe wahrer Entscheidung und somit zu wahrer Sittlichkeit zwingt? Der Tod erscheint von hier aus wie eine der positiven, gestaltenden Kräfte des irdischen Daseins, eine Macht, die dem irdischen Tun erst sein Ewigkeitsgewicht verleiht (p. 68)."

Even from the side of God in the dialogue with humans, human limitations and suffering are perceived as the forum for communication. In his treatment of the 'perfectibility of man' in *Man in History* (London: 1982), BALTHASAR juxtaposes the christian attitude towards mortality with that of 'the escape through appearance' and with 'the way of the tragic conflict'.

"The decisive difference, however, has still not been mentioned: namely, that the salvation event, by means of which man achieves a redemptive relationship to God, occurs in history, that God does not set a sign or speak a word to man, but uses man in all his existential doubtfulness and fragility and imperfectibility as the language in which he expresses the world of redemptive wholeness. God, therefore, uses existence extended in time as the script in which to write for man and the world the sign of a supratemporal eternity" (p. 63).

A concomitant aspect of death nonetheless renders its presence a dark, and mysterious enigma. For BALTHASAR, death retains an irreducible ambiguity of naturalness and unnaturalness. "Death is neither an external accident, nor is it comprehensible — in its opposition to the sense of life — as a constituent element of being, however desperately one may try to show this" (p. 49).

"So steht Tod zwischen Natur und Unnatur, und zwar unentwirrbar. Alle theologische Versuche, die negative Unnatur des Todes von einer positiven Naturhaftigkeit zu trennen, die dem nicht sündigen «Adam» zugekommen wäre, bleiben in hohem Grade phantastisch" (H.U. von BALTHASAR, *Theodramatik*, III, p. 111).

This remains true for the author of Wis as well. But in Wis the source for the unnaturalness of death is underscored and expressed through the false reasoning of the wicked. The truly tragic and sinister experience of death is intimately bound to the injustice which issues from a praxis that reduces life to an arbitrary nihilism. For the just, the manifestations of mortality are conditions that require the placing of one's hope and trust in God. The just, the sterile woman, the eunuch, the childless, the perfected youth all are described as being faithful in their virtuous lives within the context of the human limitations and mortality they face.

[6] In several studies, Karl RAHNER addresses the theological significance of death as well as the essential characteristics of human freedom. K. RAHNER, "The Dignity and

argumentation of the author, mortality is seen from two opposing perspectives, from that of the wicked and from that of the just. Mortality as such remains inherently ambiguous; it is open to different assessments. For the author, it is a condition from which the just realize their union with God through a virtuous life; for the wicked it is a condition which signifies ultimate meaninglessness.

The author of Wis never explicitly states that mortality is part of the original state of human beings. But neither does the author postulate clearly that it was not. However, the author's positive treatment of the mortality of the just, along with the positive treatment of Solomon's mortality, common to all, renders the former position which suggests an original, harmonious mortal state more consistent with the argumentation of the author.

Freedom of Man", *Theological Investigations*, Vol. 2, pp. 235-263; *On the Theology of Death*, trans. C.H. HENKEY, New York: 1961, [*Zur Theologie des Todes: Mit einem Exkurs über das Martyrium*, Freiburg: 1958]; "The Scandal of Death", *Theological Investigations*, Vol 7, 140-144; "Ideas for a Theology of Death", *Theological Investigations*, Vol. 13, pp. 169-186. Here too, RAHNER speaks of finite, limited being which is open to the transcendent as a condition for the possibility of freedom and hope.

"And so freedom is possible only where there is a transcendental openness to the infinite God, that is to say in the spiritual person. Freedom is self achievement of the person using a finite material, before the infinite God" ("The Dignity and Freedom of Man", *Theological Investigations*, Vol. 2, pp. 246-247).

"We shall now attempt to show that this situation of death constitutes precisely the true and necessary situation of Christian hope. And the first point to emphasize is that the state of hopelessness or (in order to avoid unnecessary verbal conflicts) the radical inescapability of this situation of death constitutes precisely the prior condition which makes hope in the strictly theological sense possible" ("Ideas for a Theology of Death", *Theological Investigations*, Vol. 13, p. 181).

For RAHNER, traditional theology has always maintained a natural aspect of mortality even while emphasizing its radical collusion with sin through the universal reality of original sin.

"It is in fact a doctrine of faith that death is also a natural event, when considered in itself; that is, it is a necessary consequence of the constitution of man as a body and spirit" (K. RAHNER, *On the Theology of Death*, p. 43).

This positive aspect to death does not take away from human mortality its problematic dimension. In so far as it signifies non-being, death remains incomprehensible. But mortality is also in relation to being in so far as it signifies a condition for openness to transcendence. This positive aspect does not neutralize death so as to render it irrelevant to man's spiritual and supernatural existence. On the contrary, the positive aspect of mortality consists in its perennial pointing to the irreducibility of human self-realization to the self. It is a constitutive element of becoming which structurally opens the self to transcendence. Mortality is a constant reminder that self-achievement is impossible exclusively for, by and in the self. And it is this natural aspect that makes it possible for a death to be the supreme act of redemption in the case of Christ and a decisive and ultimate moment of salvation or condemnation in the case of humans (see K. RAHNER, *On the Theology of Death*, pp. 46-54).

The mortality of the just is viewed positively in relation to God as a final moment of self-surrender to the divine. In their false reasoning, mortality is judged by the wicked to be the ultimate, destructive fate of human destiny from which no value can be derived. The ironic twist in the wicked's reasoning, as the author presents it, is that by their own decisions they bring on the very fate which they so much despise and mask. By despising weakness and mortality, the wicked receive the sentence of an ultimate death which is far more tragic than even their original ruminations on their fate suggest [7].

E-4.2 **Physical death as punishment**

On the surface level of the argumentation, physical death is not explicitly developed or elaborated as a punishment for the wicked [8]. Rather it is developed on a secondary level, requiring the deduction on the part of the reader in the flow of the argument. The movement of the author's argument on death stretches from the introduction of the dark image of death in the opening exhortation (1:12) to the punishment and demolition of wickedness through divine judgment of cosmic and apocalyptic proportions (5:17-23).

The death to be avoided and the death which the wicked bring upon themselves through their false reasoning is an ultimate death which denotes their separation from God and the cosmos. Precisely because it is ultimate death which the author judges and presents as the catastrophe to be avoided, physical death as a punishment receives a secondary position. But by secondary I do not intend an idea of less importance. The connection between the sin of the wicked and their punishment is subtly drawn by the author. Physical death as punishment constitutes an aspect of ultimate death.

---

[7] The reason the author makes this rather unique and creative critique of a negative view of mortality can be found in the main purpose of the entire work. If the scope of the work is to bolster the faith of a community under attack, a community that suffers limitations in rights and prestige, then such a critique becomes eminently intelligible. The author is dissuading those in the Jewish community who are drawn to the privileges of the Hellenists by abandoning their faith and tradition. The work bolsters the faith of those who choose to live according to the Law and consequently suffer the ostracism of the powerful. By uncovering the moral shallowness of a judgment and decision that reduce mortality to tragedy and elevate power to an illusory absolute, the author focuses on the heart of the matter within a community under attack.

[8] This has been noted particularly by those who interpret death in Wis primarily as a spiritual death which has a concomitant implication of physical death as punishment.

"... even now, it (physical death) can still be regarded as the result of sin, and its punishment, though this is a very secondary thought on the part of our author" (R.J. TAYLOR, *The Eschatological Meaning of Life and Death*, p.108).

The author inserts a qualifying phrase in the first diptych which refers to the punishment of the wicked. "The godless will receive punishment according to their reasoning" (3:10). The experience of mortality by the wicked will be experienced as a punishment because of their false reasoning[9]. It is on a secondary level of reflection in the author's argument, that the author draws the reader to understand the physical death of the wicked to be a punishment.

What the author establishes in the phrase of 3:10 is the inner connection between the false reasoning of the wicked in which they judge mortality to be a disastrous and final end of human destiny, and their experience of mortality which consequently becomes a disastrous reality. Since the reasoning of the wicked revolves around their negative judgment on their own mortality, they will experience their own death according to their judgment, namely as a punishment and as a tragic entrance to ultimate death.

For the wicked, physical death is experienced as a punishment because they had judged and decided that human mortality destroys any value or meaning for virtuous life. According to the author, they have locked themselves into their own fate. In their ruminations on their destiny during their confession, the wicked depict their futile lives with similar transient imagery as earlier, but the difference is in their lack of virtue. It is their lack of virtue which makes their experience of physical death tragic. Their very rejection of mortality, weakness and suffering renders all of these human experiences tragic. On the contrary, because of their virtue, the just experience physical death as a passage to divine beatitude.

It is in the latter part of the work, in the interpretation of the Exodus event with the digressions on false worship where the author treats the physical death of Israel's enemies explicitly as punishment[10]. And this

---

[9] For the context and interpretation of this explanatory phrase in 3:10 on the punishment of the wicked, see the above section of chapter 3 which treats Wis 3:10-12. This principle contained in 3:10 which enunciates an inner connection between the manner of wickedness and the type of punishment to be experienced becomes a major interpretive principle of the author in developing the punishments of the enemies of Israel in the third section of the book (false worship, 11:16; 12:23; 14:30-31, animal worship of the Egyptians, 15:6,18–16:1; 18:4-5). The connection in the first diptych stresses the *reasoning* of the wicked as an explanation of the punishment. Punishment is not something extraneous to the subject, but bears an inherent connection to the sin of the wicked.

[10] R.J. TAYLOR notes the different contexts for the term, θάνατος, in the first section of Wis (1–2) and in the latter part (12–19). Whereas in the first part, death is viewed with more emphasis on the ultimate quality of alienation from God, in the latter section death is viewed more concretely as a specific punishment for sin (12:20; 16:13; 18:12,16,20; 19:5), with the possible exception of 16:13 where the author simply asserts God's power over life

certainly confirms the author's adherence to a common biblical truth, where physical torment and death may be a punishment for sin. As with the author's critique of the wicked in the first part, physical death as punishment in the midrash on Exodus is strictly linked to wickedness. A difference in the author's presentation of punishment in the latter part is the additional motivation of punishment to elicit conversion (Wis 12:20,26; 16:6).

In the critique of the animal worship of the Egyptians, the author notes how the Egyptians were punished and tormented by animals, as a result of the source of their very sin of animal worship. They deserved death (Wis 12:20) and as a result of resisting conversion during the punishments of torture by such animals which they worshipped, the utmost condemnation is reserved for them (Wis 12:27).

The punishment of physical death for the enemies of the Israelites is developed primarily from the plague of death on the first born inflicted by God through the destroyer in Exodus (Exod 11:4-6; 12:12-13,23,29-30)[11]. The author of Wis emphasizes the connection between the death of the first born of the Egyptians and their killing of the infants of the holy ones (Wis 18:5). The image of the dreadful experience of death among the Egyptians, in slave and master, is presented as punishment and penalty.

> The slave was punished with the same penalty as the master
> and the common man suffered the same loss as the king
> and all together in the one name of death
> they had uncountable corpses (18:11-12).

The destroyer who inflicts the punishment is described as a warrior filling all things with death (18:15).

It is interesting to note how the author attributes death as punishment also to the righteous. The author has been comparing and contrasting the Egyptians and the Israelites in the struggle of the departure from Egypt. In having presented death as punishment for the Egyptians, the author feels compelled to meet a possible objection and recognize the punishment of death among the righteous as well and to explain its difference from that of the Egyptians.

---

and death. For TAYLOR, this in no way supposes a different optic on death from the part of the author if one understands the ultimate death stressed in the first section as being the final outcome of physical death experienced as a punishment. R.J. TAYLOR, *The Eschatological Meaning of Life and Death*, p. 102.

[11] For a thorough study of the employment and development of the last plague in Wis see M. PRIOTTO, *La prima pasqua in Sap 18,5-25*, Bologna: 1987.

"The experience of death (πεῖρα θανάτου) touched also the righteous" (18:20) [12]. The author is referring to the destruction of the rebels of Korah and those who subsequently murmured against Moses and Aaron, all of whom sinned and who experienced death as punishment in the desert (Num 16:25-35, 17:1-15). Physical death as punishment remains connected to wickedness and rebellion. This accounts for the experience of death touching Israel in the desert [13]. But it is precisely as a community that Israel survives, saved by the intercession of Aaron who appeals to the oaths of the covenant promises (Wis 18:21). The Egyptians, in their enmity against the just, experience death as punishment, and this death will be experienced by the wicked among the righteous as well.

A major difference of argumentation between the first and latter sections of Wis is the perspective of the community [14]. In the first part of the work, the author concentrates on the ethical conditions for a blessed immortality and for a tragic ultimate death. These ethical conditions

---

[12] PRIOTTO prefers to understand the phrases, πεῖρα θανάτου (Wis 18:20), and πεῖρα τῆς ὀργῆς (Wis 18:25) as 'the test of death' and 'the test of wrath' rather than 'the experience of death' and 'the experience of wrath' (M. PRIOTTO, *La prima pasqua in Sap 18,5-25*, pp. 180-181, 223-225. Both interpretations of experience and testing are possible given the nuances of the verb, πειράζω (experience - Wis 2:24, 12:26, 19:5, test - 3:5, 11:9). But what is important in the Wis author's argument with the plagues is the quality of punishment that is meant to elicit conversion (as implied in 18:11-12). This nuance of death as punishment is experienced by the righteous, but it was not followed by a definitive judgment against all of Israel because of the intercession of Aaron. What the author highlights in the description of the plague on the Israelites in the desert is the saving quality of Aaron's intercession who appeals to the covenant promises.

[13] The author recognizes and concedes that individuals among the Israelites have sinned. But these individual sins do not destroy the righteousness of those who remain under the bond of the covenant. "For even if we sin we are thine, we acknowledge thy sovereignty, but we will not sin, because we know that we are accounted thine" (15:1-2), (see M. GILBERT, *La critique des dieux*, pp. 181-186). This is the author's manner of handling the objection that surfaces in the contrast of the experience of the holy ones and the Egyptians, when one recognizes that also individuals and groups among the Israelites have suffered death as punishment.

[14] In the first part of Wis, the critical challenge in the trial scene is the prospective death of the single just one. Even though the rebuttal of the author in four diptychs focuses on the situation of the just in general, it is clear that the operative concern is the fate of this individual who represents all those who align themselves with justice (the just, the virtuous sterile, the virtuous youth). This contrast between the individual and the community in apocalyptic presentations is well noted. See J.J. COLLINS, "Apocalyptic Eschatology as the Transcendence of Death", *CBQ* 36 (1974) 21-43. "In classical biblical prophecy the issue had always been the life of the nation. Apocalyptic still deals with a communal context, whether it be the nation or, more often, the just. However, its concern has extended to the life of the individual... It is this hope for the transcendence of death which is the distinctive character of apocalyptic over against prophecy" (p. 30). Cf. R. NORTH, "Prophecy to Apocalyptic via Zachariah", VTSup 22 (1972) 47-71.

remain operative in the interpretation of the exodus event under its communal aspect. Individuals who are disobedient suffer death as punishment.

The Israelites as a community experience an extraordinary salvific event in the exodus while the Egyptians because of their continual rebellion meet ultimate tragedy — a strange death (19:5). Physical death is retained as a punishment for wickedness, an aspect of the ultimate and decisive death which is a final alienation from God [15].

E-4.3 Ultimate death

We have had numerous occasions to encounter this key image of the author in the unfolding of his argument in presenting mortality and physical death as punishment. Early in the opening exhortation, the author creates a tension between wickedness and injustice, on the one hand, and God, wisdom, and justice on the other. The tension comes to its critical point in the presentation of the prime negative motive for loving justice and seeking God, the avoidance of death. The two moments in the author's argument where the concept of ultimate death can be focused are at the beginning and the end of the metaphorical trial scene, namely in the introduction of the dark image of death and in the apocalyptic judgment which presents the alienation from God that the wicked have brought on themselves.

The author presents the dark image of death as the antithesis to the divine. If the divine presents the culmination of blessing for the just, then death as the absence of divine blessing presents the ultimate curse for the wicked.

---

[15] The author does not enter into the discussion of the sinfulness and conversion of the righteous in the first part of the book. A progressive conversion of the just or their growth into unity with the divine is only hinted at in the image of gold being purified in fire (3:6), and the youth perfected in a short time (4:13). The reason for this is understandable given the contrast the author builds between the wicked and just in the scene of a trial. However, the internal connection that the author draws between the wicked's reasoning on mortality and their experience of suffering and mortality as punishment is applicable to the just as well, as in the case of the rebels among the Israelites (Wis 18:20).

In this light, it is interesting to note the reaction to death of the sixth and seventh sons of the faithful mother in 2 Macc 7:18-19, 32-34. They recognize their experience of suffering and physical death as a purifying punishment for their sins even as they place their trust in God's judgment: "For we are suffering because of our own sins. And if our living Lord is angry for a little while, to rebuke and discipline us, he will again be reconciled with his own servants" (2 Macc 7:32-33). This reflection on the part of the righteous sons before their own death would not be foreign to the author of Wis.

In this contrast, death is presented as a state of complete separation from God. God did not intend such death for humans nor delights in such destruction that involves separation from both God and creation (1:13-14). The main reasons for deducing that the death under discussion by the author is much more than the experience of mortality or physical death as punishment is the apocalyptic judgment in which the just are rewarded and the wicked are punished. In this judgment, the ultimate state of death for the wicked is alienation from God and the cosmos and for the just it becomes clear that their physical death is their passage to final beatitude.

The prime elements which constitute the tension are God and death. Union with God is achieved through wisdom and justice, death is brought on through false reasoning and injustice. It is a rather straightforward relational scheme which the author presents at the outset for the setting of his argument. The author works out this tension between God and death for the reader dramatically through the trial scene between the just and the wicked. And this takes place as we have seen under an analysis of the false reasoning of wickedness and in the presentation of the vindication of the virtue of the just.

The author presents the end result of the trial of the wicked with the imagery of an apocalyptic judgment. The wicked are forced to admit to the error of their lives both in their reasoning and in their positions of injustice. The confession is not a sign of conversion. They make no address to the just nor to God. The confession of the wicked simply confirms their incorrect reasoning and the correct reasoning of the author within the metaphor of the trial scene. The imagery of a cosmic judgment adds finality to the state of complete separation between the wicked and the divine. As the forces of the cosmos had been declared to be in relation to the divine, so too do these forces combat with God against the wicked in the ultimate judgment (1:14; 5:17-23). This apocalyptic judgment vindicates the reasoning of the author against the reasoning of the wicked. It is this death the reader is exhorted to avoid through correct reasoning on mortality in the light of faith. The analysis which operated during the trial scene to disprove the wicked's reasoning on mortality and power is to be applied finally to one's concrete life in self-governance (6:1-21).

As was noted during the analysis of the dynamic of the author's argument, the author does not denote with precision his teleological positions regarding the 'where and when' of the survival of the person after physical death. But this does not interfere with the emphasis the author places on avoiding such a negative sentence as ultimate death. In light of the author's reasoning, the ultimate death described through apocalyptic imagery signifies the death that is to be avoided — a death that represents complete separation from God and the cosmos.

Even though this death for the wicked denotes a quality of separation from God that only 'an ultimate judgment' can express, the author acknowledges that it is brought on through concrete judgments and decisions. It exerts its own attractive force to interpret the human condition of mortality as a hopeless and tragic human destiny (1:16; 2:21-24). Death has entered the cosmos through the envy of the adversary, but it is not a constitutive force of the cosmos. This death, which is a separation from God, exerts its power in the lives of humans by provoking a nihilistic view of mortality that issues in a dynamic of evil. The cosmos remains wholesome and creative in defending the cause of the just during life and in the apocalyptic judgment.

Throughout the study of the dynamic of the author's argument and the critique of the interpretations of death, the difficulty of interpreting the dark image of death as human mortality has been touched upon. It may be helpful to summarize the indications the author has formulated in his argumentation to restrict the dark image of death to ultimate death. There are four major reasons within the author's over arching argumentation, that lead to an understanding of ultimate death as the death which God did not make. 1) The death which is introduced as the negative motive for loving justice and seeking God is placed in complete antithesis to God. However, the author presents God as the true protagonist in the mortality experienced by the just (3:1-9) and by the perfected youth (4:13-15). 2) The two phrases which qualify the type of person who brings on this death place the responsibility on the wicked (1:16, 2:24). Such qualifications would be superfluous and inconsistent to the author's argument if mortality had been strictly implied in the dark image of death. 3) The author treats the mortal condition of the just and of Solomon not as punishment but as an indication of the human condition which by its very limitations elicits the desire to seek the aid of God. To include mortality as a human condition that God did not create or intend in the dark image of death hurls against the difficulty of the author's interpretation of the mortal condition of the just and Solomon. 4) It is the wicked's nihilistic judgment on their mortal condition which they deny to be open to a divine being that unleashes their flight to illusion, power and violence; it is not their wickedness, nor the first occurrence of wickedness that causes their mortal condition.

The apocalyptic judgment that represents the ultimate death which the author postulates as the negative motive for loving justice and seeking God is duplicated in the conclusion of the book. The interpretation of the plagues and the crossing of the sea is presented in apocalyptic fashion with the imagery of the changing of the elements [16]. It provides a parallel

---

[16] The idea that the cosmos is inherently fashioned according to the wisdom of God and therefore structurally promotes justice is a unitive principle of the work as a whole. It

in the closing of the book to the apocalyptic judgment against the wicked. The parallel has a way of confirming for the reader the apocalyptic judgment against the wicked. The ultimate judgment against the Egyptians who are presented as an enemy of God and Israel is an expression in Israel's history of the ultimate judgment against wickedness. Through a reflection on history, the reality of an ultimate judgment is confirmed[17].

In his extended contrast of the plagues of the Egyptians to the blessings of the Israelites which lead to the final critical point, the author accentuates the function of punishment to elicit conversion. In this battle against wickedness, the elements of the cosmos are presented as combatting on the side of the Lord in favor of the just.

> For the creation, serving you, its maker,
> exerts itself in punishments over the unrighteous,
> and in kindness relaxes on behalf
> of those who trust in you (Wis 16:24)[18].

The punishments accompany the Egyptians to the bitter end because they do not repent (Wis 12:26; 19:4). The final outcome of the tension

---

is an idea present in all three major parts of Wis. See J.J. COLLINS, "Cosmos and Salvation: Jewish Wisdom and Apocalyptic in the Hellenistic Age", *HR* 17 (1977) 121-142.

"It appears then that the Wisdom of Solomon presents a coherent theology throughout the book. God is encountered through the cosmos, by wisdom. History illustrates the structure of the universe, and eschatology is also built in to that structure. The human way to salvation is by understanding the structure of the universe and adapting to it in righteousness" (p. 128).

[17] In his thorough study of the sixth diptych, Wis 18:5-25, M. PRIOTTO notes the similarity of the vocabulary to denote the destruction of the wicked between 5:17-23 and 18:15-16. For PRIOTTO the author of Wis consciously draws a parallel between the destruction of the wicked and the last plague of the Egyptians in order to highlight the eschatological significance of the judgment.

"Sap 5,17-23 descrive tramite l'immagine tradizionale del guerriero l'intervento risolutore e definitivo di Dio, intervento che provocherà un totale sconvolgimento cosmico e la sconfitta definitiva degli empi. Nella rilettura dell'ultima piaga egiziana lo PseudoSalomone non solo si rifà all'evento storico, ma, tramite l'uso del medesimo vocabolario e della medesima immagine di Sap 5,17-23, invita verosimilmente ad interpretare questo evento storico come segno ed anticipazione del giudizio finale" (M. PRIOTTO, *La prima pasqua in Sap 18,5-25*, pp. 134-135, see also the concluding summary pp. 228-229).

[18] Whereas in the apocalyptic judgment of the wicked (Wis 5) the cosmos is said to combat with God against wickedness, in the final section of the book, the cosmos combats both in favor of the righteous and against the wicked (16:17; 19:6). The reason for this double function of the cosmos in the latter section is the comparison and contrast of the plagues of Egypt and the blessings of Israel. The positive function of the forces of the cosmos in favor of the righteous in the midrash is an expression of the author's assertion in the first section that the forces of the cosmos are wholesome (1:14).

between the Egyptians and God's people is an extraordinary passage for
Israel and a terrible judgment against Egypt.

> ... that your people might experience an extraordinary passage
> and that they might find a strange death (Wis 19:5).

In the descriptions of the judgment against Egypt in favor of the righteous, the author emphasizes the role of the elements of creation. "For the
whole creation in its nature again was fashioned anew" (Wis 19:6). The
Egyptians meet their strange death and the righteous their deliverance.

E-5 The Relationship between Mortality, Physical Death as Punishment and Ultimate Death

The unity of the author's argumentation in Wis 1–6 is sustained on
the formal level through the concentric structure and on the internal level
through the trial structure. These structures underscore the priority given
to the unity of the argument. The reader is led through the complex
reasoning of the author with the aid of such orientation.

What the author is arguing is not obvious, nor simple. The
interaction of appearance and reality in the argumentation emphasizes
differing viewpoints to the single reality of mortality. The main thrust of
the author's exhortation and argument can be summarized in the
following manner. If you want to have life, love justice and seek God. Do
not be led into the illusion of considering human weakness, suffering and
mortality as the annihilators of meaning. On the contrary, it is such a
judgment on the human condition, which deprecates human limitations
and extols power as an illusory escape from such limitations, that
unleashes a life of injustice which destroys the self. The true death to be
avoided as an enemy is not mortality which all human beings experience,
it is the death that results in an ultimate condemnation by God through
the cosmos for injustice and the absence of virtue. Life in God is attained,
despite whatever appearances to the contrary may suggest, through a life
of virtue guided by God's spirit and wisdom.

In the final analysis, the author's line of argument draws a very
definite relation among the three aspects of death presented throughout
the argumentation. The author's explanation of the cause for ultimate
death on the part of the wicked is their false reasoning and injustice.
Though this death exerts an attracting force, it is the wicked who bear
responsibility of bringing it on themselves through their reasoning and
acting. This much is clear from the author's tenacious effort to separate

God from the responsibility of the ultimate death that the author presents as the real enemy to be avoided.

But where the author is particularly creative in the presentation of the source of death is in the explanation of the dynamic of evil. In this explanation of the dynamic of evil converge mortality, physical death as punishment and ultimate death. The source of their evil is traced to the origins of the wicked's false reasoning on human mortality which culminates progressively in the project to inflict physical death on the just. Their false reasoning on mortality, in which the wicked judge physical death to be the ultimate tragedy of human beings, unleashes their escape to illusion through youthful pleasures, through power and through violence. Whereas for the just, their faith in God guides them in a life of virtue that conducts them to a union with the divine which goes beyond their suffering, weaknesses and death.

Therefore, in the author's reasoning, it is not mortality which is the result of wickedness. Rather the opposite is the case. It is the rejection of the limitations implied in mortality which unleashes injustice. Injustice in turn brings on the ultimate death in the apocalyptic judgment according to the scheme of the trial. Though the blatant expression of injustice is manifested finally in the wicked's project to kill the just, the origin of such injustice is traced to the wicked's nihilistic assessment and rejection of mortality. By rejecting weakness and mortality, the wicked are rejecting their limitations, common to all human beings, which orient humans to seek completion in relation to the divine. Solomon's sober reflection on his own weakness constitutes a counterpoint to the negative judgment of mortality by the wicked. Solomon's reflection leads to openness and hope in the divine; the wicked's judgment leads to despair and escape into illusion.

Physical death as punishment remains related to mortality and to ultimate death. But their relationship is rather unique in the author's reasoning. The relationship is subtly implied in the author's assertion during the refutation of the wicked's project that the wicked will be punished according to their reasoning (3:10). The point of this assertion is not simply to predicate punishment of the wicked. It implies that the punishment will have an internal relationship to the source of their wickedness. Since in their reasoning the wicked had pronounced a negative judgment on their mortality, their experience of physical death will bear the characteristics of their fears and rejection. Physical death for them will be a punishment, suffered in despair and hopelessness, just as they had declared mortality to signify. This physical death experienced as a punishment will be the entrance into the ultimate death which signifies complete separation from God in a final judgment.

The author deliberately introduces the negative antithesis to the divine with an ambiguous term, death. It is only after following the author's argumentation that a clarification of the author's concept of death is possible for the reader. Once the relationship between the three aspects of death is apprehended from the author's argumentation, a reassessment and clarification of the opening dramatic phrases on death follows. The death that God did not make and the death which entered the cosmos through the devil's envy does not refer to the human condition of mortality. Rather this antithesis to the divine refers to the ultimate death which separates humans from God. The alienation from God interprets mortality as the despairing destiny of human beings. It renders the experience of mortality as punishment for the wicked. It is this myopic vision of reality which rejects mortality and creatureliness through a flight to illusion, power and violence that is part of the antithesis to the divine. Its end result which renders the experience of creatureliness not as openness to God but as punishment and disaster was never willed by God. It is this death which remains the real enemy to be avoided by loving justice and seeking God, and not the illusory enemy of mortality [19].

E-6   Reasons for the Author's Sustained Ambiguity of Death

One of the reasons for the multiple interpretations of the author's notion of death by scholars is the sustained ambiguity of death on the surface level of the text. An operating principle of interpretation in this study has focused on the importance of the author's argumentation as a whole. The unity of the argument is sustained through the intricate concentric structure and through the recurring image of the trial scene. It

---

[19] The interpretation of several scholars, as we had seen, which includes mortality in the death that God did not make, was motivated primarily to include physical death as punishment. The distinction between mortality and physical death as punishment was not drawn and integrated from the author's argumentation. As a result, the insights the author presents on the source of injustice in the wicked's reasoning and judgment on mortality had been overlooked. It should be noted that such an interpretation which rigorously includes mortality (without drawing the distinction between mortality and physical death as punishment) as the death that God did not make comes dangerously close, at least on the surface, to the very position on mortality the author is severely critiquing. The human experience of limitation, according to the author, which is sublimely represented in mortality is not the tragic destiny of human beings. It is a reality which leads the just to place their trust in God. It spurs Solomon to seek the wisdom that comes from above. Mortality becomes tragic under the lack of vision caused by sin and wickedness which issues in an ultimate death that is the true tragedy the author exhorts the reader to avoid.

is only through an attentive reading and re-reading of the argument in its entirety, which the concentric form and trial scene elicit structurally, that the three aspects of mortality, physical death as punishment and ultimate death emerge with growing clarity.

On the surface level of the text, the author does not draw clear, unequivocal distinctions between the notions of death[20]. This lack of precision through distinctions of terms is partly accounted for by the literary form which does not highlight philosophical accuracy as much as it utilizes a dramatic situation of tension and crisis to unfold an argument.

Nonetheless, the lack of formal distinctions on the various aspects of death that become crucial in the central argument of the text needs to be explained. The author's use of surface ambiguity explains a pedagogical procedure that is consistent with sapiential writing. Through surface ambiguity the author draws the reader into the argumentation of various perspectives on mortality and death according to the ambiguity inherent in the phenomenon of mortality itself.

This creative function of ambiguity as a literary technique has been touched upon in certain literary circles, but has not been greatly developed in biblical criticism or applied to biblical texts[21]. An early advocate of several diverse types of ambiguity was W. Empson who

---

[20] Even though it must be maintained that the author does not denote precise, differentiating terms for mortality, physical death as punishment and ultimate death, it is also true that the term, θάνατος, for the most part, represents death in its dark aspect. A. Schmitt goes so far as to limit the term, θάνατος, to a negative, ethical death.

"Die Tatsache, daß θάνατος als (Straf-)Tod eindeutig negative besetzt ist, zeigt sich darin, daß für die Gerechten dieses Nomen und ebenso ἀποθνῄσκειν (sterben) vermieden werden. Statt dessen Euphemismen: 2,17b; 3,2b.3a; 4,7.10-11.16-17. Nur 2,20 (im Mund der Frevler) und 18,20 (Tod als Strafe für das Murren des Volkes in der Wüste) verwendet Weish θάνατος bezüglich der Gerechten" (A. Schmitt, *Das Buch der Weisheit*, p. 86). But through the employment of the term, θάνατος, for the physical death of the just which is not a punishment (2:20) and also in 16:13 where God is said to have power over life and death, the ambiguity of the term is sustained.

[21] The literary function of ambiguity for eliciting reflection and clarification on the part of the reader has been noted by J.-N. Aletti in a short study of the seduction phraseology in Prov. Aletti recognizes in the confusion the author creates by using the same ambiguous terms in the speech of the seductress and in lady wisdom a deliberate ambiguity that precedes clarification.

"Prov. i 22-23 nous a donc permis de repérer une double opération qui se répète tout au long des neuf chapitres: d'une part un brouillage axiologique repérable grâce à l'usage ambigu d'un certain nombre de termes, d'autre part une clarification et une présentation des vraies valeurs à l'aide d'antithèses lexématique et schématique. Et c'est la répétition de ce phénomène *stylistique* de confusion puis de clarification qui seule permet de comprendre le rapport que le texte fait exister entre séduction et parole et que nous analyserons du point de vue de la connotation." J.-N. Aletti, "Séduction et parole en Proverbes I–IX", *VT* 27 (1977) pp. 133-134.

provided a stock of examples from Classical and English literature[22].
P. RICŒUR had provided a quasi philosophical basis for the function of
the ambiguity of metaphor[23]. L. ALONSO SCHÖKEL has noted the creative
use of paradox, double meaning and ambiguity in a few biblical passages
in order to record the technique in the manual on Hebrew poetics[24].

E - 6.1   The inherent ambiguity of mortality

The ambiguity of death on the surface level of the text, where
mortality, physical death as punishment and ultimate death remain
undifferentiated through a lack of technical terms, reflects the inherent
ambiguity of mortality itself. The author of Wis recognizes and utilizes
this inherent ambiguity of mortality in the different perspectives on
mortality represented by the reasoning of the wicked and the just.
Mortality remains a human condition that is fundamentally open to
different interpretations. It represents for the believing and unbelieving
human being an unknown, a condition that evokes ultimate questions
which need to be resolved. But the manner in which the question of
mortality is resolved has an effect of vital importance according to our
author. If the question of mortality is resolved in faith, it leads to a
virtuous life which is crowned with eternal life. If the question of
mortality is resolved by reducing the meaning of life to nihilism, it leads
to a life of injustice that culminates in ultimate death. The surface
ambiguity of death in the opening exhortation of Wis reconstructs the
ambiguity of death that a person must face in life. The author conducts
the reader through a trial scene that focuses on the meaning of death to
elicit from the reader an understanding of mortality and ultimate death
based on faith, in order to prepare the reader for the contemplation of
the wisdom that comes from God.

Two attitudes which the author relates in the unfolding of his
argument on mortality are despair and trust. The wicked despair in their
own mortality; the just trust in God from within their mortality. As we
have seen, the author unravels the thread which leads from a despair of
mortality to a life of illusion, power, violence and finally to ultimate
death. Whereas a life of trust in God leads to eternal life and immortality.

---

[22] W. EMPSON, *Seven Types of Ambiguity*, New York: 1963.

[23] P. RICŒUR, *La métaphore vive*, Paris: 1975; *The Symbolism of Evil*, trans.
E. BUCHANAN, Boston: 1970; "Biblical Hermeneutics", *Semeia* 4 (1975) 29-145;
"Philosophical Hermeneutics and Theological Hermeneutics", *Studies in Religion/
Sciences Religieuses* 5 (1975) 14-33; "Philosophy and Religious Language", *JR* 54 (1974)
71-85;

[24] L. ALONSO SCHÖKEL, *A Manual of Hebrew Poetics*, Subsidia Biblica 11, Rome:
1988, pp. 161-162, 182-194.

The ambiguity of mortality is compounded by the inclusion of physical death as punishment and ultimate death as final separation from God, both of which are related to the despair of mortality in the wicked.

By presenting a contrast of the effects of these two attitudes to mortality, the author conducts an analysis of the dynamic of evil. The author engages the reader in this analysis with a view to critique what he considers a false view of mortality which leads to an ultimate death. Within the larger spectrum of the general exhortation, the author considers this false view of mortality the main obstacle to loving justice, to seeking God. The critique of the false view of death is the preparation for the eulogy of wisdom and the praise of its positive effects for a full life.

E - 6.2 Ambiguity as a catalyst for reflection

Not only does the surface ambiguity of death correspond to the inherent ambiguity of mortality itself, it also functions as a catalyst for engaging the reader in the difficult argumentation conducted in the trial scene. The reader is addressed as a ruler who judges (Wis 1:1) as one who is to verify the contradicting arguments presented in favor of different positions. But the reader is also addressed as a king (Wis 6:1), as one who governs the self, in order that the analysis of mortality be applied to one's own life.

The surface ambiguity of death in the scene of a trial elicits reflection on the validity of appearances, on the hidden quality of reality, on the results of truth and falsehood. The dissuasion from bringing on death in the opening exhortation (1:12) introduces an image that conjures up an issue of vital importance. Death is an image that is charged with a meaning of finality, whether it refers to mortality, physical death as punishment or ultimate death. By introducing qualifying phrases that delimit the notion of death to a restricted meaning, the author engages the reader in the reflection on the ramifications of ultimate death.

The ambiguity of death is worked over by the author through the image of a trial scene in the analysis of appearances and reality. What appears as death in one case is not death, what appears as life in another is not life. Concretely, in the case of the wicked, their apparent exultation in youthful pleasures, their exercise of power over the weak, their temporal successes are not a sign of true power and life. Their injustice stamps their lives with the seal of God's ultimate judgment. Their temporal success is only an appearance, a futile and transient escape from the mortality they fear. In the case of the just, their physical death through violence or through natural causes and their lack of temporal success are not a sign of death. Their trust in God stamps their mortal lives with the eternity of God's fidelity. Their lack of temporal success is only an appearance in the face of the riches of their virtue.

The effect of the analysis of mortality from the perspective of the wicked and the author has a bearing on the opening dissuasion from death. The author is transferring the fear of natural death to a justified fear of ultimate death. Or, from another point of view, the author is specifying what one should fear exactly regarding the condition of mortality. Not the condition of mortality itself which remains open to eternal life through trust in God's fidelity. Rather, one should fear ultimate death which has its origins in the rejection of the human condition of mortality in despair [25].

The ambiguity surrounding the notion of death accentuates the need for the reader's reflection on appearance and reality, on truth and falsehood. The author's analysis of the origin of ultimate death in the rejection of mortality and creatureliness explains how the wicked's stance towards life shelters only appearances of success. Their adherence to youthful pleasures, to power over the weak and to temporal successes are simply appearances, a momentary escape from the end result of their mortality — ultimate death. The blatant sign of their ultimate death, that unmasks their temporal success as appearance, is their injustice, particularly their violent project to kill the just one. With the reader's appropriation of this dissuasion from bringing on ultimate death through injustice that stems from a false view of mortality, the author then conducts the reader in the second part of Wis to a contemplation of the beauty of God's wisdom in life.

---

[25] The author's analysis of human limitation, weakness and mortality manifests a consistent and intelligible position for a community that is under attack, that feels threatened by the successes of surrounding cultures or communities. In the context of the Jewish community at Alexandria, the author is addressing the community, perhaps the youth of his time, who no doubt are attracted to the successes of Hellenism, culturally and philosophically at the expense of the Jewish tradition which at the time may appear weak and powerless. The author is addressing a root question. What is the significance of human limitations and mortality? What meaning is to be attributed to this human condition? The author attacks a position that interprets human weakness, limitation and ultimately mortality as the final tragic realities of life. On the contrary, the author sustains that it is precisely such a despair in the human condition that elicits an escape to the illusion of success and power which ultimately brings injustice and death. In the first part of Wis the author intricately probes into the dynamic of evil in order to unmask for the reader the facade of a false power that thrives on injustice. Once the tragic mask placed on mortality by the false reasoning of the wicked is lifted, the reader is prepared to appreciate the positive attributes and values of the wisdom that come from God and that are proven in history.

CONCLUSION

Since this work was undertaken with a specific task in mind, it would not be out of order to consider in summary fashion the results of the interpretation of the text of Wis in light of its literary structure. The re-reading of the text with careful attention to its literary unity uncovered the author's sustained employment of a subtle image of a trial. It is not as if this image is perceivable simply in light of the literary structure. But the parallelism of units within the concentric structure encourages a reading and re-reading of the passages with a view to grasp their similarities and differences. Therefore it is the attention the reader pays to the concentric structure that highlights the palpability of images that are presented to induce a concrete effect.

Both the literary unity of the first part of Wis together with the sustained employment of the trial scene point to the importance of grasping the argument that the author unfolds concretely in its unity. What the author argues for in the opening exhortation is by no means simple. For this reason, the author's treatment of death and life has been considered philosophical (B.R. GAVENTA, 1987). But this philosophical discourse of the author on the issue of life and death is not presented through an objective, philosophical discussion. Rather, the author chooses the dramatic background scene of a trial through which to present issues and perspectives of vital importance.

The image of the trial was a felicitous choice for the author's quasi philosophical treatment of death. First of all, by their very nature of assessing culpabibilty and innocence, the proceedings of a trial accommodate the dramatic issues of life and death.

Secondly, since the author's treatment of mortality and death involves misinterpretations that have serious consequences of illusions and injustice, the debate form of sifting the evidence within the trial background accommodates the author's treatment of different perspectives and judgments on mortality.

Thirdly, the author presumes and understands the underlying ambiguity of death. The trial debate accommodates the viewing of events and their interpretations in their ambiguity. The crucial difference between appearances and reality is an issue of importance in a trial. The task at hand in a trial is to go to the heart of the matter and to establish the facts, going beyond appearances and intentionality. The author's argumentation on death in the central diptychs hinges on the motive to reverse the different perspectives on the appearance of human mortality, suffering and limitations in order to establish the truth.

The effect of the author's reasoning throughout the debate is a penetration into the source of a death that is tragic and ultimate. It is not the mortality of a virtuous human existence that constitutes a disastrous and impoverished synthesis of the meaning of human life and death. For the virtuous, mortality is ultimately conceived as a testing and a passage to divine life. The sinister death that the author dissuades the reader from bringing on through folly and injustice is an ultimate separation from both God and the cosmos.

Ironically, this ultimate death originates in the very negative judgment and nihilistic assessment of the condition of human mortality. Such nihilism unleashes an escape to illusion, power and violence that leaves in its wake the victims of its reasoning. Mortality is not the result of sin. It is sin and folly that views the condition of mortality as absolutely tragic. Such a position towards life envisages a justification of its own tragic view of suffering and mortality in its perpetration of violence through power. For the author, ultimate death is the result of rejecting the human condition of limitations and weakness that ultimately and foundationally are constituted for a total surrender to God in life as exemplified in the lives of the virtuous.

The author sustains an operative function of death's ambiguity throughout the argumentation. The ambiguity of death stems from two different perspectives regarding the understanding of mortality. This first level of ambiguity constitutes a phenomenological source, for the reality of physical death is open to diverse interpretations and attitudes. It solicits a response on the part of each individual. A second level of ambiguity arises from the author's own employment of the terms for death with different connotations, namely that of mortality, physical death as punishment and ultimate death.

There are two responses that the ambiguity of death evokes in the unfolding of the author's argumentation. The natural fear of physical death is transferred in the course of the argument to a fear of ultimate death. This ultimate death is the real negative motive the author presents for mobilizing the reader's attention to love justice and to seek God.

Secondly the metaphor of the trial scene explains the author's pedagogical reason for sustaining a surface ambiguity of death. The surface ambiguity within the sustained image of a trial challenges the reader to look behind the appearances of physical death. The exhortation is constructed with the metaphor of a trial scene in order to lead the reader into a critical examination of the negative force that hinders loving justice and seeking God — a fear and rejection of mortality that leads to ultimate death, the privation of divine life. The reality of ultimate death casts a shadow that deceives humans to fear mortality by escaping into illusion, power and violence. The author constructs the argument to free the reader from this false view of mortality and to promote a vision of life rooted in a trust in God.

By engaging the reader as a judge who follows the proceedings of a trial in order to arrive at a judgment, the author draws the reader into a critical examination of a fundamental and crucial issue. Once the reader appropriates the author's insight into the illusion of injustice built on a decision that views mortality as nihilistic, the author then leads the reader into an appreciation of the practical values and aesthetic beauty of the wisdom that comes from God.

There is a minimal effect that I hope the results of this study will bring to bear on exegetical and theological scholarship regarding Wis. This effect is to question critically the reduction that has often been made of the author's memorial citations on death as referring to the idea of mortality being the result of sin. The author is far from referring to mortality as a human condition when commenting on 'the death that God did not make' and when stating that 'through envy of the adversary death has entered the cosmos'. This death, on the contrary, refers to mortality experienced as punishment by the unjust precisely because of their rejection of human limitations as tragic. This experience of death constitutes an ultimate death. For the author, its presence in the cosmos is one of deceiving humans to despair in their mortality, to blind them from the truth that their creatureliness ultimately and foundationally is open to immortality in relation to God.

But beyond this minimal effect, there are three areas in contemporary theology where the Wis author's rather unique treatment of death may contribute to the discussion of significant issues.

1) The author's presentation of the reasoning of the defendants of injustice offers a unique view of the dynamic of evil. The power and subtlety of the dynamic consists in the fact that it originates innocuously in what appears as a sober assessment of life, but progressively leads to tragic, self-justifying violence. The origin of ultimate and tragic injustice lies in the rejection of mortality as a constituent of becoming and as a sign of creatureliness. Life positions that follow from such a radical negative judgment issue in an attempt to escape from the presentient manifestations of mortality into illusion, into power over others, and finally into the self-justifying position of violence. The underlying motive throughout this dynamic is a despair in the self which is tragically manifested in blatant injustice.

Does this presentation of the dynamic of evil not echo the denial of death which Ernest BECKER catalogued in his psycho-philosophical analysis of Western culture (E. BECKER, *The Denial of Death*, New York: 1973)? With a critical eye, BECKER analyzes the manners in which Western societies deny the reality of death, ranging from philosophical positions to funeral rites. The analysis had a tremendous popular success, for it charts the process within a concrete stance towards life that attempts to avoid the reality of the final void towards which human life precipitates [1].

But the analysis remains undifferentiated. No functional distinction is offered between authentic transcendence of death and unauthentic escaping from death. Ultimately, BECKER's analysis leaves one with the impression that any position whatsoever, even one which attempts to postulate a hope of transcending death, is precluded to be an escape from the void of death. The Wis author's analysis of the dynamic of evil presents a distinction between an unauthentic denial of death and an authentic transcendence of death which accepts the condition of creatureliness in relation to God [2].

2) A corollary to the author's analysis of the dynamic of evil is the implication of a positive aspect to mortality as being a constitutive element of common humanity. Human finitude is a constituent that orients the person to seek realization beyond the self. The virtuous life, according to the author of Wis, seeks to transcend the limitations of human existence specifically in the recognition of one's completion and realization in God achieved through the practice of virtue.

This positive view of the condition of mortality has not been sufficiently integrated in contemporary Christian theology. G. MARTELET recently has noted the urgent need to integrate this positive perspective of mortality, human finitude and creatureliness, in Christian theology. The lack of such a re-integration could have the serious consequence of rendering ineffective to our contemporaries the Christian comprehension and understanding of human life and death [3]. The Wis author's triple

---

[1] In a rather short span of time, considering the complexity and extent of the argument, BECKER published a series of works that review the nature of human beings from a psychological point of view. The idea of escaping or avoiding the void of human existence takes on the quality of an interpretive key in this philosophy. E. BECKER, *The Revolution in Psychiatry, the new understanding of Man*, New York: 1974; *Angel in Armor, a post-freudian perspective on the nature of man*, New York: 1975; *Escape from Evil*, New York: 1975.

[2] H.U. von BALTHASAR treats philosophical and religious attempts to overcome the reality of death that flounder in unauthenticity as opposed to authentic transcendence (see *Man in History: a theological study*, London: 1968,1982, "The Perfectibility of Man", pp. 43-72).

[3] MARTELET stresses the importance of reviewing the formulation of Christian anthropology in light of the immersion of our societies in the technical sciences

distinction between mortality, physical death as punishment and ultimate death provides a biblical perspective for viewing and assessing a positive view of human finitude in distinction to the tragedy of injustice.

3) Finally, both the dynamic of evil and the perspective of a human finitude open to immortality, as presented by the author of Wis, contain important psychological clues as to why the death of Christ has the extraordinary force to free humans from the power of death. How is it that a tragic death, even that of the Son of God, can save and liberate a person? The juridical overtones within a theology of redemption do not exhaust the expressions of the liberating powers of Christ's sacrificial act.

The power of death, in the case of the defendants of injustice in Wis, stems from the assessment and judgment that human mortality is the tragic end of human life. It is the deceiving quality of such a position that reduces human life to despair. As a self-evident proof of their position, they plan to inflict this disastrous expression of mortality on one who expresses hope of life beyond human limitations. The confrontation of the blessedness of the just and the wicked elicits an unmasking of the entire dynamic of evil among the defendants.

There are analogies that can be drawn between the context of the projected death of the just in Wis and the death of Christ in the NT. An obvious difference between the two is the salvific motivation in the death of Christ. What does it mean that Christ *freely* took on the subjection to a shameful death that was being imposed upon him to destroy his presence and the presence of his word? The resurrection of Christ, in light

---

(G. MARTELET, *Libre réponse à un scandale*, Paris: 1986). This short, impressive work constitutes an attempt to integrate the positive quality of human finitude within the larger perspective of Christian anthropology. Two quotations from the 'avant-propos' and the 'introduction' will suffice to note the urgency MARTELET postulates for a re-integration of the positive aspect of human finitude in Christian theology. Biblical exegesis must play a crucial role in such an integration.

"Il faut réinterpréter la Genèse, l'Epître aux Romains, le concile de Trente, sans les fausser bien sûr, mais en tenant compte exact des données de la science concernant l'évolution, la paléontologie, la préhistoire, la naturalité de la mort. Ce dernier point est capital et fort peu intégré encore par la théologie. C'est un fait pourtant: la mort appartient par essence à la vie. Point n'est donc besoin du péché pour expliquer que vivre et mourir ne font qu'un. Il est donc aussi impensable que la Bible ignore ou nie un tel fait" (p. 5).

"Alors que l'exégèse, tardivement d'ailleurs, ne s'est pas sentie obligée de soutenir le caractère historique des onze premiers chapitres de la Genèse, la dogmatique, celle de la création de l'homme, et du péché originel notamment, ne semble pas avoir compris dans son ensemble le défi que lui lance la science des origines de l'homme; du moins le grand public chrétien n'en a-t-il pas senti encore tous les effets. Cette quasi-surdité ou ce retard à intégrer ce qu'un enfant apprend désormais dès l'éveil scolaire de son intelligence ont eu des conséquences graves" (p. 7).

of the giving up of his life, unmasks the dynamic of evil that everyone shares when they reject the finitude of human existence as being ultimately condemned to tragedy and despair. The power of the free death of Christ is two-fold. On the one hand, Christ's death becomes a spoken word that unmasks the lie of reducing the meaning of human life to a tragic judgment on finitude. At the same time, because of Christ's free acceptance of the test, it becomes a personal word of forgiveness for the infliction of a tragic and unjust test of death. On the other hand, the death and resurrection of Christ becomes a restoring word of salvation by its manifestation of the openness of human finitude to the embracing of divine transcendence. The death of Christ can liberate humans from the lie of a rejection of human limitations and can restore the hope of transcendence for those created in the image and likeness of God.

BIBLIOGRAPHY

For a detailed bibliography on the Book of Wisdom from commentaries to articles published up to 1982, compiled by Maurice GILBERT, one may consult C. LARCHER, *Le Livre de la Sagesse ou la Sagesse de Salomon*, Paris: 1983, pp. 11-48.

Entries for this bibliography are extended up to 1984 in M. GILBERT, "Sagesse de Salomon (ou livre de la Sagesse)", *DBS* 11 (1986) cols. 114-119.

SELECTED BIBLIOGRAPHY ON THE BOOK OF WISDOM

M. ADINOLFI, "Il messianismo di Sap 2,12-30", *AttiSettBibl* 18 [1964], Brescia: 1966, 205-217.

L. ALONSO SCHÖKEL, *Ecclesiastes y Sabiduría, Los Libros Sagrados*, 17, Madrid: 1974.

Y. AMIR, "The Figure of Death in the 'Book of Wisdom'", *JJS* 30 (1979) 154-178.

Y. AMIR, "The Wisdom of Solomon and the Literature of Qumran", [Proceedings of the Sixth World Congress of Jewish Studies, Vol. III, Jerusalem, 1977] 329-335.

D. BARSOTTI, *Meditazione sul Libro della Sapienza, Bibbia e Liturgia* 18, Brescia: 1976.

A. BARUCQ, "La gloire des justes (Sg 3,1-9)", [*AS* 96, Paris: 1967] 7-17.

P. BEAUCHAMP, "Le salut corporel des justes et la conclusion du livre de la Sagesse", *Bib* 45 (1964).

P. BIZZETI, *Il Libro della Sapienza*, SRivB 11, Brescia: 1984.

BONAVENTURE, *Commentarius in librum Sapientiae*, [Opera Omnia I-X, ed. Quaracchi, 1893] VI, 139-171.

S. BRETON, "¿Libro de la Sabiduría o Libro de la Justicia? El tema de la justicia en la interpretación del Libro de la Sabiduría", *CuadBíbl* 1 (1978) 77-104.

H. BÜCKERS, *Die Unsterblichkeitslehre des Weisheitsbuches*, Münster: 1938.

B. CELADA, "El libro de la Sabiduría, recuperado para la causa de la justicia", *CuBibl* 37 (1980) 43-55.

J.J. COLLINS, "Jewish Apocalyptic against its Hellenistic Near Eastern Environment", *BASOR* 222 (1975) 27-36.

J.J. COLLINS, "The Root of Immortality: Death in the Context of Jewish Wisdom (Sir WisSol)", *HTR* 71 (1978) 177-192.

M. CONTI, "L'umanismo aeo nel libro della Sapienza", *Anton* 49 (1974) 423-447.

R. CORNELY, *Commentarius in librum Sapientiae*, published posthumously by F. ZORELL, *Cursus Scripturae Sacrae*, VT II, V, Paris: 1910.

W.J. DEANE, *The Book of Wisdom*, Oxford: 1881.

M. DELCOR, "L'immortalité de l'âme dans le Livre de la Sagesse et dans les documents de Qumrân", *NRT* 77 (1955) 614-630.

É. Des Places, "Le Livre de la Sagesse et les influences grecques", *Bib* 50 (1969) 536-542.

A.A. Di Lella, "Conservative and Progressive Theology: Sirach and Wisdom", *CBQ* 28 (1966) 139-154, also in *Studies in Ancient Israelite Wisdom*, ed. J.L. Crenshaw, New York: 1976, 401-416.

A.-M. Dubarle, "La tentation diabolique dans le Livre de la Sagesse (2,24)", [Mélanges E. Tisserant, I, Rome: 1964] 187-195.

A.-M. Dubarle, "Le péché originel dans les livres sapientiaux", *RThom* (1956) 597-619.

W. Dulière, "Antinoüs et le livre de la Sagesse", *ZRGG* 11 (1959) 201-227.

A. Dupont-Sommer, "Les «impies» du Livre de la Sagesse ne sont-ils pas des Épicuriens?", *RHR* 111 (1935) 90-109.

F. Feldmann, *Das Buch der Weisheit*, HS VI, 4, Bonn: 1926.

J. Fichtner, *Weisheit Salomos*, HAT II, 6, Tübingen: 1938.

F. Focke, "Synkrisis", *Hermes* 58 (1923) 327-368.

F. Focke, *Die Entstehung der Weisheit Salomos. Ein Beitrag zur Geschichte des jüdischen Hellenismus*, FRLANT, n.s.5, Göttingen: 1913.

E. Gärtner, *Komposition und Wortwahl des Buches der Weisheit*, Schriften der Lehranstalt für die Wissenschaft des Judentums II, 2-4, Berlin: 1912.

B.R. Gaventa, "The Rhetoric of Death in the Wisdom of Solomon and the Letters of Paul", [K.G. Hoglund, E.F. Huwiler, J.T. Glass, R.W. Lee, eds., *The Listening Heart*, JSOTSupS 58 1987, in honor of Roland E. Murphy] 127-145.

A. Gelin, *Les idées maîtresses de l'Ancien Testament*, LD 2, Paris: 1959.

D. Georgi, *Weisheit Salomos*, (*Jüdische Schriften aus hellenistisch-römischer Zeit*, III, 4, pp. 391-478), Gütersloh: 1980.

M. Gilbert, "Gn 1–3 dans le livre de la Sagesse", [*La Création dans l'Orient ancien*, LD 127 (1987)] 323-344.

M. Gilbert, "Il cosmo secondo il Libro della Sapienza", [*Il cosmo nella Bibbia*, ed. G. De Gennaro, Napoli: 1980] 189-199.

M. Gilbert, "Il giusto sofferente di Sap 2:12-20", [*L'antico testamento interpretato dal nuovo: il messia*, ed. G. De Gennaro, Napoli: 1985,] 193-218.

M. Gilbert, "L'adresse à Dieu dans l'anamnèse hymnique de l'Exode", [*El misterio*, Fest. L. Alonso Schökel, 1983]. M. Gilbert, "La figure de Salomon en Sg 7-9", [*Études sur le Judaïsme Hellénistique*. LD 119 [1984] 225-250.

M. Gilbert, "La nuit pascale Sg 18,6-9", *AS* 50 (1974) 52-57.

M. Gilbert, "La structure de la prière de Salomon (Sg 9)", *Bib* 51 (1970) 301-331.

M. Gilbert, "Le juste traqué (Sg 2,12.17-20)", *AS* 56 (1974) 30-35.

M. Gilbert, "Sagesse de Salomon (ou Livre de la Sagesse)", *DBS* 11 (1986) cols. 58-119.

M. Gilbert, *La critique des dieux*, AnBib 53, Rome: 1973.

A.T.S. Goodrick, *The Book of Wisdom*, The Oxford Church Bible Commentary, London: 1913.

P. Grelot, "L'Eschatologie de la Sagesse et les apocalypses juives", [*À la rencontre de Dieu*, Mém. A. Gelin, Le Puy, 1961] 165-178; [*De la mort à la vie éternelle*, LD 67, 1971] 187-199.

C.L.W. GRIMM, *Das Buch der Weisheit, Kurzegefasstes exegetisches Handbuch zu den Apokryphen des Alten Testaments VI*, Leipzig: 1860.

I. HEINEMANN, "Synkrisis oder äußere Analogie", *TZ* 5 (1948) 241-252.

P. HEINISCH, *Das Buch der Weisheit*, Münster: 1912.

S. HOLMES, "Wisdom of Solomon", [R.H. CHARLES, ed. *The Apocrypha and Pseudepigrapha of the Old Testament*, I, Oxford: 1913] 518-568.

A. HULSBOSCH, "De Eschatologie van het Boek der Wijsheid", *StudCath* 27 (1952) 113-123.

A.-M. LA BONNARDIÈRE, "Le «juste» défié par les impies (Sap 2,12-21) dans la tradition patristique africaine", [*La Bible et les Pères*, ed. A. BENOIT, Paris: 1971] 161-186.

M.J. LAGRANGE, "Le Livre de la Sagesse, sa doctrine des fins dernières", *RB* 4 (1907) 85-104.

C. LARCHER, *Études sur le Livre de la Sagesse*, Paris: 1969.

C. LARCHER, *Le Livre de la Sagesse ou la Sagesse de Salomon*, vol. 1-3, ÉtBN 1,3,5, Paris: 1983-1985.

W.H.A LEAROYD, "The Envy of the Devil in Wisdom 2,24", *ExpTim* 51 (1939-1940) 154-178.

I. LORINUS, *Commentarius in Librum Sapientiae*, Lyon: 1607.

F. LUCIANI, "Il significato di *teleo* in Sap 4,16", *BbbOr* 20 (1978) 183-188.

S. LYONNET, "Le sens de *peirazein* en Sap 2,24 et la doctrine du péché originel", *Bib* 39 (1958) 27-36.

L. MARIÈS, "Remarques sur la forme poétique du livre de la Sagesse (1:1-9:17)", *RB* 5 (1908) 251-257.

L. MARIÈS, "Rythmes quantitatifs dans Le Livre de la Sagesse", *CRAI*, 1935, pp. 104-117.

A. MATTIOLI, "Felicità e virtù. La dottrina della Sapienza nel brano macarico per le sterili e gli eunuchi (Sap 3,13-4,6)", [Gesù Apostolo e Sommo Sacerdote. In Memoria di P.T. BALLARINI, Casale: 1984] 23-49, reprinted in "Possibilità sia per le sterili che gli eunuchi di essere pienamente felici", [*Le realtà sessuali nella Bibbia*, Casale Monferrato: 1987] 189-204.

R.E. MURPHY, "«To Know Your Might is the Root of Immortality» (Wisd 15,3)", *CBQ* 25 (1963) 88-93.

U. OFFERHAUS, *Komposition und Intention der Sapientia Salomonis*, Diss. Bonn 1981.

A. PELLETIER, "Ce n'est pas la Sagesse mais le Dieu sauveur qui aime l'humanité", *RB* 87 (1980) 397-403.

F. PERRENCHIO, "Struttura e analisi letteraria di Sapienza 1,1-15", *Sales* 37 (1975) 289-325.

F. PERRENCHIO, "Struttura e analisi letteraria di Sapienza 1,16–2,24 e 5,1-23", *Sales* 43 (1981) 3-43.

M. PHILONENKO, "Le Maître de justice et la Sagesse de Salomon", *TZ* 14 (1958) 81-88.

M. PRIOTTO, *La prima pasqua in Sap 18,5-25*, SRivB, 15, Bologna: 1987.

J.M. REESE, "Can Paul Ricœur's Method Contribute to Interpreting the Book of Wisdom?", [*La Sagesse de l'Ancien Testament*, BETL 51 ed. M. GILBERT, Louvain-Gembloux: 1979] 384-396.

J.M. Reese, "Plan and Structure in the Book of Wisdom", *CBQ* 27 (1965) 391-399.

J.M. Reese, *Hellenistic Influence on the Book of Wisdom and its Consequences*, AnBib 41, Rome: 1970.

G. Scarpat, "La morte seconda e la duplice morte", *Paideia*, 42 (1987) 55-62.

G. Scarpat, "Note a tre passi della Sapienza (Sap 2,16; 2,24; 4,19)", [*Testimonium*, Fest. V. Dupont, 1985] 453-464.

G. Scarpat, "Una speranza piena di immortalità (Sap 3,4)", *RivB* 36 (1988) 487-494.

J. Schaberg, "Major Midrashic Traditions in Wisdom 1,1–6,25", *JSJ* 13 (1982) 75-101.

A. Schmitt, *Das Buch der Weisheit*, Würzburg: 1986.

R. Schütz, *Les idées eschatologiques du Livre de la Sagesse*, Paris-Strasbourg: 1935.

A. Sisti, "La figura del giusto perseguitato in Sap 2,12-20", *BbbOr* 19 (1977) 129-144.

A. Sisti, "La morte prematura in Sap. 4,7-17", *RivB* 31 (1983) 129-146.

A. Sisti, "Vita e morte nel libro della Sapienza", *BbbOr* 25 (1983) 49-61.

P.W. Skehan, "Isaiah and the Teaching of the Book of Wisdom", *CBQ* 2 (1940) 289-299.

P.W. Skehan, "Text and Structure of the Book of Wisdom", *Traditio* 3 (1945) 1-12.

E. Stein, "Ein jüdisch-hellenistischer Midrasch über den Auszug aus Ägypten", *MGWJ* 78 (1934) 558-575.

M.J. Suggs, "Wisdom of Solomon II, 10-V: A Homily Based on the Fourth Servant Song", *JBL* 76 (1957) 26-33.

R.J. Taylor, "The Eschatological Meaning of Life and Death in the Book of Wisdom I–V", *ETL* 42 (1966) 72-137.

F.R. Tennant, "The Teaching of Ecclesiasticus and Wisdom on the Introduction of Sin and Death", *JTS* 6 (1905) 232-237; see also *JTS* 2 (1901) 207-223.

H.ST.J. Thackeray, "Rhythm in the Book of Wisdom", *JTS* 6 (1905) 232-237.

J. Vílchez, "El binomio justicia-injusticia en el Libro de la Sabiduría", *CuadBibl* 7 (1981) 1-16.

W. Weber, "Die Composition der Weisheit Salomos", *ZWT* 47 (1904) 145-169.

W. Weber, "Die Unsterblichkeit der Weisheit Salomos", *ZWT* 48 (1905) 409-444.

J.P. Weisengoff, "Death and Immortality in the Book of Wisdom", *CBQ* 3 (1941) 104-133.

J.P. Weisengoff, "The Impious in Wisdom 2", *CBQ* 11 (1949) 40-65.

D. Winston, *The Wisdom of Solomon*, AnchorB 43, New York: 1979.

A.G. Wright, "Numerical Patterns in the Book of Wisdom", *CBQ* 29 (1967) 524-538.

A.G. Wright, "The Structure of the Book of Wisdom", *Bib* 48 (1967) 165-184.

A.G. Wright, "The Structure of Wisdom 11–19", *CBQ* 27 (1965) 28-34.

A.G. Wright, "Wisdom", *The Jerome Biblical Commentary*, Englewood Cliffs, NJ: 1968, pp.556-568.

J.-K. Zenner, "Der erste Theil des Buches der Weisheit", *ZKT* 22 (1898) 417-431.

J. Ziegler, *Sapientia Salomonis (Septuaginta, Vetus Testamentum Graecum, XII, 1)*, Göttingen, 1962, 1980.

G. Ziener, "Weisheitsbuch und Johannesevangelium", *Bib* 38 (1957) 396-418, and *Bib* 39 (1958) 37-60.

GENERAL BIBLIOGRAPHY

J.-N. Aletti, "Séduction et parole en Proverbes i–ix", *VT* 27 (1977) 129-144.

L. Alonso Schökel, "La réponse de Dieu", *Concilium*, 189 (1983) 75-84.

L. Alonso Schökel, "Sapiential and Covenant Themes in Genesis 2–3", [*Studies in Ancient Israelite Wisdom*, ed. J.L. Crenshaw, New York: 1976] 468-480.

L. Alonso Schökel, *A Manual of Hebrew Poetics*, Subsidia Biblica 11, Rome: 1988.

L. Alonso Schökel, J.L. Sicre Diaz, *Job*, Nueva Biblia Española, Madrid: 1983.

E. Babini, *L'antropologia teologica di Hans Urs von Balthasar*, Milano: 1988.

L.R. Bailey, *Biblical Perspectives on Death*, Philadelphia: 1979.

H.U. von Balthasar, *Christlicher Stand*, Einsiedeln: 1977.

H.U. von Balthasar, *Man in History*, London: 1982.

H.U. von Balthasar, *Theodramatik*, "Die Handlung", Vol. III, Einsiedeln: 1980.

H.U. von Balthasar, *Theodramatik*, "Prolegomena", Vol. I, Einsiedeln: 1973.

P. Beauchamp, "Création et fondation de la loi en Gn 1,1-2,4a", in *La création dans l'Orient ancien*, LD 127 (1987) 139-182.

M.A. Beavis, "The Trial before the Sanhedrin (Mark 14:53-65): Reader Response and Greco-Roman Readers", *CBQ* 49 (1987) 581-596.

E. Becker, *Angel in Armor, a post-freudian perspective on the nature of man*, New York: 1975.

E. Becker, *Denial of Death*, New York: 1973.

E. Becker, *Escape from Evil*, New York: 1975.

E. Becker, *The Revolution in Psychiatry, the new understanding of Man*, New York: 1974.

G. Bertram, "*Zoê* and *Bios* in the Septuagint", *TDNT*, pp. 851-854.

P.-M. Bogaert, "La «seconde mort» à l'époque des *Tannaïm*", [*Vie et survie dans les civilisations orientales*, ed. A. Théodoridès, P. Naster, J. Ries, *Acta Orientalia Belgica* 3, Louvain: 1983] 199-207.

H. Bois, *Essai sur les origines de la philosophie judéo-alexandrine*, Toulouse, 1890.

W. Booth, *The Rhetoric of Fiction*, Chicago: 1970.

P. Bovati, *Ristabilire la giustizia*, AnBib 110, Rome: 1986.

R.H. Charles, *Eschatology. The Doctrine of a Future Life in Israel, Judaism and Christianity. A critical History*, New York: 1963.

A.H. Chroust, *Aristotle: Protrepticus, A Reconstruction*, Notre Dame: 1964.

J.J. Collins, "Apocalyptic Eschatology as the Transcendence of Death", *CBQ* 36 (1974) 21-43.

J.J. Collins, "Cosmos and Salvation: Jewish Wisdom and Apocalyptic in the Hellenistic Age", *HR* 17 (1977) 121-142.

J.L. Crenshaw ed., *Studies in Ancient Israelite Wisdom*, New York: 1976.

R. Detweiler ed., *Reader Response Approaches to Biblical and Secular Texts*, Semeia 31, 1985.

L. DI FONZO, *Ecclesiaste*, Rome: 1967.

O.A.W. DILKE, *Mathematics and Measurements*, London: 1987.

J.G. EICHHORN, *Einleitung in die Apokryphen des Alten Testaments*, Leipzig: 1803.

W. EMPSON, *Seven Types of Ambiguity*, New York: 1963.

A.-M. DUBARLE, *Le péché originel dans l'écriture*, LD 20 (1958).

R.M. FOWLER, "Who Is 'the Reader' in Reader Response Criticism?" *Semeia* 31 (1985) 5-23.

R. GARLAND, *The Greek Way of Death*, London: 1985.

P. GIBERT, *Bible, mythes et récits de commencement*, Paris: 1986.

M. GILBERT, "La description de la vieillesse en Qohelet xii 1-7, est-elle allégorique?", VTSup 32 (1981 96-109.

W. GOOSENS, "Immortalité corporelle", *DBS* 4 (1949) 298-317.

P. GRELOT, *De la mort à la vie éternelle*, LD 67 (1971).

H. HAAG, "Der 'Urstand' nach dem Zeugnis der Bibel", *TQ* 148 (1968) 385-404.

M. HADAS, *Hellenistic Culture: Fusion and Diffusion*, New York: 1972.

E. HATCH, H.A. REDPATH, *A Concordance to the Septuagint*, Graz: 1975.

J.H. HAYES, C.R. HOLLADAY, *Biblical Exegesis*, Atlanta: 1982.

M. HENGEL, *Jews, Greeks and Barbarians*, trans. J. BOWDEN [*Juden, Griechen und Barbaren*, Stuttgarter Bibelstudien, 76, Katholisches Bibelwerk, Stuttgart: 1976], Philadelphia: 1980.

M. HENGEL, *Judaism and Hellenism*, trans. J. BOWDEN [*Judentum und Hellenismus*, WUNT 10, Tübingen: 1973] vol I-II, Philadelphia: 1974.

A. HULSBOSCH, "Conceptus Paulini vitae et mortis", *DivThom* 47-49 (1944-46) 43.

P. HUMBERT, *Études sur le récit du Paradis et de la chute dans la Genèse*, Neuchâtel: 1940.

R. JACOBSON, "Linguistics and Poetics", [*Style in Language*, ed. T.A. SEBEOK, Cambridge: 1960] 350-377.

O. KAISER, E. LOHSE, *Tod und Leben*, Stuttgart: 1977, {*Death and Life*, trans. J.E. STEELY, Nashville: 1981}.

H.A. KENIK, *The Design for Kingship: The Deuteronomistic Narrative Technique in 1 Kings 3:4-15*, Chico, CA: 1983.

M. KRIEG, *Toderbilder im Alten Testament oder: 'Wie die Alten den Tod gebildet'*, ATANT 73 (1987).

M.-J. LAGRANGE, "La paternité de Dieu dans l'Ancient Testament", *RB* 5 (1908) 482-499.

B.C. LATEGAN, "Current issues in the hermeneutical debate", *Neot* 18 (1984) 1-17.

X. LÉON-DUFOUR, *Face à la mort, Jésus et Paul*, Parole de Dieu 18, Paris: 1979 [*Life and Death in the New Testament*, trans. T. PRENDERGAST, San Francisco: 1986].

I. LORINUS, *Commentarius in Librum Sapientiae*, Lyon: 1607.

A. MARCHADOUR, *Mort et vie dans la bible*, CahÉv 29, 1979.

H.I. MARROU, *Histoire de l'éducation dans l'antiquité*, Paris: 1948.

G. MARTELET, *Libre réponse à un scandale*, Paris: 1986.

R. MARTIN-ACHARD, *De la mort à la résurrection d'après l'Ancien Testament*, Neuchâtel: 1956.

R. MARTIN-ACHARD, *La mort en face: selon la Bible hébraïque, Essai biblique* 15, Geneva: 1988.

G. MASPERO, *Études égyptiennes*, I, Paris: 1886.

G.W.E. NICKELSBURG, *Resurrection, Immortality, and Eternal Life in Intertestamental Judaism*, Cambridge: 1972.

R. NORTH, "Prophecy to Apocalyptic via Zachariah", VTSup 22 (1972) 47-71.

B. OCH, "The Garden of Eden: From Creation to Covenant", *Judaism* 37 (1988) 143-156.

R.H. PFEIFFER, *History of New Testament Times with an Introduction to the Apocrypha*, Westport, CT: 1949.

G.G. PORTON, "Diversity in Postbiblical Judaism", [*Early Judaism and its Modern Interpreters*, eds. R.A. KRAFT, G.W.E. NICKELSBURG, Atlanta: 1986] pp. 57-80.

K. RAHNER, "Ideas for a Theology of Death", *Theological Investigations*, Vol. 13, pp. 169-186.

K. RAHNER, "The Dignity and Freedom of Man", *Theological Investigations*, Vol. 2, pp. 235-263.

K. RAHNER, "The Scandal of Death", *Theological Investigations*, Vol. 7, pp. 140-144.

K. RAHNER, *Zur Theologie des Todes: Mit einem Exkurs über das Martyrium*, Freiburg: 1958, {*On the Theology of Death*, trans. C.H. HENKEY, New York: 1961}.

P. RICŒUR, "Biblical Hermeneutics", *Semeia* 4 (1975) 29-145.

P. RICŒUR, "Philosophical Hermeneutics and Theological Hermeneutics", *Studies in Religion/Sciences Religieuses* 5 (1975) 14-33.

P. RICŒUR, "Philosophy and Religious Language", *JR* 54 (1974) 71-85.

P. RICŒUR, *La métaphore vive*, Paris: 1975.

P. RICŒUR, *The Symbolism of Evil*, trans. E. BUCHANAN, Boston: 1970.

J. RIES ed., *La Mort selon la Bible, dans l'Antiquité classique, et selon Manichéisme*, CCL 5, Louvain: 1983.

S. SAPORTA, "The Application of Linguistics to the Study of Poetic Language", [*Style in Language*, ed. T.A. SEBEOK, Cambridge: 1960].

J. SCHREINER, "Gen 6:1-4 und die Problematik von Leben und Tod", [*De la Tôrah au Messie*, Mélanges Henri CAZELLES, Paris: 1981] 65-74.

E. STANKIEWICZ, "Linguistics and the Study of Poetic Language", [*Style in Language*, ed. T.A. SEBEOK, Cambridge: 1960] 69-81.

J. STARCKY, "Les Quatre Étapes du Messianisme à Qumrân", *RB* 70 (1963) 484-505.

H.B. SWETE, *An Introduction to the O.T. in Greek*, Cambridge: 1902.

V. TCHERIKOVER, *Hellenistic Civilization and the Jews*, New York: 1970.

N.J. TROMP, *Primitive Conceptions of Death and the Nether World in the Old Testament*, BibOr 21 (1969).

E.E. URBACH, *The Sages: their concepts and beliefs*, Jerusalem: 1975.

A. VANHOYE, *La structure littéraire de l'épître aux Hébreux*, Studia Neotestamentica 1, Paris: 1963.

G. VERMES, *The Dead Sea Scrolls*, Sheffield: 1987³.

H. VORGRIMLER, ed., *Commentary on the Documents of Vatican II*, vol. 5; "Pastoral Constitution on the Church in the Modern World", Part I, Chapter I, J. RATZINGER, trans. W.J. O'HARA, Freiburg: 1969.

L. WÄCHTER, *Der Tod im Alten Testament*, Stuttgart: 1967.

H. WAHLE, "Die Lehren des rabbinischen Judentums über das Leben nach dem Tod", *Kairos* 14 (1972) 291-309.

C. WESTERMANN, *Genesis 1-11*, trans. J.J. SCULLION, [Genesis 1-11, *Biblischer Kommentar*, Neukirchen-Vluyn, 1974], London: 1984.

C. WESTERMANN, *Praise and Lament in the Psalms*, trans. K.R. CRIM and R.N. SOULEN, Edinburgh: 1981.

H.W. WOLFF, *Anthropologie des Alten Testaments*, Munich: 1973, {*Anthropology of the Old Testament*, trans. M. KOHL, London: 1981}.

J. ZANDEE, *Death as an Enemy According to Ancient Egyptian Concepts*, New York: 1977.

J. ZIEGLER, *Isaias, Echter-Bibel*, Würzburg: 1948.

Sources for translations:

Translations to the classical authors are cited from the *Loeb Classical Library* with the respective versification of each work, unless otherwise indicated.

Translations to the pseudepigrapha are cited from *The Apocrypha and Pseudepigrapha of the Old Testament*, ed. R.H. CHARLES, 2 vols, London: 1983-1985.

Translations to the Qumran texts are cited from G. VERMES, *The Dead Sea Scrolls*, New York: 1979.

ABBREVIATIONS OF PERIODICALS AND COLLECTIONS

AnBib	—	Analecta Biblica
AnchorB	—	*Anchor Bible*
Anton	—	*Antonianum*
AS	—	*Assemblées du Seigneur*
ANET	—	J. B. PRITCHARD ed., *Ancient Near Eastern Texts*
ATANT	—	Abhandlung zur Theologie des Alten und Neuen Testaments
AttiSettBibl	—	*Atti della Settimana Biblica*
BASOR	—	*Bulletin of the American Schools of Oriental Research*
BbbOr	—	*Bibbia e Oriente*
BETL	—	Biblioteca Ephemeridum Theologicarum Lovaniensium
Bib	—	*Biblica*
BibOr	—	Biblica et Orientalia
CahÉv	—	*Cahiers Évangile*
CBQ	—	*Catholic Biblical Quarterly*
CCL	—	Collection Cerfaux-Lefort
Concilium	—	*Concilium*
CRAI	—	*Comptes rendus de l'Académie des Inscriptions et Belles-Lettres*
CuadBibl	—	*Cuadernos Bíblicos*
CuBíbl	—	*Cultura Bíblica*
DBS	—	*Dictionnaire de la Bible, Supplément*
DivThom	—	*Divus Thomas*
ÉtBN	—	Études Bibliques, Nouvelle Série
ETL	—	*Ephemerides Theologicae Louvanienses*
ExpTim	—	*Expository Times*
FRLANT	—	Forschungen zur Religion und Literatur des Alten und Neuen Testaments
HAT	—	Handbuch zum Alten Testament
Hermes	—	*Hermes*
HR	—	*History of Religions*
HS	—	*Die Heilige Schrift des Alten Testaments*
HTR	—	*Harvard Theological Review*
JBL	—	*Journal of Biblical Literature*
JJS	—	*Journal of Jewish Studies*
JR	—	*Journal of Religion*
JSJ	—	*Journal for the Study of Judaism*
JSOT	—	*Journal for the Study of the Old Testament*
JSOTSupS	—	Journal for the Study of the Old Testament, Supplement Series
JTS	—	*Journal of Theological Studies*
Judaism	—	*Judaism*
Kairos	—	*Kairos*

LD — Lectio Divina
MGWJ — *Monatsschrift für Geschichte und Wissenschaft des Judentums*
Neot — *Neotestamentica*
NRT — *Nouvelle Revue Théologique*
Paideia — *Paideia*
RB — *Revue Biblique*
RHR — *Revue de l'Histoire des Religions*
RivB — *Rivista Biblica*
RSPT — *Revue des sciences philosophiques et théologiques*
RThom — *Revue Thomiste*
Sales — *Salesianum*
Semeia — *Semeia*
SR — *Studies in Religion/Sciences Religieuses*
SRivB — Supplementi alla Rivista Biblica
StudCath — *Studia Catholica*
TDNT — G. Kittel and G. Friedrich (eds.), *Theological Dictionary of the New Testament*
TQ — *Theologische Quartalschrift*
Traditio — *Traditio*
TZ — *Theologische Zeitschrift*
VT — *Vetus Testamentum*
VTSup — Vetus Testamentum, Supplements
WUNT — Wissentschaftliche Untersuchungen zum Neuen Testament
ZKT — *Zeitschrift für katholische Theologie*
ZRGG — *Zeitschrift für Religions- und Geistesgeschichte*
ZWT — *Zeitschrift für wissentschaftliche Theologie*

INDEX OF SUBJECTS

AUTHORS CITED

SCRIPTURE REFERENCES

Because I have
loved life
so much
I know I will
love death
as well

(R. TAGORE, *Song Offerings*, 95)